LEVEL
2

SPORT

JENNIFER STAFFORD-BROWN

SIMON REA

HODDER
EDUCATION
AN HACHETTE UK COMPANY

In order to ensure that this resource offers high-quality support for the associated BTEC qualification, it has been through a review process by the awarding body to confirm that it fully covers the teaching and learning content of the specification or part of a specification at which it is aimed, and demonstrates an appropriate balance between the development of subject skills, knowledge and understanding, in addition to preparation for assessment.

While the publishers have made every attempt to ensure that advice on the qualification and its assessment is accurate, the official specification and associated assessment guidance materials are the only authoritative source of information and should always be referred to for definitive guidance.

No material from an endorsed textbook will be used verbatim in any assessment set by BTEC.

Endorsement of a textbook does not mean that the textbook is required to achieve this BTEC qualification, nor does it mean that it is the only suitable material available to support the qualification, and any resource lists produced by the awarding body shall include this and other appropriate resources.

Orders: please contact Bookpoint Ltd, 130 Milton Park, Abingdon, Oxon OX14 4SB. Telephone: (44) 01235 827720. Fax: (44) 01235 400454. Lines are open from 9.00–5.00, Monday to Saturday, with a 24-hour message answering service. You can also order through our website www.hoddereducation.co.uk

If you have any comments to make about this, or any of our other titles, please send them to educationenquiries@hodder.co.uk

British Library Cataloguing in Publication Data

A catalogue record for this title is available from the British Library

ISBN: 978 1 444 1 86581

Published 2013

Impression number   10 9 8 7 6 5 4 3 2 1

Year   2016 2015 2014 2013

Cover photo © Fuse / Getty Images

Typeset by Integra Software Services Pvt. Ltd., Pondicherry, India.

Printed in Italy for Hodder Education, an Hachette UK Company, 338 Euston Road, London NW1 3BH

Contents

Introduction

Welcome to *BTEC Sport Level 2*. We hope that you will find this textbook interesting and useful as you study your course. After the success of the London Olympic Games and Paralympics in 2012, sport has never been more popular in the UK than it is today. We are never far from the next major sports event whether it is Wimbledon, football, cricket and rugby World Cups or Olympic, Paralympic and Commonwealth Games. Studying sport is also becoming increasingly important as we need people who have knowledge of sport to help coach, instruct, manage and participate.

You have probably played sports for several years but this may be the first time you have studied a sports course. This book is designed to help you in your study of sport. It will provide information that will develop your understanding of sport and help you to complete your assignment work.

BTEC courses are split up into units of study. Amongst these units you will study important subjects such as anatomy and physiology, psychology of sport, fitness and training in sport and practical sport performance. You will also participate in a range of team and individual sports.

Each unit will be assessed either through written assignments prepared by your teachers or by an onscreen test. The activities in the book will help to prepare you for these assessments.

BTEC courses are aimed at developing skills and knowledge needed in work. You will be able to make links between the information presented in the book and areas of work that you are interested in. We provide some examples of how people in various occupations have used their knowledge in their jobs.

We hope you enjoy reading this book and that your course will inspire you to discover more and more about sport and sports performance.

How to use this book

This book will give you all of the knowledge you will need for the BTEC Sport Level 2 qualification. The layout and language is aimed specifically at Level 2 students and each learning aim is clearly set out so that you can find the information that you need.

Tick the boxes to track your progress through each topic.

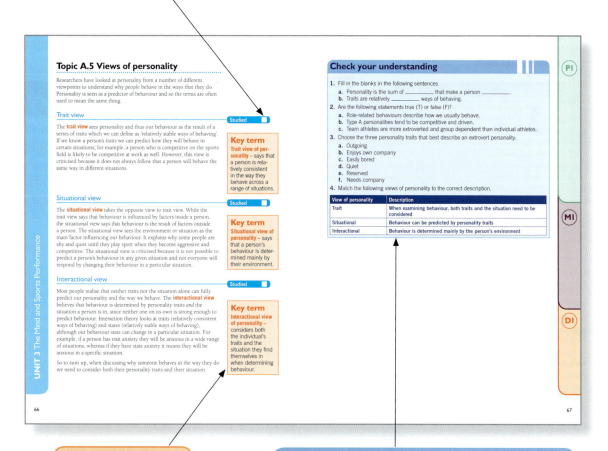

Key term

Check important words and what they mean.

Check your understanding

Use these questions at the end of each topic to make sure that you have understood the main points.

How to use this book

Real world connection

Find out more about sport through real life case studies.

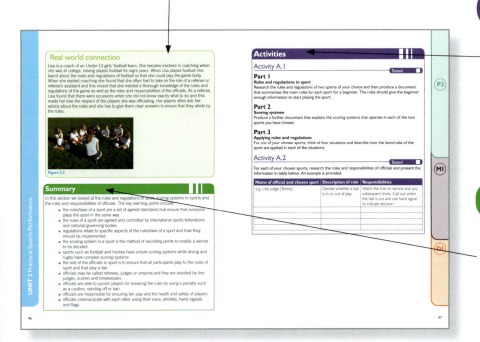

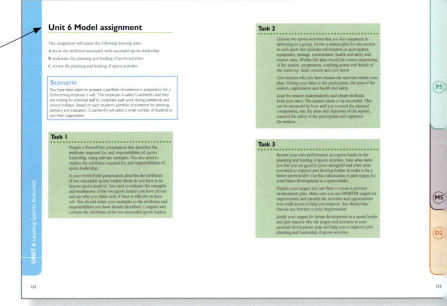

Activities

Test your understanding of the subject with activities which give you examples of what you need to know to meet pass, merit and distinction criteria.

Summary

Summaries of the key knowledge for each learning aim, with tick boxes for you to check off which subjects you have revised.

Model assignment

At the end of each unit you'll find a Model Assignment that will give you the opportunity to generate the evidence you need.

Unit 1

Fitness for Sport and Exercise

In order for a person to perform to the best of their ability, they must have high levels of the appropriate components of fitness. Different sports also have differing fitness requirements. There are lots of different training methods that can be used in fitness training programmes and these will be explored in this unit, together with the principles of fitness training. Fitness testing for different components of fitness will also be looked at as well as the advantages and disadvantages of each of the different tests.

Learning aims

By the end of this unit you will:

✓ know about the components of fitness and the principles of training

✓ explore different fitness training methods

✓ investigate fitness testing to determine fitness levels.

Topic A.1 Components of physical fitness

There are six components of physical fitness:

1. aerobic endurance
2. muscular endurance
3. flexibility
4. speed
5. muscular strength
6. body composition.

Aerobic endurance

Aerobic endurance is the ability of the cardiorespiratory system to work efficiently in order to supply nutrients and oxygen to working muscles during sustained physical activity. Other names for this component of physical fitness are cardiorespiratory fitness, cardiorespiratory endurance or aerobic fitness.

The **cardiorespiratory system** consists of the cardiovascular system which includes the heart, blood and blood vessels, and the respiratory system which includes the lungs and airways.

The cardiorespiratory system is responsible for taking in and using oxygen from the air that is breathed in and transporting nutrients and oxygen around the body. It also removes waste products such as carbon dioxide and lactic acid.

> **Key terms**
>
> **Aerobic endurance** – the ability of the cardiorespiratory system to work effectively.
>
> **Cardiorespiratory system** – the cardiovascular system and the respiratory system, which together transport nutrients and oxygen around the body and remove waste products.

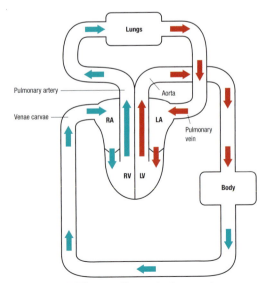

Figure 1.1 The cardiorespiratory system

Muscular endurance

Studied ☐

Muscular endurance is the ability of the muscular system to work efficiently. A person with muscular endurance is able to have their muscles continue contracting over a period of time against a light to moderate fixed resistance load.

> ## Key term
> **Muscular endurance** – the ability of the muscular system to work effectively and to be able to contract for a period of time against a light to moderate fixed resistance load.

Flexibility

Studied ☐

Flexibility means having an adequate range of motion in all joints of the body so that you are able to carry out all of the movements that are required every day. It also means the ability to move a joint fluidly through its complete range of movement.

> ## Key term
> **Flexibility** – having sufficient range of motion in all of the body's joints and being able to move a joint fluidly through its range of movement

Speed

Studied ☐

Speed is the distance a person travels divided by the time taken to travel that distance. Speed is measured in metres per second (m/s). The faster an athlete is able to run over a set distance, the greater their speed.

> ## Key term
> **Speed** – distance divided by the time taken.

The main types of speed are:

- accelerative speed – sprints up to 30 metres
- pure speed – sprints up to 60 metres
- speed endurance – sprints with a short recovery period in-between each sprint.

Muscular strength

Studied ☐

Muscular strength is the maximum force (in kg or N (newtons) that can be generated by a muscle or muscle group.

Body composition

Studied ☐

Body composition refers to the relative ratio of fat mass to fat-free mass (e.g. vital organs, muscle and bone) in the body.

> ## Key terms
> **Muscular strength** – the maximum force that can be generated by a muscle or muscle group.
>
> **Body composition** – the relative ratio of fat mass to fat-free mass.

Topic A.2 Components of skill-related fitness

- **Agility** refers to the ability of a sports performer to quickly and precisely move or change direction without losing their balance or decreasing their time.
- **Balance** is the ability to maintain centre of mass over a base of support. There are two types of balance static balance and dynamic balance.
- **Coordination** is the smooth flow of movement needed to perform a motor task efficiently and accurately.
- **Power** is the product of strength and speed and is expressed as the work done in a unit of time.
- **Reaction time** is the time taken for a sports performer to respond to a stimulus and the initiation of their response.

Key terms

Coordination – balanced or skilful movement to perform a motor task effectively.

Power – the result of the combination of strength and speed and is the amount done in a given amount of time.

Reaction time – how quickly a sports performer responds to a stimulus.

Key terms

Agility – being able to move or change direction quickly and accurately without losing your balance or affecting your time.

Balance – being able to preserve your centre of mass over a support base. In sports there are two types of balance – static, where the sports performer remains still, and dynamic, where the sports performer is able to perform a controlled movement.

Topic A.3 Why fitness components are important for successful participation in given sports

Having high levels of each of the required fitness components for a specific sport will enable you to successfully meet the physical demands of your sport and reach your highest levels of performance.

Sports rely on high levels of skill, too, and having high levels of each of the required skill-related components is also essential to achieve success.

The right combination of physical and skill-related fitness will lead to efficient performance, which is important so that energy is not wasted.

In some sports, different members of a team may require varying types of physical fitness and skill-related fitness, for example, a goal keeper in football will require high levels of power, speed, strength, fast reaction times and good coordination in order to perform their role well. A striker, however, will need high levels of muscular endurance, aerobic endurance, speed, power and agility to perform well in their position.

Topic A.4 Exercise intensity and how it can be determined

For your external assessment you will need to know how to be able to measure heart rate (HR) and apply HR intensity to fitness training methods.

Training intensity calculations

Intensity is how hard an individual trains. Individuals should train at different training intensities depending upon the fitness results that they want to attain. The different training levels are called **training zones** and these can be used to work out **target zones** and **training thresholds**.

For your external assessment you need to be able to explain what is meant by training zones, target zones and training thresholds and be able to calculate training zones.

How to calculate a training zone

First work out the maximum heart rate (HR max) for an individual:

HR max = 220 – age (years)

So, for a 16 year old, HR max = 220 – 16 = 204 beats per minute (bpm)

A 60–85% HR max is the recommended training zone for cardiovascular health and fitness.

You will need to be able to calculate the 60–85% HR max for people of different ages.

To work out the training zone at 60–85% of maximal heart rate for an 18 year old:

HR max = 220 –18 = 202 bpm

Training range is:

60% HR max x 60/100

202 x 60/100 = 121 bpm

85% HR max x 85/100

202 x 85/100 = 172 bpm

The training zone for an 18 year old is therefore 121–172 beats per minute. This means the individual should make sure their heart rate is between these numbers to ensure that they are training at the correct intensity.

> **Key terms**
>
> **Training zone** – this is the heart rate range to work out in order to gain a specific training effect
>
> **Target zone** – this is the heart rate range that a person should be aiming to work at in order to gain a training effect
>
> **Training threshold** – this is the minimum heart rate that a person should be working at in order to improve physical fitness.

Figure 1.2 Intensive training

Always include the units in your answer if you have the option – this may give you extra marks!

Always round up or down to a whole number – bpm are in whole numbers – there are no 0. beats per minute!

Borg Rating of Perceived Exertion (RPE) scale

Studied ☐

The RPE scale is used as a measure of exercise intensity. The scale ranges from 6 (rest) to 20 (exhaustion) (see Table 1.1).

Table 1.1 Borg RPE Scale

Rating of Perceived Exertion (RPE) Scale	
6	No exertion at all
7	Extremely light
8	
9	Very light
10	
11	Light
12	
13	Somewhat hard
14	
15	Hard (heavy)
16	
17	Very hard
18	
19	Extremely hard
20	Maximal exertion

RPE and heart rate

The number stated on the RPE scale can be multiplied by 10 to obtain an estimate of heart rate during a workout:

RPE x 10 = HR (bpm)

If an individual is working at level 15 on the RPE scale, their HR would be calculated as follows:

15 x 10 = 150 bpm

Topic A.5 The basic principles of training (FITT)

FITT is an acronym for the different principles of training that should be used when designing personal training programmes.

Frequency: the number of training sessions completed over a period of time, usually per week.

Intensity: how hard an individual will train; this is usually expressed as a percentage of maximum intensity.

Time: how long an individual will train for each session.

Type: how an individual will train by selecting a training method to improve a specific component of fitness and/or their sports performance.

The FITT principles in a training programme therefore ask the following questions:

- How often?
- How hard?
- How long?
- How will you train?

For your external assessment, you will need to be able to apply the FITT principles to training methods, regimes and given exercise situations.

Topic A.6 Additional principles of training

Progressive overload

Overload is where an athlete continually works harder than previously to gain increasing fitness and performance. This continued increase in intensity (how hard the athlete works) is called **progressive overload**.

> **Key term**
> **Progressive overload** – in order to progress, training must be demanding enough to cause the body to adapt, thereby improving performance.

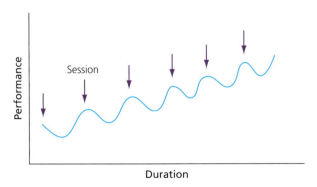

Figure 1.3 Progressive overload

Specificity

Studied ☐

Specificity refers to the fact that any fitness gain will be specific to the muscles or systems to which the training is applied. As different types of training will produce different results, it is important to make sure that training is specific to the sport that an individual is competing in. For example, if a person is training for a marathon, they will need to include lots of distance running in their training programme; they will not improve their running performance if their training only included swimming!

Key term

Specificity – training should be specific to the individual's sport, activity or physical/skill-related fitness goals.

Individual differences/needs

Studied ☐

The training programme should be designed to meet the sports performer's **individual differences and needs**. These are determined from their personal goals and competition goals.

Key term

Individual differences/needs – developing a training programme that suits the performer's personal and competition goals.

Adaptation

Studied ☐

Adaptation is where the body changes to cope with the extra loads and stresses applied to the body systems during training (see Figure 1.4). Adaptation occurs during the recovery period after the training session is completed. Most athletes will have at least one rest day a week to give their body time to adapt to the training that they have completed.

Key term

Adaptation – how the body reacts to training loads by increasing its ability to cope with those loads. It occurs during the recovery period after a training session has finished.

Adaptation after a training session.

Figure 1.4 Adaptation occurs after a training session

UNIT 1 Fitness for Sport and Exercise

Reversibility

Studied

If training stops, or if the intensity of training is not sufficient to cause adaptation, then the training effects are reversed and the body will return to its previous fitness level. This **reversibility** is sometimes referred to as 'use it or lose it'.

> **Key term**
>
> **Reversibility** – occurs when training stops or when training is not sufficient to cause adaptation. It is a reverse of the effects of training.

Variation

Studied

It is important to include **variation** in the training regime otherwise the individual may become bored, making it difficult for them to maintain their enjoyment and motivation to train.

Although training is mostly specific to the competition sport, the occasional exercise that is not specific to the sport can also be included in a training programme for variation. This also helps to improve some components of physical fitness, for example, yoga is good for flexibility training and swimming helps with aerobic endurance.

For the external assessment, you will need to be able to apply the principles of training to different training methods, different training regimes and different exercise settings.

> **Key term**
>
> **Variation** – varying the training regime will prevent boredom and help the sports performer to continue to enjoy their training.

Rest and recovery

Studied

An athlete needs rest to give their body a chance to recover from training and give their body time to adapt to the training (see adaptation on the previous page).

Check your understanding

1. Match the definitions to the component of fitness they describe.

Component of fitness	Definition
1. Aerobic endurance	**a.** the product of strength and speed
2. Muscular endurance	**b.** the ability of a sports performer to move quickly and precisely or change direction without losing their balance or reducing their time
3. Strength	**c.** the ability of the cardiorespiratory system to work efficiently, supplying nutrients and oxygen to working muscles during sustained physical activity
4. Speed	**d.** the ability of the muscular system to work efficiently, so that a muscle can contract over a period of time against a light to moderate fixed resistance load
5. Agility	**e.** the maximum force in kg or N that can be generated by a muscle or muscle group
6. Power	**f.** distance divided by time taken

Summary

In this section we looked at the components of physical and skill-related fitness and why fitness components are important for successful participation in sports. We also looked at how exercise intensity can be determined and the basic principles of training (FITT) as well as additional principles of training. The key learning points include:

- aerobic endurance (also known as cardiorespiratory fitness/endurance and aerobic fitness) is the ability of the cardiorespiratory system to work efficiently
- the cardiorespiratory system consists of the heart, blood, and blood vessels together with the lungs and airways.
- the cardiorespiratory system takes up oxygen from the air we breathe, transports nutrients and oxygen around the body and removes waste products such as carbon dioxide
- the components of physical fitness are aerobic endurance, muscular endurance, flexibility, speed, muscular strength and body composition
- the components of skill-related fitness are agility, balance, coordination, power and reaction time
- successfully meeting the physical and skill-related demands of a sport means you can reach your optimal performance, perform efficiently and decide which aspect of the sport or position suits you best
- being able to measure your heart rate (HR) and apply your HR intensity to your fitness training methods
- understanding target zones and training thresholds will enable you to calculate training zones and apply HR max to training
- the FITT principles (frequency, intensity, time and type) should always be applied to training methods, regimes and exercise situations
- the additional principles of training include progressive overload, specificity, individual differences/needs, adaptation, reversibility and variation
- rest and recovery are important for the body to recover from the training and to allow adaptation to occur.

Activities

Activity A.1

Tested

Part 1

Components of physical and skill-related fitness

Consider each of these sports performers.

- Bradley Wiggins
- Mo Farrah
- Beth Tweddle
- Wayne Rooney
- Jessica Ennis

Select one of the sports performers and decide which are the three most important components of physical fitness and the three most important components of skill-related fitness for that sports performer and place them in the table below. Explain why each component is important for that sports performer.

Component of physical fitness	Why is it important?

Component of skill-related fitness	Why is it important?

Part 2

Exercise intensity

Write an example of a week's training programme for your selected athlete, making sure you include the FITT principles and the additional principles of training.

Activity A.2

Tested

Match the principles of training to their correct description.

Description	Principles of training
1. The time length of each session	**a.** Type
2. Doing more than the body is used to	**b.** Frequency
3. The number of training sessions per week, month or year	**c.** Reversibility
4. The amount of effort expended in each training session	**d.** Specificity
5. Targeting the component of fitness you wish to improve	**e.** Time
6. If you do not use a fitness gain you will lose it	**f.** Intensity
7. Choosing muscular endurance, strength or flexibility	**g.** Overload

Learning aim B: Explore different fitness training methods

Topic B.1 Requirements for fitness training methods

This topic looks at the key requirements for different training methods that you need to be aware of.

Safe, correct use of equipment:

Failure to use training equipment safely and correctly could lead to injuries. It is important to use the correct equipment so that training is performed effectively.

Safe, correct use of training technique:

If a training technique is not carried out correctly, this can result in the training not providing the correct intensity or training aim and could also result in injury.

Requirements for undertaking the fitness training method:

A warm up and cool down are essential parts of a training session. The warm up helps to prepare the body for exercise so that there is a reduced risk of injury, such as a muscle strain. Once the training session has been completed, a cool down should be carried out to help the body recover from the exercise session by helping it to rid itself of lactic acid and to stretch out muscles.

Application of the basic principles of training (FITT) for each fitness training method:

In order to develop a safe and effective training programme you need to consider the basic principles of training. These principles are a set of guidelines to help you understand the requirements of programme design. The principles of training are:

Frequency – how often the sports performer will train each week.

Intensity – how hard the sports performer will work (usually expressed as a percentage of maximum intensity).

Time – indicates how long the sports performer will train for in each session.

Type – indicates what sort of training will be performed; it must be specific to each sports performer.

Linking each fitness training method to the associated health-related/skill-related component of fitness:

Different training methods are linked to different physical or skill-related components of fitness. Some training methods will link to a number of different physical and skill-related components of fitness. You need to be able to link each fitness training method to its associated health-related or skill-related component of fitness for your external assessment – this is explored in more detail in Topic B.3 of this unit.

Topic B.2 Additional requirements for each of the fitness training methods

Advantages and disadvantages:

You need to know the advantages and disadvantages of each of the fitness training methods that are described in this unit. How appropriate the method of training is to the actual sport the performer is taking part in is very important when considering fitness training methods. For example, a football player will need to be able to go from a jog to a sprint in order to intercept a ball so acceleration sprint training would be appropriate for them as this incorporates the rolling start.

Factors such as the equipment required, the cost of equipment and the ease of carrying out the method of training must all be considered as well.

Application of exercise intensity to fitness training methods:

You need to know that in order for specific fitness training methods to be effective, such as interval or fartlek training, they must be performed at the appropriate intensities.

Application of principles of training to fitness training methods:

You must be able to apply both the FITT principles and the additional principles of training to the various fitness training methods.

Appropriate application of fitness training method(s) for given situation(s):

You will need to be able to apply appropriate fitness training methods for individuals who are training for a particular sport or specific component of physical or skill-related fitness.

Appropriate application of fitness training method(s) to given client needs/goals/aims/objectives:

You must be able to select appropriate training methods for an individual who has a specific target they wish to achieve, such as preparing for a competition or improving one or more components of fitness.

Topic B.3 Fitness training methods

Flexibility training

The main types of flexibility training are:

- static
- ballistic
- proprioceptive neuromuscular facilitation (PNF) technique.

Static

Active static stretching is where the sports performer applies internal force from another muscle group to stretch and lengthen the muscle. This involves actively doing something to produce the stretch, for example, holding your arm across your body to stretch your deltoids (see Figure 1.5).

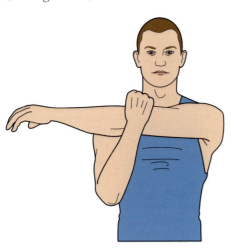

Figure 1.5 Active static stretching

Passive static stretching is also called assisted stretching. This is where the help of another person or an object such as a wall or bench is used for the stretch. The other person/object applies external force, causing the muscle to stretch (see Figure 1.6).

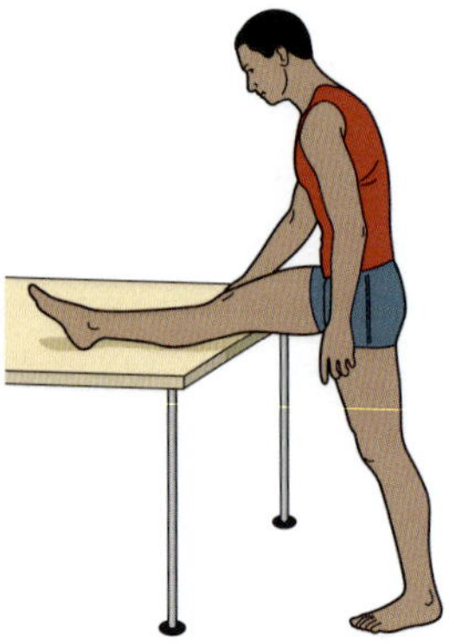

Figure 1.6 Passive static stretching

> **Key terms**
>
> **Active static stretching** – performed independently and requires the sports performer to apply internal force to stretch and lengthen the muscle.
>
> **Passive static stretching** – requires the help of another person or an object to apply external force, causing the muscle to stretch.

UNIT 1 Fitness for Sport and Exercise

Ballistic

Ballistic stretching is where the performer carries out fast, bouncing, jerky movements through the range of motion of their joints (see Figure 1.7). This type of stretching is specific to the movement pattern of the sport or activity that is to be performed. Ballistic stretching can cause muscle strains so it must be carried out carefully. It is usually only used in sports where the sports performer already has high levels of flexibility, such as gymnastics or ballet.

Figure 1.7 Ballistic stretching is bouncy stretching!

Proprioceptive neuromuscular facilitation (PNF) technique

This type of stretching is used to develop mobility, strength and flexibility and can be performed in the cool-down part of a training session to develop the length of the muscle. The **proprioceptive neuromuscular facilitation technique** of stretching requires the help of a partner or an immovable object to provide resistance.

With a partner, the performer warms up and then stretches their muscle to the greatest range of their movement. Their partner helps them to hold the muscle in an isometric contraction for around 6–10 seconds. They then relax the muscle and the partner stretches the muscle further (this is static passive stretching) to allow the muscle to stretch even further.

The PNF technique works by stopping the stretch reflex from happening.

Key terms

Ballistic stretching – fast, jerky movements through the complete range of motion.

Proprioceptive Neuromuscular Facilitation (PNF) technique – a stretching technique that inhibits the stretch reflex.

Figure 1.8 PNF technique

Strength, muscular endurance and power training

Studied ☐

The main types of strength, muscular endurance and power training methods are:

- circuit training
- free weights
- plyometrics.

Circuit training

Circuit training involves the performer moving around different stations or exercises that involve resistance-based training to develop strength, muscular endurance and power. Circuit training can involve the use of dumb-bells, free weights or body weight as in press-ups. The stations or exercises are organised so that the individual going around the circuit uses different muscle groups at each station to avoid fatigue. Figure 1.9 describes a typical circuit.

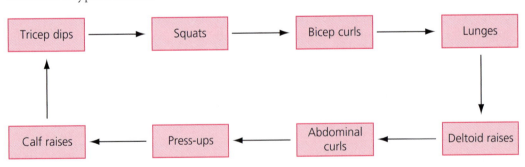

Figure 1.9 Circuit training

Free weights

A free weight is one that is not attached to machinery. Examples of free weights are barbells (Figure 1.10) and dumb-bells (Figure 1.11).

Barbells and dumb-bells are used to perform dynamic exercises to strengthen different muscle groups, for example, bicep curls are used to strengthen the biceps.

Figure 1.10 Barbell

- Order of strength, muscular endurance and power exercises: the order in which exercises are carried out is important – core exercises should be carried out before assistance exercises.
  - **Core exercises** are the major lifts such as squats and bench press, using the major muscle groups.
  - **Core conditioning exercises** are those that work the core muscles of the body, including those in the back and stomach which help to stabilise the spine and pelvis.
  - **Assistance exercises** are those that use the minor muscle groups or those associated with the performer's particular sport. If a performer is not training for a specific sport they will need to perform exercises which alternate between upper and lower body and also alternate push and pull exercises.

Figure 1.11 Dumb-bells

- Intensity of exercise: this is worked out as a percentage of the one repetition maximum (1RM) which is the maximum amount of weight that can be lifted for one repetition. So, if a performer can lift 50 kg for 1RM in the bicep curl, 50 per cent of their 1RM is 25 kg.
- **Reps and sets**: the number of repetitions (reps) is one complete movement of the exercise. A set is how often you complete a group of reps. For example, you may do two sets of 10 reps on bicep curls.
- **Maximum strength training**: this involves producing a single movement against a resistance or load. It requires the performer to do a series of repetitions in sets, followed by a rest period. It involves low reps and high loads, for example 90 per cent 1RM and 1–6 reps.
- **Strength endurance training**: this involves repetitive movements of a muscle or muscle group. It involves high reps and low loads, for example, 50–60 per cent 1RM and 20 reps.

- **Elastic strength training**: this involves producing movements in very close succession, for example 75 per cent 1RM and 12 reps. This type of training is performed by gymnasts, for example.

Plyometrics

This type of training is used to develop explosive power and strength that is specific to a particular sport. **Plyometrics** involves maximal lengthening (eccentric action) followed by maximal shortening (concentric action) of a muscle (see Figure 1.12).

During the exercise, landing produces maximal lengthening of a muscle while jumping up produces maximal shortening of a muscle. Examples of plyometric exercises include lunging, bounding, barrier hopping and jumping.

The amounts of force produced on the muscles in this type of training mean that it can cause muscle soreness or injury.

Plyometric training is used by sports performers such as sprinters, hurdlers and netball, volleyball and basketball players.

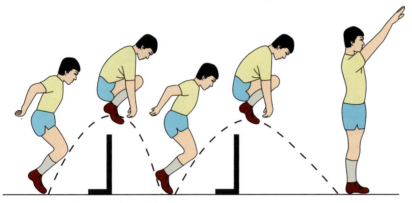

Figure 1.12 Plyometric training

Aerobic endurance training

Studied ☐

The main types of aerobic endurance training are:

- continuous
- fartlek
- interval
- circuit.

Continuous training

Continuous training requires the performer to exercise at a steady pace and moderate intensity for a minimum period of 30 minutes, for example, jogging or cycling for at least 30 minutes.

Fartlek training

In this type of training the intensity is varied by running at different speeds or over different terrain such as up and down hills. The training is continuous with no rest period. Equipment such as a harness, running with weights or running with a weighted backpack can also be used in **fartlek training** to increase the intensity.

Key terms

Elastic strength training – involves movements in quick succession.

Plyometrics – exercises which produce maximal force as the muscle lengthens (eccentric action) before an immediate maximal force as the muscle shortens (concentric action).

Key terms

Continuous training – training at a steady pace for at least 30 minutes.

Fartlek training – changing the intensity of training by varying the speed or terrain.

Interval training

Interval training involves exercising followed by a rest or recovery period. The typical exercise time can vary from 30 seconds to five minutes, followed by recovery periods which can involve complete rest or exercising at a very low intensity such as walking or light jogging. To increase aerobic endurance, the number of rest periods is decreased and work intensity is decreased to around 60% of a person's maximum oxygen uptake.

Circuit training

Circuit training involves different stations or exercises that are all aerobic endurance based. The exercises are performed using longer time periods and in steady rhythmical movements – usually 45 seconds work and 15 seconds rest. Exercises are chosen that work the larger muscle groups. The stations or exercises are organised so that the individual going around the circuit uses different muscle groups at each station to avoid fatigue (see Figure 1.13).

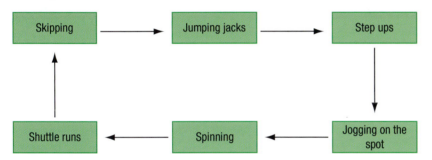

Figure 1.13 Circuit training

Speed training

Studied ☐

The main methods for speed training are:

- hollow sprints
- acceleration sprints
- interval training.

Hollow sprints

Hollow sprints are a series of sprints separated by a 'hollow' period of jogging or walking between each sprint (see Figure 1.14).

Figure 1.14 Hollow sprints

Acceleration sprints

In **acceleration sprints**, the individual starts from standing or walking then increases their stride so that they accelerate up to their maximum sprint pace. This is then followed by a rest or recovery period followed by more sprints.

Key terms

Interval training – the sports performer carries out a period of training followed by a rest or recovery period.

Circuit training – different stations or exercises are used to develop aerobic endurance.

Key terms

Hollow sprints – a series of sprints separated by a 'hollow' period of jogging or walking.

Acceleration sprints – involve the pace gradually increasing from a standing or walking start.

Different drills can be included, such as hill sprints and resistance drill using sleds and chutes to increase resistance.

Interval training

Interval training involves exercising followed by a rest or recovery period. For speed training, the work intervals are shorter than for aerobic endurance training and will be of a much higher intensity – close to maximum levels, for example, work 10 seconds and rest 60 seconds. To develop speed the rest intervals are increased and the intensity is increased.

Some training methods sound very similar. They can be used in different ways to train different components of fitness. Table 1.2 gives some examples.

Table 1.2 Different types of training

Type of training	Component of Fitness	Component of Fitness
Circuits	Strength	Aerobic endurance
	Resistance-based exercises	Aerobic exercises
Free weights	Strength	Muscular endurance
	High load, low reps	Low load, high reps
Interval training	Speed	Aerobic endurance
	Increase rest periods, increase intensity	Decrease rest periods, decrease intensity

Check your understanding

1. Match the training method to the component of fitness.

Component of fitness	Training method
Flexibility	Plyometrics
Strength	Hollow sprints
Power	Continuous training
Aerobic endurance	Heavy weights with low repetitions
Muscular endurance	75% 1RM and 12 reps
Speed	Low weights with high repetitions
Elastic strength	PNF

Summary

In this section we have looked at the fitness training methods for flexibility, strength, speed, muscular endurance, aerobic endurance and power training. The key learning points include:

- the use of correct and safe equipment and training technique is essential
- a fitness training method must always include a warm-up and cool down and the basic principles of training (FITT) should be applied
- each fitness training method has its advantages and disadvantages and consideration should be given to whether it is appropriate for the given situation and the needs of the sports performer
- there are two types of static flexibility training – active and passive
- ballistic flexibility training involves bobbing or bouncing movements
- proprioceptive neuromuscular facilitation (PNF) technique develops mobility, strength and flexibility
- circuit training, free weights and plyometrics are all techniques for increasing strength, muscular endurance and power training
- methods of aerobic endurance training are continuous training, fartlek training, interval training and circuit training
- speed training includes using hollow sprints, acceleration sprints and interval training.

Activity

Think of a sport that you like to take part in or watch and answer the questions below.

a) State the components of fitness that are required for this sport.
b) Describe the different training methods that you can use to train each of the identified components of fitness.
c) What are the advantages and disadvantages of each of the training methods that you have described?
d) Explain what training intensity a performer needs to work at for each of the identified training methods.

Learning aim C: Investigate fitness testing to determine fitness levels

Fitness tests are carried out to determine the fitness level of sports performers. The tests must be valid and reliable in order to provide useful data. Validity means asking 'does the test actually test for the component of fitness that I need to measure?' For example, a speed test using shuttle runs will test the performer's ability to *turn* more than their actual speed, so would not be a valid test for speed. Reliability means asking 'if the test is repeated, do I get the same results?'

The conditions of the test must always be identical so that it is possible for the same results to be produced. This includes not only the temperature and the environment but also the equipment to ensure that it is calibrated and working properly. This is important so that any changes in the test results are due to changes in the fitness of the performer taking part in the test and not due to errors in the measurements.

Topic C.1 Fitness test methods for components of fitness

This topic looks at the fitness tests you need to know about:

- flexibility
- strength
- aerobic endurance
- speed
- speed and agility
- anaerobic power
- muscular endurance
- body composition.

For each test, the following information is provided:

- what the test measures
- the equipment required for the test
- how the test is carried out
- the units that the results of the test are usually measured in
- the advantages and disadvantages of the test
- the validity and reliability of the test.

Flexibility test

Test name	Sit and reach test
Equipment	Sit and reach box
	Figure 1.15
Purpose	Measures the flexibility of the muscles in the lower back and hamstrings.
Protocol	Ask the performer to warm up with five minutes' jogging or cycling.
	Ask the performer to take off their shoes and any clothing which will restrict movement.
	The performer sits with their legs straight and their feet against the board. Their legs and back should be straight.
	The performer reaches as far forward as they possibly can and pushes the marker forward.
	Record the furthest point the marker reaches.
	Repeat the test and record the best score.
Unit of measurement	Centimetres or inches
Advantages	Quick and easy to perform
	Equipment is inexpensive.
Disadvantages	This test is safe to perform unless the athlete has a lower back injury, particularly a slipped disc.
Validity	This test only measures the flexibility of the lower back and hamstrings. It does not test the flexibility of all of the joints in the body.
Reliability	This depends upon how much time has been spent on the warm up. It is best to have the same warm up before the test is taken in order to increase the reliability of the test. The test must be carried out slowly and steadily with no ballistic, bouncy movements.

Table 1.3 Results of sit and reach test (cm)

Gender	Excellent	Above average	Average	Below average	Poor
Male	>35	28–34	23–27	16–22	<16
Female	>37	33–36	29–32	23–28	<23

Test name	Grip dynamometer
Equipment	Hand grip dynamometer
	Figure 1.16
Purpose	A static test to assess muscular strength in the lower arm and hand muscles.
Protocol	Adjust the handle to fit the size of the performer's hand.
	The performer holds the dynamometer in their stronger hand and keeps their arm hanging by their side with the dynamometer by their thigh.
	The performer squeezes the dynamometer as hard as they can for around 5 seconds.
	Record the results and repeat after about a minute.
	Use the performer's best result.
Unit of measurement	KgW
Advantages	Requires very little equipment.
	Quick and easy test to carry out.
Disadvantages	Only measures the strength in the lower arm and hand muscles. Does not give any indication of the strength of other muscle groups.
	The dynamometer needs to be adjusted properly for the performer's hand size. If this is not done properly the test results may not be accurate.
Validity	The test does not provide a measure of general strength as the strength of the forearms and hand does not always represent the strength of different muscle groups.
	If a person is right or left handed this can affect the results because the stronger hand/arm is usually the dominant one.
Reliability	The dynamometer needs to be calibrated before use to ensure that it provides reliable data.
	The technique to perform the test needs to remain the same and the same rest periods between each test need to be given in order to compare results.

Table 1.4 Results of grip dynamometer (kg)

Rating	Excellent	Very good	Above average	Average	Below average	Poor	Very poor
Males	>64	56–64	52–56	48–52	44–48	40–44	<40
Females	>38	34–38	30–34	26–30	22–26	20–22	<20

Aerobic endurance test – Forestry step test

Test name	Forestry step test
Equipment	Bench Height for males = 40 cm Height for females = 33 cm Metronome
Purpose	Predicts aerobic endurance levels.
Protocol	Set the metronome at 90 beats per minute. The performer stands in front of the bench. The stop watch is started and the performer starts stepping at a rate of 22.4 steps per minute in time with the metronome. The performer continues stepping for 5 minutes then sits down immediately. The performer finds their pulse and after 15 seconds of sitting down they count their pulse for 15 seconds. The tables available at www.hodderplus.co.uk/btecsport show how to work out the results for the test.
Unit of measurement	ml/kg/min
Advantages	Quick and easy to perform. The equipment is not expensive. A number of people can perform the test at the same time.
Disadvantages	Different height benches are required for males and females. Taller people will find the test easier than shorter people.
Validity	Research has shown that this is a valid test for aerobic endurance.
Reliability	If the test protocol is followed appropriately then the test is reliable.

Aerobic endurance test – Multi stage fitness test

Studied ☐

Test name	Multi stage fitness test (also known as the bleep test)
Equipment	Pre-recorded CD or tape of bleep sounds
	Flat area of 20 metres
	Cones
	Tape measure
	Flat running surface
Purpose	Estimation of VO$_2$ max for aerobic endurance.
Protocol	Mark out a length of 20 metres with cones.
	Start the CD or tape. The performers run when the first bleep sounds. They must run the distance of 20 metres before the second bleep sounds.
	When this bleep sounds they turn around and run back.
	As the performers continue to do this, the time between the bleeps gets shorter and shorter so that they have to run faster and faster.
	If a performer fails to get to the other end before the bleep on three consecutive occasions, they are out.
	Record at what point the athlete dropped out.
	Use Table 1.6 to assess the predicted VO$_2$ max.
Unit of measurement	ml/kg/min
Advantages	This test can be used with large groups, as all the performers run together.
	Equipment is not expensive.
Disadvantages	Performers have to be highly motivated and must exercise to exhaustion in order to obtain the required data.
	The test is not recommended for people with health problems, injuries or low fitness levels as it is a maximal test.
Validity	This test is good for performers whose sports require lots of running, but for a swimmer or cyclist this test is less useful because it uses running to test aerobic fitness.
	Because sport is specific, the test should involve movement in the main sport that the individual takes part in.
Reliability	The following can all affect the reliability of this test: running surface, climate, wind speed, whether the test is performed indoors or outdoors, motivation levels of performers and group dynamics.

Table 1.6 Results of multi stage fitness test (adapted from Baechle and Earle, 2000)

Category	Extremely high	Very high	High	Above average	Average
Males (s)	70	63–69	57–62	52–56	44–51
Females (s)	60	54–59	49–53	44–48	35–43

Speed test

Test name	35 m sprint
Equipment	Flat running surface
	Tape measure
	Stop watch
Purpose	To measure the straight running speed of a performer.
Protocol	The performer warms up for several minutes.
	The performer then does the 35 m run at less than their maximum speed.
	The performer starts the test behind the line with one or two hands on the ground.
	The trainer shouts 'go' and the athlete sprints the 35 m as quickly as possible.
	The run should be repeated after 2–3 minutes and the average of two or three runs taken.
	Use Table 1.7 to assess the results.
Unit of measurement	Usually measured in seconds.
Advantages	Quick and easy to perform.
	Does not require expensive equipment
Disadvantages	The performer's footwear and test surface can affect the results of this test. If there is insufficient grip then the performer will not do so well in the test.
Validity	Is a valid test for sprinting speed in a straight line.
Reliability	The individual should have at least a 3 minute recovery period between each run.
	The trainer must be accurate and must stop the stop watch as soon as the athlete crosses the 35 m line.

Table 1.7 Results of 35 m sprint test

Rating	Excellent	Good	Average	Fair	Poor
Males (s)	<4.80	4.80–5.09	5.10–5.29	5.30–5.60	5.6+
Females (s)	<5.30	5.30–5.59	5.60–5.89	5.90–6.20	6.2+

Speed and agility test

Test name	Illinois agility run test
Equipment	Cones
	Stopwatch
	Measuring tape
	Flat non-slip surface
	Figure 1.17 Layout for the Illinois agility run test
Purpose	Test for running agility.
Protocol	Mark out the test so that the length of the test is 10 metres and the distance between the start and finish points is 5 metres.
	Use four cones to mark the start, finish and the two turning points.
	Use another four cones, spaced out 3.3 metres apart down the centre of the route.
	The performer lies on their front with their head to the start line and their hands by their shoulders.
	The trainer starts the stop watch and shouts 'go'. The performer gets up as quickly as possible and runs around the course, without knocking the cones over, to the finish line. The trainer stops the stopwatch when the performer reaches the finish line.
Unit of measurement	Usually measured in seconds.
Advantages	Requires very little equipment.
	Test is quick and easy to administer.
Disadvantages	The test does not distinguish if the performer is better at turning right or left.
Validity	This is a valid test for sports performers who need to run and change direction in their sport, such as in dodging or intercepting an opponent in football, etc.
Reliability	The performer's footwear and test surface can affect the results of this test. If there is insufficient grip then the performer will not do so well in the test.

Table 1.8 Results of Illinois agility test

Rating	Excellent	Good	Average	Fair	Poor
Males (s)	<15.2	16.1–15.2	18.1–16.2	18.3–18.2	>18.3
Females (s)	<17.0	17.9–17.0	21.7–18.0	23.0–21.8	>23.0

Anaerobic power

Test name	Vertical jump test
Equipment	Wall Ruler/tape measure Chalk **Figure 1.18**
Purpose	Test of anaerobic power by measuring how high a performer can jump.
Protocol	The performer rubs chalk on their fingers and stands approximately 15 cm away from the wall. With their feet flat on the floor, the performer reaches as high as they can and makes a mark on the wall. The performer rubs more chalk on their fingers, then bends their knees to 90 degrees and jumps as high as they can up into the air. At the top of their jump they make a second chalk mark with their fingertips. The trainer measures the difference between their two marks; this is their standing jump score. This test is best done three times so the performer can use the results of the best of their three jumps (see Table 1.9 to calculate performance).
Unit of measurement	cm or kgm/s
Advantages	The test is quick and easy to perform. It does not require any expensive equipment.
Disadvantages	The jumping technique can have an effect on performance rather than just the power of the legs. The test only measures power in the legs and does not test for upper body power.
Validity	The test is valid for measuring the power of the lower body.
Reliability	Jumping technique can affect the results – it is important that the individual has a number of practice jumps so that improvements in power are shown in the test rather than improvements in jumping technique.

Table 1.9 Results of the vertical jump test

Rating	Excellent	Very good	Above average	Average	Below average	Poor	Very poor
Males	>70	61–70	51–60	41–50	31–40	21–30	<21
Females	>60	51–60	41–50	31–40	21–30	11–20	<10

Muscular endurance tests

Test name	One-minute press-up test
Equipment	Mat
	Stopwatch
Purpose	Test of muscular endurance of the arms and chest.
Protocol	The performer lies in a press-up position with their back straight, toes tucked under, their elbows straight and hands shoulder width apart.
	On the command of 'go' the performer bends their elbows to lower their chest to the floor.
	They return to the start position by straightening their elbows – this constitutes one repetition.
	The performer does as many repetitions as they can in one minute (see Table 1.10)
	Females can use the adapted press-up position where the knees are bent and the lower legs are in contact with the floor (see Table 1.11).
Unit of measurement	Number of press-ups per minute.
Advantages	Requires very little equipment.
	Large groups can be tested at the same time.
Disadvantages	Only tests for the endurance of the arms and the chest.
	The test requires high levels of motivation so that the maximum number of repetitions is completed.
Validity	This is a good test for muscular endurance but is only specific to the chest and the arms.
Reliability	The test requires high levels of motivation so performers have to be highly motivated to obtain reliable results. The trainer must ensure that the press-ups are carried out using the correct technique.

Table 1.10 Results of the one-minute press-up test – full body press-up

Age	Excellent	Good	Average	Fair	Poor
20–29	>54	45–54	35–44	20–34	<20
30–39	>44	35–44	25–34	15–24	<15
40–49	>39	30–39	20–29	12–19	<12
50–59	>34	25–34	15–24	8–14	<8
60+	>29	20–29	10–19	5–9	<5

Table 1.11 Results of the one-minute press-up test – adapted press-up position

Age	Excellent	Good	Average	Fair	Poor
20–29	>48	34–38	17–33	6–16	<6
30–39	>39	25–39	12–24	4–11	<4
40–49	>34	20–34	8–19	3–7	<3
50–59	>29	15–29	6–14	2–5	<2
60+	>19	5–19	3–4	1–2	<1

Test name	One-minute sit-up test
Equipment	Mat
	Stopwatch
Purpose	Test of muscular endurance of the abdominals
Protocol	The performer lies on the floor with their fingers on their temples and their knees bent.
	On the command of 'go', the performer sits up until their elbows touch their knees.
	They return to the start position with the back of their head touching the floor. This constitutes one repetition.
	The performer does as many sit-ups as they can in one minute.
Unit of measurement	Number of sit-ups per minute.
Advantages	Requires very little equipment.
	Large groups can be tested at the same time.
Disadvantages	Only tests for endurance of the abdominals.
	The test requires high levels of motivation so that the maximum number of repetitions is completed.
Validity	A full sit-up also uses the hip flexor muscles, so the muscular endurance of the hip flexor muscles is also tested.
Reliability	The test relies on high levels of motivation so individuals have to be highly motivated to obtain reliable results.

Table 1.12 Results of the one-minute sit-up test – Males

Age	Very poor	Poor	Fair	Good	Excellent	Superior
Under 20	<36	36–40	41–46	47–50	51–61	>61
20–29	<33	33–37	38–41	42–46	47–54	>54
30–39	<30	30–34	35–38	39–42	43–50	>50
40–49	<24	24–28	29–33	34–38	39–46	>46
50–59	<19	19–23	24–27	28–34	35–42	>42
60+	<15	15–18	19–21	22–29	30–38	>38

Table 1.13 Results of the one-minute sit-up test – Females

Age	Very poor	Poor	Fair	Good	Excellent	Superior
Under 20	<28	28–31	32–35	36–45	46–54	>54
20–29	<24	24–31	32–37	38–43	44–50	>50
30–39	<20	20–24	25–28	29–34	35–41	>41
40–49	<14	14–19	20–23	24–28	29–37	>37
50–59	<10	10–13	14–19	20–23	24–29	>29
60+	<3	3–5	6–10	11–16	17–27	>27

Body composition

Test name	Body mass index (BMI)
Equipment	Weighing scales Stadiometer
Purpose	To calculate whether a person is overweight.
Protocol	Ask the person to remove their shoes, then measure their standing height and record the measurement in metres. Again with shoes off and wearing only light clothing, weigh the person on weighing scales and record their weight in kilograms. To calculate the person's BMI, use the following equation: Weight (kg) ÷ (Height (m) x Height (m)) = BMI
Unit of measurement	kg/m^2
Advantages	Requires very little equipment. It is a quick and easy test to perform. The individual does not have to remove any clothing so it is less embarrassing than the skin fold test.
Disadvantages	This test can be used for the average adult. It cannot be used for pregnant women, children, very muscular athletes or people over the age of 60.
Validity	It does not take into account the actual body composition. A person may have a lot of muscle tissue and very little body fat but still gain a score of being overweight/fat on the BMI. The test does not measure body composition.
Reliability	As long as body weight and body height are measured correctly, the test is reliable.

You must know how to work out a person's BMI from their weight in kilograms and their height in metres. For example, Sam is 152 cm tall and weighs 56 kg. What is her BMI?

Answer: $56 ÷ 1.52^2 = 56 ÷ 2.31$ = BMI of 24

Always show your working out as you may get extra marks for this!

Table 1.14 BMI classifications

Classification	Obesity class	BMI (kg/m^2)
Underweight		18.5
Normal		18.5–24.9
Overweight		25–29.9
Obesity	I	30–34.9
Obesity	II	35–39.9

Test name	Bioelectrical impedance analysis (BIA)
Equipment	Bioelectrical impedance analysis analyser Bed or mat Alcohol pads Weighing scales Tape measure or other means of measuring height Detection electrode Current source electrode **Figure 1.19**
Purpose	Used to predict the percentage of body fat.
Protocol	Ask the performer to remove the shoe and sock on their right foot. Ask the performer to lie on a bed or mat and swab their right hand and right foot with an alcohol wipe. Place the electrodes of the BIA on their right hand and right foot and move their legs and arms away from their body. A very small electrical current is then passed through the body.
Unit of measurement	Percentage of body fat.
Advantages	The individual does not have to remove any clothing so the test is not as embarrassing as the skin fold test.
Disadvantages	The equipment is quite expensive. The individual must ensure they are well hydrated and have not consumed alcohol in the 48 hours prior to the test or taken part in high intensity exercise in the 12 hours prior to the test. A person with a pacemaker or a pregnant woman should not be tested.
Validity	It is not as accurate at the skin fold measurements. The scores are influenced by how well hydrated a person is – if a person is dehydrated, their percentage of body fat will be overestimated.
Reliability	The individual must be properly hydrated prior to the test and must follow all the pre-test guidelines to ensure the results are reliable.

This test works because fat-free tissue such as muscle and bone are good conductors of electrical current, whereas fat is not. The amount of resistance to the electrical current is related to the amount of fat-free tissue in the body and so can be used to estimate the percentage of body fat.

Table 1.15 Body fat percentages comparison table

Fat level	Very low	Low	Average	High	Very high
Males (%)	7–10	10–13	13–17	17–25	Above 25
Females (%)	14–17	17–20	20–27	27–31	Above 31

Test name	Skinfold testing using the Jackson-Pollock nomogram method
Equipment	Skinfold callipers 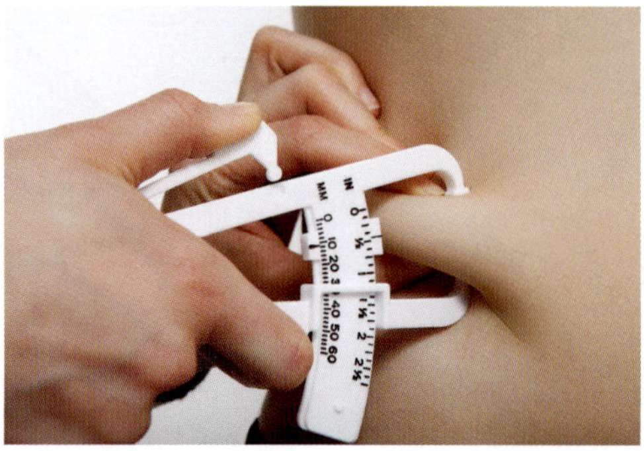 **Figure 1.20** Jackson-Pollock nomogram method of calculating percentage of body fat
Purpose	To predict percentage of body fat.
Protocol	Test sites for males: chest, abdomen and thigh. Test sites for females: triceps, suprailiac and thigh. Take the measurements on the right hand side of the body. Mark the client up accurately. Pinch the skin 1 cm above the marked site. Pull the fat away from the muscle. Place the callipers halfway between the top and bottom of the skinfold. Allow the callipers to settle for 1–2 seconds. Take the reading and wait 15 seconds before repeating for accuracy. Add up the total of the three measurements in mm. Plot the age of the individual and the sum of the three skinfolds (mm) on the nomogram. Use a ruler to join up the two plots – percentage body fat can be seen where the two lines cross over the percentage body fat lines to the closest 0.5%, according to gender (see Figure 1.21). 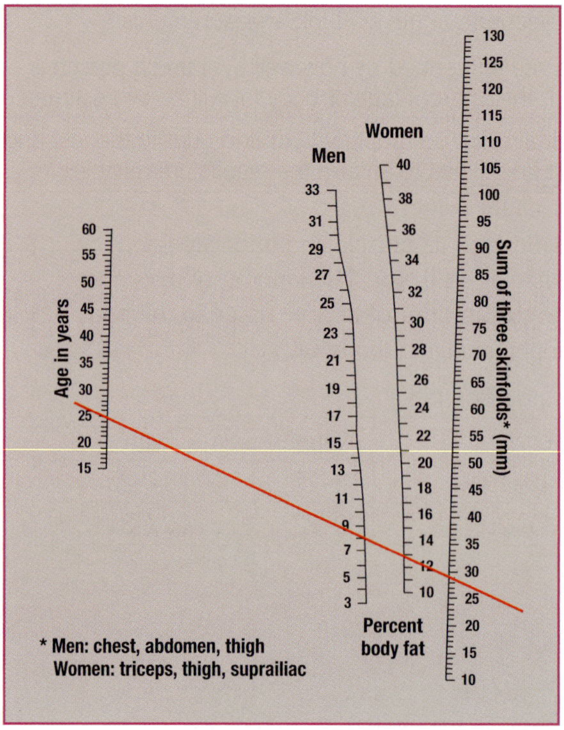 **Figure 1.21** An example of a Jackson-Pollock nomogram

Unit of measurement	Percentage of body fat
Advantages	It provides a good estimation of a person's body fat.
Disadvantages	The person being tested has to remove or adjust their clothing and have parts of their body 'pinched' by the test, which can be embarrassing.
Validity	This is one of the most valid tests for estimating body fat percentage.
Reliability	The body parts must be tested in the same places in order to get reliable results. This relies to some extent on the skill of the trainer to identify the correct sites.

Table 1.16 Comparison table of body fat percentages calculated using the Jackson-Pollock nomogram method

Results (16–29 years)	Males	Females
Very low fat	<7	<13
Slim	7–12	13–20
Ideal	13–17	21–25
Overweight	18–28	26–32
Obese	29+	33+

Summary of fitness tests

Studied ☐

Table 1.17

Component of fitness	Fitness test
Flexibility	Sit and reach
Strength	Grip dynamometer
Aerobic endurance	Multi-stage fitness test
	Forestry step test
Speed	35 m sprint
Speed and agility	Illinois agility run test
Anaerobic power	Vertical jump test
Muscular endurance	One-minute press-up test
	One-minute sit up test
Body composition	Body mass index
	Bioelectrical impedance analysis
	Skinfold testing – Jackson-Pollock nomogram method

Topic C.2 Importance of fitness testing to sports performers and coaches

Fitness tests are used by sports performers and coaches to give baseline data for monitoring/improving performance. Fitness tests are taken regularly to monitor if a training programme is producing the desired results. Training programmes can be changed or modified depending on the results from the fitness tests. The results can also give a performer something to aim for and help them with setting goals, for example, they may want to achieve level 15 on the multi-stage fitness test in their next fitness test.

Topic C.3 Requirements for administration of each fitness test

Pre-test procedures

Studied ☐

When testing sports performers it is important that the tests are safe and that the test conditions are consistent and stable.

The sports performer must:

- have medical clearance for any health conditions
- be free of injuries
- wear appropriate clothing
- avoid eating a heavy meal three hours before the test
- ensure they have had a good night's sleep
- avoid training on the day of the test and be fully recovered from previous training
- avoid stimulants such as tea, coffee or nicotine for two hours before the test.

The area where the tests are performed should be:

- at room temperature (around 18 degrees)
- well ventilated
- clean and dust-free.

Medical referral

Studied ☐

A sports performer should not be tested and should be referred to a doctor if they are experiencing any of the following:

- muscle injuries
- chest pain or tightness
- light-headedness or dizziness
- irregular or rapid pulse

- joint pain
- headaches
- shortness of breath.

Safety of the sports performer is of the utmost importance and although it is valuable to get good results, this must not be at the cost of the performer's health. It is also important to check that the sports performer does not experience any of the above symptoms after the test has been conducted.

Informed consent

Studied ☐

An informed consent form makes the sports performer aware of what is involved in the exercise testing and any risks there may be. Once they are aware they can then give their agreement or consent to undertake the tests and the risks which are involved. An informed consent form provides documented evidence that the sports performer has been given all the necessary information to undertake the test.

The informed consent form confirms that the individual:

- understands the test method
- knows exactly what is required of them during testing
- has fully consented to their participation in the fitness test
- knows that they are able to ask any questions relating to the test
- understands that they can withdraw their consent at any time.

The consent form should be signed and dated by the sports performer, the tester and by a tutor if you are performing the tests at school/college. If the participant is under 18 years of age a parent or guardian will also be required to give their consent to the participation.

Calibration of equipment

Studied ☐

Calibration is the process of checking (and if necessary adjusting) the accuracy of fitness testing equipment before it is used, by comparing it to a recognised standard. Testing equipment must always be carefully checked before use. If equipment isn't correctly calibrated it could lead to inaccurate (invalid) results.

Topic C.4 Interpretation of fitness test results

For your external assessment you must be able to interpret sets of results from fitness tests.

You will need to compare fitness test results to normative published data. This means you will need to be able to find a person's score on the fitness table and find out what that score means – average, good, poor – compared to other people.

You will also compare one set of fitness test results to another.

You must be able to draw conclusions from sets of results, for example, did the results show the need to improve some components of fitness?

You must be able to analyse and evaluate test results. This means you will need to explain why the results were what they were. For example, if you take part in lots of flexibility exercises such as yoga then you will probably get a high score on the sit and reach test.

You will need to be able to suggest and justify appropriate recommendations for improvements to fitness for a given purpose/situation/participant. You will need to be able to compare the fitness test results to the normative data and work out which components of fitness need to be improved upon in comparison to the other fitness test results. For example, if there are high scores in aerobic endurance, speed and power, but very low scores in flexibility, the flexibility training will need to be improved because having low levels of flexibility can lead to muscle strains, etc.

You also need to be able to suggest and justify appropriate fitness training methods that could be used for a given purpose/situation/participant.

Check your understanding

Consider the components of fitness required for the sport that you take part in or a sport that you enjoy watching and answer the following questions.

1. Which fitness tests would be suitable to measure the components of fitness required for this sport?
2. What equipment would you need for each of these tests?
3. Explain how reliable and valid each of these tests are.

Real world connections

Harry has always enjoyed sports and studied BTEC National Sport at college. He decided that he wanted to coach football and took a number of coaching qualifications to help him to become the assistant coach for of a semi-professional football team. His role involves helping the team to improve their playing ability, which includes not only developing their football skills and techniques but also their fitness so that the whole team is able to play to the best of their ability for the duration of the match. While most matches last 90 minutes, the aerobic endurance of the team is really challenged when they go into extra time, so Harry has made sure that continuous exercise training methods are incorporated into the team's training programme, as well as the other physical fitness and skill-related components of fitness required for football. Harry knows that the fitness of the team is important to reduce the risk of injury due to such factors as lack of flexibility or muscle imbalances.

Summary

In this section we looked at different fitness testing methods, why fitness testing is important to sports performers and coaches and the requirements for the administration of each type of fitness test. The key learning points include:

- tests are used to establish fitness levels, including those that measure flexibility (sit and reach test), strength (grip dynamometer), aerobic endurance (multi-stage fitness test), speed (sprint test), speed and agility (Illinois agility run test), anaerobic power (vertical jump test), muscular endurance (press-ups and sit-ups) and body composition (body mass index, bioelectrical impedance analysis and skinfold testing)
- fitness testing is important because it gives baseline data for monitoring and improving a sports performer's performance and the results can be used to design training programmes
- before a fitness test can be carried out you must make sure the participant understands what is involved in the test so that they can give their informed consent and equipment must be calibrated to ensure its accuracy
- the results of fitness tests must be accurately measured and recorded in the appropriate units so that they can be interpreted accurately and compared to published data tables as well as the results of the sports performer's peers.

Complete the table to check your knowledge of the tests for the different components of fitness and their advantages and disadvantages. The first row has been completed for you.

Component of fitness	Possible test for the component of fitness	Strengths of the test	Weaknesses of the test
Flexibility	Sit and reach test. The performer sits with their feet against a board and legs straight. They slowly bend forwards to see how far they can reach.	Easy to use and does not require expensive equipment. Easy to explain and for the participant to perform. Safe test that gives quick results.	The score only measures flexibility in the back, hamstrings and calves. It cannot be used to identify the range of movement in one specific area or any other joint/ muscle in the body. It gives a general measure of flexibility but lacks specificity.
Strength			
Aerobic endurance			
Speed			
Anaerobic endurance			
Muscular endurance			
Body composition			
Agility			

Unit 2

Practical Sports Performance

Participation in sport continues to grow as people are inspired by the performances of the 2012 British Olympians and Paralympians and they see the fun and enjoyment of playing sport. There are many opportunities for playing sport in Britain and most people understand the health benefits that physical activity brings. This unit focuses on increasing your understanding of how sports are played and officiated and also the development and improvement of your own performance in sports.

Learning aims

By the end of this unit you will:

- ✓ understand the rules, regulations and scoring systems for selected sports
- ✓ practically demonstrate skills, techniques and tactics in selected sports
- ✓ be able to review sports performance.

Assessment criteria

Assessment and grading criteria		
To achieve a **PASS** grade the evidence must show that the learner is able to:	To achieve a **MERIT** grade the evidence must show that the learner is able to:	To achieve a **DISTINCTION** grade the evidence must show that the learner is able to:
P1 Describe the rules, regulations and scoring systems of two selected sports	**M1** For each of two selected sports, explain the role and responsibilities of officials and the application of rules, regulations and scoring systems	**D1** Compare and contrast the roles and responsibilities of officials from two selected sports, suggesting valid recommendations for improvement to the application of rules, regulations and scoring systems for each sport
P2 Apply the rules of a selected sport in four specific situations		
P3 Describe the roles and responsibilities of officials from two selected sports		
P4 Describe the technical and tactical demands of two selected sports		
P5 Use relevant skills, techniques and tactics effectively, in two selected sports, in conditioned practices	**M2** Use relevant skills, techniques and tactics effectively, in two selected sports, in competitive situations	
P6 Independently produce an observation checklist that can be used effectively to review own performance in two selected sports		
P7 Review own performance in two selected sports, describing strengths and areas for improvement	**M3** Explain strengths and areas for improvement in two selected sports, recommending activities to improve own performance	**D2** Analyse strengths and areas for improvement in two selected sports, justifying recommended activities to improve own performance

Learning aim A: Understand the rules, regulations and scoring systems for selected sports

Topic A.1 Rules (or laws)

The **rules** of a sport, or laws as they are called in some sports, like football and cricket, are a set of agreed standards that ensure that a sport is played the same way by everyone. The rules of a sport are agreed and controlled by international sports federations (ISFs) and national governing bodies (NGBs). The following are some examples of international sports federations:

- FIFA – Fédération Internationale de Football Association
- ITF – International Tennis Federation
- BWF – Badminton World Federation

These federations have agreed the rules of their sport and review them regularly, making changes if necessary. National governing bodies are local to each country and they ensure that the rules are implemented at all levels of the sport. They are also responsible for training officials to uphold the rules in competitions.

> **Key term**
>
> The **rules** of a sport are the agreed standards that have been set by a national or international governing body for the sport. Rules ensure that everyone taking part in a sport plays the same way.

Topic A.2 Regulations

Regulations relate to specific aspects of the rules or laws and are concerned with how the rule should be implemented. For example, there are regulations regarding what can and cannot be worn in relation to clothing, jewellery and studded boots or spiked running shoes. In swimming, high-tech swimsuits were banned in 2010 and running tracks have regulations on the length and shape of track spikes. Most sports have regulations regarding banned substances and have testing procedures to ensure athletes do not use such substances. Other regulations will relate to equipment used, playing surface, facilities, time, health and safety and the officials involved in the sport, such as the referee, umpire, judge, starter or timekeeper.

> **Key term**
>
> **Regulations** – particular aspects of rules and how a rule should be implemented.

Topic A.3 Scoring systems

Every sport has a method of recording points and being able to judge a winner. These methods range from very simple methods, such as scoring goals, to the very complex where there are different numbers of points for different methods of scoring, as in rugby union and basketball, for example.

Hockey, football, handball and netball all award one point for each goal scored and the winner is the team with the most goals. Badminton and table tennis award one point for each play won, with the winner being decided as the first player to a set number of points. Athletics and swimming races are decided by the fastest times.

In cricket the team with the most runs wins but there are different numbers of runs awarded and a player can be awarded a four if they hit the ball to the boundary or a six if they hit the ball over the boundary.

The most complex **scoring systems** are found in sports where judges decide who will be the winner. For example, gymnastics, figure skating and diving have judges that award points when they see different skills being performed and the quality of the skill being performed.

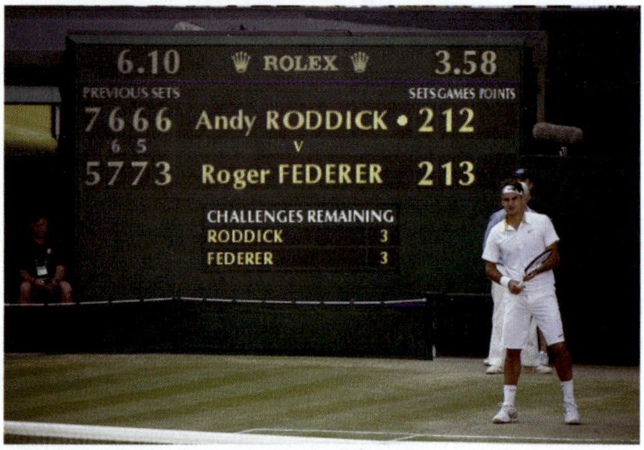

Figure 2.1 Tennis uses a complex scoring system

> **Key term**
>
> **Scoring system** – the method of recording points in order to judge a winner.

Topic A.6 Roles of officials

The role of the **officials** in sport is to ensure that all participants play to the rules of the sport and that play is fair. They are called different names in different sports, such as referee, umpire or judge and they are often assisted by timekeepers, scorers, referee's assistants, line judges and third or fourth officials. Officials often work in teams, such as in tennis, where the chair umpire is assisted by line judges and a video referee (at televised tournaments).

Officials will implement the rules of a sport and will take disciplinary action against any player who breaks the rules. The penalties available to officials differ between sports and they range from being cautioned, warned, sent off, sin binned or banned from future matches.

> **Key term**
>
> **Sport officials** – make sure participants play fairly and in accordance with the rules of the sport. They are responsible for checking the sport meets the needs of health and safety and make decisions as to whether a goal or point should be awarded.

Topic A.7 Responsibilities of officials

The officials are responsible for implementing the rules of the sport and for ensuring fair play and the health and safety of all players. They ensure the sport meets health and safety requirements by checking the playing surfaces, equipment and the players' footwear and clothing. Increasingly technology is being made available to assist officials with their decision making. A video referee is used in rugby to decide whether a try should be awarded and umpires' decisions in cricket can be checked by a third official who also deals with player referrals.

Figure 2.2 Officials have to control players and implement the rules

Officials have agreed methods of communicating with each other and use whistles, flags and hand signals to pass information between themselves, particularly when there is a distance between the officials. Some officials are able to use their voices to convey information but it is often combined with hand signals so that the other officials, players and crowd know the decision that they have made.

Officials have a responsibility to ensure they are equipped to fulfil their role effectively, by having the correct qualifications, being dressed appropriately and having the required level of fitness.

Check your understanding

1. Fill in the blank spaces in the following sentences:
   a. The rules of sport are a set of _____ _____ to ensure a sport is played _____.
   b. The rules of a sport are set down by _____ _____ _____.
2. Place a tick in the appropriate column to decide whether the following sports have simple or complex scoring systems.

Sport	Simple scoring system	Complex scoring system
Tennis		
Swimming		
Synchronised swimming		
Hockey		
Golf		

3. Name three officials who may assist the main official in a sport of your choice.
4. Give three methods officials use to convey information.

Real world connection

Lisa is a coach of an Under-13 girls' football team. She became involved in coaching when she was at college, having played football for eight years. When Lisa played football she learnt about the rules and regulations of football so that she could play the game fairly. When she started coaching she found that she often had to take on the role of a referee or referee's assistant and this meant that she needed a thorough knowledge of the rules and regulations of the game as well as the roles and responsibilities of the officials. As a referee, Lisa found that there were occasions when she did not know exactly what to do and this made her lose the respect of the players she was officiating. Her players often ask her advice about the rules and she has to give them clear answers to ensure that they abide by the rules.

Figure 2.3

Summary

In this section we looked at the rules and regulations of sport, scoring systems in sports and the roles and responsibilities of officials. The key learning points include:

- the rules/laws of a sport are a set of agreed standards that ensure that everyone plays the sport in the same way
- the rules of a sport are agreed and controlled by international sports federations and national governing bodies
- regulations relate to specific aspects of the rules/laws of a sport and how they should be implemented
- the scoring system in a sport is the method of recording points to enable a winner to be decided
- sports such as football and hockey have simple scoring systems while diving and rugby have complex scoring systems
- the role of the officials in sport is to ensure that all participants play to the rules of sport and that play is fair
- officials may be called referees, judges or umpires and they are assisted by line judges, scorers and timekeepers
- officials are able to punish players for breaking the rules by using a penalty such as a caution, sending off or ban
- officials are responsible for ensuring fair play and the health and safety of players
- officials communicate with each other using their voice, whistles, hand signals and flags.

Activities

Activity A.1

Tested

Part 1

Rules and regulations in sport

Research the rules and regulations of two sports of your choice and then produce a document that summarises the main rules for each sport for a beginner. The rules should give the beginner enough information to start playing the sport.

Part 2

Scoring systems

Produce a further document that explains the scoring systems that operate in each of the two sports you have chosen.

Part 3

Applying rules and regulations

For *one* of your chosen sports, think of four situations and describe how the laws/rules of the sport are applied in each of the situations.

Activity A.2

Tested

For each of your chosen sports, research the roles and responsibilities of officials and present the information in table below. An example is provided.

Name of official and chosen sport	Description of role	Responsibilities
e.g. Line judge (Tennis)	Decide whether a ball is in or out of play	Watch the line on service and any subsequent shots. Call out when the ball is out and use hand signal to indicate decision.

Learning aim B: Practically demonstrate skills, techniques and tactics in selected sports

Topic B.1 Technical demands

Every sport is made up of different skills and techniques and these are described as the **technical demands** of that sport. Skills are the different aspects of a sport that you need to learn and practise to enable you to play the sport well. The skills of a sport vary depending upon its demands. For example, to play basketball you need to learn the following skills:

- Passing: moving the ball to another teammate
- Receiving: being able to receive the ball at different heights and different speeds from another teammate
- Shooting: aiming at the basket and then propelling it in the right direction, at the right speed
- Dribbling: moving with the ball at speed in close contact to your body
- Intercepting: anticipating where the ball is going to be thrown and then moving into that space before your opponent.

Techniques refer to how well particular skills are undertaken or played. A basketball player who is able to pass well or shoot well is said to have 'good technique' in those skills.

Key terms

Technical demands – the different skills and techniques required to play the sport.

Techniques – how skills are undertaken or played.

Continuous, serial and discrete skills

`Studied ☐`

Skills are classified in relation to how clear it is to identify the start and finish points of a movement.

A **continuous skill** is one which has no clear start or finish as the end of one cycle automatically becomes the start of the next. This is the case in skills such as running and cycling and these skills tend to be rhythmical or continuous in nature.

A **discrete skill** is one which has a clear start and a clear finish and once performed, the athlete will move onto another skill. For example, tennis is made up of discrete skills such as the serve, followed by a forehand, backhand, volley or lob. Cricket shots also involve discrete skills.

Figure 2.4 Cycling is a continuous skill

Key terms

Continuous skills – those that are continuous in nature and have no clear start or finish, such as cycling or running.

Discrete skills – have a clear beginning and end and the athlete will move onto another skill once they have performed the skill.

A **serial skill** is one which is made up of several components or parts. A good example of a serial skill is the triple jump, which is made up of three parts – the hop, the skip and the jump (see Figure 2.6). We could add the run up and the landing as extra parts. A gymnastics floor routine is another good example of a serial skill made up of several parts.

Figure 2.5 Cricket shots are examples of discrete skills

Figure 2.6 Triple jump is a serial skill

Topic B.2 Tactical demands

The **tactical demands** of a sport are the different ways that a sport can be played to increase the chances of winning. They include all the methods that can be used to gain an advantage over your opponent, including defending and attacking, choice and use of shots or strokes, use of the available space, etc. Playing tactically often means playing to your strengths or finding out and exploiting your opponent's weaknesses.

In tennis, for example, you can use attacking or defensive tactics to beat your opponent. Attacking tactics means you find opportunities to get into position where you can play winning shots; defensive tactics means you keep trying to get into positions to return the ball and wait for your opponent to make a mistake. Another tennis tactic is to place the ball on your opponent's weaker side or make them play their weaker shots. Another tactic is to get an opponent who is short on stamina to run about, remaining patient until they become tired and make mistakes.

Key terms

Serial skills – consist of a number of separate components or parts, such as a dance routine.

Tactical demands – the methods a sports performer can use to increase their chances of winning against an opponent.

Topics B.8 and B.9 Isolated and conditioned practices

Skills and techniques can be practised under different conditions. **Isolated practices** are where you take a particular skill out of a sport and practise it outside of a game situation. For example, a basketball player may practise their shooting from different positions or a tennis player may spend time practising volleys at the net.

Conditioned practices occur when a sport is changed to enable the players to focus on practising specific skills or certain tactics. For example, in football small-sided games can be used to practise passing and moving and cricket practices can be set up to only allow players to play certain shots.

Competitive situations are when the sport is played in its full form against opponents under competitive conditions with officials.

Key terms

Isolated practices – involve taking specific skills out of a sport and practising them on their own, rather than as part of a game.

Conditioned practices – involve changing a sport to allow the performers to focus on specific skills and tactics.

Key term

Competitive situations – involve playing a full-sided game against an opposition and with match officials overseeing the game.

Check your understanding

1. Fill in the blank spaces in the following sentences:
   a. Skills are different aspects of a sport that you need to _____ and _____ .
   b. A player with good technique would perform _____ _____ .
2. Classify the skills shown in the table below as discrete, continuous or serial.

Skill	Discrete	Continuous	Serial
Skipping			
Ice dance routine			
Throw-in			
10 m dive			
Rowing			
High jump			

3. What is the aim of using tactics?
4. Match the terms shown below to their appropriate description.

Terms	Description
Isolated practices	A sport is played in its full form against opponents
Conditioned practices	A skill is taken out of a sport and practised separately
Competitive situations	A sport is changed to enable players to practise certain skills or tactics

Summary

In this section we looked at the technical and tactical demands of sport and the different types of skills and practices in sport. The key learning points include:

- sports are made up of different skills and techniques which are referred to as their technical demands
- skills are the different aspects of a sport that need to be learned and practised
- techniques are how particular skills are played
- a continuous skill is one which has no clear start or finish as the end of one cycle automatically becomes the start of the next
- a discrete skill is one which has a clear start and a clear finish
- a serial skill is one which is made up of several components or parts
- the tactical demands of a sport are the different ways that a sport can be played to increase the chances of winning
- isolated practices are where you take a skill out of a sport and practise it outside of a game situation
- conditioned practices are where a sport is changed to enable the players to focus on practising specific skills or certain tactics
- competitive situations are when the sport is played competitively, in its full form, with officials.

Part 1

Skills/techniques and tactics

For two sports of your choice, identify and describe six skills/techniques and six tactics that are needed for success in each sport.

Part 2

Recording skills/techniques and tactics

Use the templates below to prepare a logbook to record the skills/techniques and tactics you used during five practical sport sessions.

Skill/technique	Session 1 Conditioned or competitive	Session 2 Conditioned or competitive	Session 3 Conditioned or competitive	Session 4 Conditioned or competitive	Session 5 Conditioned or competitive
1.					
2.					
3.					
4.					
5.					
6.					

Tactic	Session 1 Conditioned or competitive	Session 2 Conditioned or competitive	Session 3 Conditioned or competitive	Session 4 Conditioned or competitive	Session 5 Conditioned or competitive
1.					
2.					
3.					
4.					
5.					
6.					

Improving and reviewing performance

All sports performers should aim to continually improve their skills and techniques so that they can advance their performance. The alternative is to continue to perform the same skills in the same way and to obtain the same results. To make improvements performance must be constantly reviewed. This is done by gaining as much information as possible about the performance using different sources of information. The main aims of reviewing performance are to:

- establish current levels of competence
- identify what the sports performer is doing well (areas of strength)
- identify what the sports performer is doing badly (areas for improvement).

A review of performance must contain as much information as possible. Performance in sport can be broken down into the following categories:

- sport-specific skills
- sport-specific techniques
- tactical demands of the sport
- fitness demands of the sport.

An analysis may also include psychological skills, such as the ability to relax under pressure and maintain concentration.

Collecting feedback on performance

Studied ☐

You will need to collect information on performance and a good place to begin is by recording information gained from your own participation in sport, including information on:

- whether you were successful or not
- the final score or outcome achieved
- how it felt to perform the skills
- your thoughts on what went well and what went less well.

This information can be backed up by recording your performance using a video recorder. This is valuable because when you are performing you are often concentrating so hard that you are not thinking about what you are doing well or poorly. Watching and re-watching video footage enables you to analyse each part of your performance and to work out information such as how many passes you made, how many were completed successfully and how many led to attacking situations.

You can also include the views and opinions of other people in your review as they can provide important information, too. Such people include:

- your coach/teacher
- your teammates
- other participants (opponents)
- observers.

If you do include other people in your review you must let them express their opinions honestly. You also need to accept any negative comments they may make as they are telling you so that you can improve.

Topic C.1 Observation checklist

The **observation checklist** contains a list of categories that you can use for self-analysis. The checklist must contain details of the technical and tactical demands of your sport and record information about the quantity and quality of performance. See Table 2.1 below for an example of a checklist for a hockey player.

Once you have recorded your performance you can watch the video footage and then perform your review.

Table 2.1 Observation checklist for a hockey player

Skill/technique	Successful	Unsuccessful	Percentage successful	Score /10
Long passing				
Short passing				
Shooting from close range				
Shooting from long distance				
Crossing				
Tackling				
Tactic	Successful	Unsuccessful	Percentage successful	Score /10
Finding space				
Pressuring opponent				

> ## Key term
>
> **Observation checklist** – used to record information about the skills/ techniques and tactics you use when playing a sport.

Topic C.2 Review performance

Once you have completed your review you will have gained a lot of information that you will need to analyse in order to include it in your **performance review**. As you analyse your information, decide whether each skill/technique and tactic is an area of strength or an area for improvement. You can then focus on the areas for improvement. With practice, your strengths will remain your strengths but it is the areas for improvement that are of most importance.

In order to address your areas for improvement you need to:

- set short- and long-term goals
- develop activities to improve your performance.

These two activities are closely linked. For example, if your long-term goal is to improve your long-range passes, this can be stated as improving your success rate for long-range passing to 75% (it is currently 60%). An example of a short-term goal would be to undertake activities to improve passing by completing three sessions per week practising long-range passing. Other activities to improve performance could be having extra coaching, designing a new training programme or attending a course.

> ## Key term
>
> **Performance review** – involves analysing your sports performance and deciding whether each skill/technique and tactic is an area of strength or an area for improvement.

Check your understanding

1. Give three reasons why you need to review performance.
2. Give three pieces of information that could be gained from a review of performance.
3. Fill in the missing words in the paragraph using the words shown below.

analyse	teammates	successful	perform	coach	feedback	video

There are many sources of _____ about performance, including information about whether you were _____ or not and how it felt to _____ skills. _____ footage enables you to _____ your performance more deeply. Information can also be gained by talking to your _____ and _____.

4. Once you have completed your review, what two things should you do to address areas for improvement?

Summary

In this section we looked at why it is important to review performance, sources of information on performance and how to construct an observation checklist. The key learning points include:

- reviewing performance will help you make improvements
- performance is reviewed by gaining as much information as possible using different sources of information
- the aims of reviewing performance are to establish current levels of competence, identify what is being done well and what is being done less well
- performance in sport can be broken down into sport-specific skills, sport-specific techniques, tactical demands of the sport and fitness demands of the sport
- the observation checklist includes categories for the technical and tactical demands of the sport and is used to record information about the quantity and quality of performance
- when analysing information from your review, decide whether each skill/technique and tactic is an area of strength or an area for improvement
- once you have identified areas for improvement you can set short- and long-term goals and develop activities to improve your performance.

Activity

Part 1

Reviewing performance

Design an observation checklist you can complete to review your performance in two sports.

Part 2

Use a video camera to record your performance in two sports, then use the checklists you created in Part 1 above to review your performance and describe your areas of strength and areas for improvement.

UNIT 2 Practical Sports Performance

Unit 2 Model assignment

This assignment will assess the following learning aims:

A understand the rules, regulations and scoring systems for selected sports

B practically demonstrate skills, techniques and tactics in sport

C be able to review sports performance.

Scenario

You are hoping to secure a holiday job working as a coach at a sports camp for 8–13-year-olds. As part of the application process you need to be able to show to your potential employer that you have both knowledge of selected sports and expertise in performing and officiating selected sports. You have been asked to complete a series of tasks to demonstrate your skills and knowledge of two sports.

Task I

Create a handbook that describes the roles and responsibilities of officials in two sports and describes the rules, regulations and scoring systems in your two selected sports. You need to explain the roles and responsibilities of officials and the application of rules, regulations and scoring systems. You also need to compare and contrast the roles and responsibilities of officials for two selected sports and make valid recommendations for the improvement of the application of the rules, regulations and scoring system for each sport.

Present observation records, witness statements or video evidence to show that you have been able to apply the rules in a selected sport in four different situations.

Task 2

Produce an A3 sized poster describing the technical and tactical demands of two selected sports.

Present observation records, witness statements or video evidence to demonstrate that you are able to use effectively relevant skills, techniques and tactics in two selected sports in conditioned practice. You need to demonstrate these relevant skills, techniques and tactics in two selected sports in competitive situations.

Task 3

Using your knowledge of effective performance in two sports, independently produce a checklist that can be used to review your own performance in each of the sports.

Use your checklist to review your performance and describe your strengths and areas for improvements in each of your two selected sports. You need to explain your strengths and areas for improvement in your two selected sports and recommend activities that you can do to improve your own performance. You also need to analyse your strengths and areas for improvement in your two selected sports and justify the activities you have recommended to improve your own performance.

Unit 3

The Mind and Sports Performance

Although the study of sport examines all the factors that influence performance, it has traditionally focused on the physical requirements for sports performance. However, at all levels of sport it has now been recognised that being the fittest or most talented is not enough; control over the mind and thoughts is also necessary for success. This unit examines the mind and sports performance through an exploration of subjects such as personality, motivation, self-confidence and anxiety control.

Learning aims

By the end of this unit you will:

✓ investigate personality and its effect on sports performance

✓ explore the influence that motivation and self-confidence have on sports performance

✓ know about arousal and anxiety, and the effects they have on sports performance.

Assessment criteria

Assessment and grading criteria

To achieve a **PASS** grade the evidence must show that the learner is able to:	To achieve a **MERIT** grade the evidence must show that the learner is able to:	To achieve a **DISTINCTION** grade the evidence must show that the learner is able to:
P1 Using relevant examples, describe personality, including methods of measurement and three different views	**M1** Explain three different views of personality, and how personality can affect sports performance	**D1** Analyse three different views of personality, and how personality can affect sports performance
P2 Describe types and views of motivation and the benefits motivation and self-confidence have on sports performance	**M2** Discuss the benefits motivation and self-confidence have on sports performance	**D2** Analyse the benefits motivation and self-confidence have on sports performance
P3 Summarise, with relevant examples, methods to increase self-confidence in sport		
P4 Describe, using relevant examples, factors that influence self-efficacy in sport		
P5 Describe goal setting, different types of goals that can be set, and how these can influence sports performance and motivation	**M3** Discuss how goal setting can influence motivation and the roles of the different types of goals that can be set	
P6 Describe, using relevant examples, different types of anxiety	**M4** Assess, using four theories, the effect arousal and anxiety have on sports performance and their control	**D3** Evaluate imagery and relaxation techniques as methods of controlling arousal and anxiety, and in improving sports performance
P7 Describe, using four theories, the effect arousal and anxiety have on sports performance and their control		

Learning aim A: Investigate personality and its effect on sports performance

Topic A.1 Definition of personality

In sport we see performers with different personalities, for example, Mo Farah or Bradley Wiggins, and if we wanted to describe their personalities we would use labels to describe them. We might say that Mo Farah is quiet, confident and driven, while Wiggins is outgoing, calm and optimistic. We are able to make distinctions between the personalities of these two athletes and if you compared your personality to them, you would probably find that you had some personality traits (characteristics) that were similar to them and some that were different.

This uniqueness of personality is something that psychologists agree upon and an accepted definition of personality is:

> *'Personality is the sum of the characteristics that make a person unique.'*
>
> (Weinberg and Gould, 2007:28)

Characteristics, also known as personality traits, refer to the relatively consistent way that people behave or the labels that we give people. We can only say relatively consistent because people do not always behave in the same way. For example, an outgoing person may have times when they like to be quiet and have time on their own. One way to understand personality better is to look at its structure or its layers.

Topic A.2 Structure of personality

Rainer Martens (1975) saw personality as having three different depths or layers, as shown in Figure 3.1.

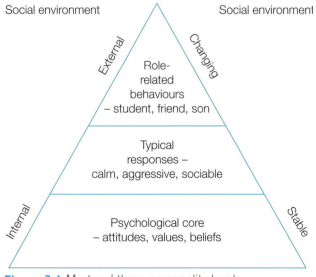

Figure 3.1 Martens' three personality levels

61

- Level 1: this is the psychological core. It is the deepest part of our personality and is described as 'the real us'. It includes our feelings, attitudes and values and we show it to very few people except those closest to us.
- Level 2: these are the typical responses that we show and are the traits that describe how we usually behave and respond to situations. Typical responses would be the labels 'happy', 'outgoing' or 'quiet' that we use to describe people.
- Level 3: these are our role-related behaviours and they are the shallowest part of our personality. They explain how we change our behaviour depending on the situation that we find ourselves in – the 'roles' that we play each day. For example, throughout the day we may play the role of student, friend or sportsperson, and we change our behaviour slightly to adapt to each situation. It could explain why some people may be quiet in the classroom but loud and lively on the sports field. We change our behaviour to fit into the situation we find ourselves in.

Topic A.3 Personality types

Introverts versus extroverts

Research into personality has tried to categorise people into **personality** types so that they can see how they behave when playing sport and whether certain personality types are more successful than others. One method has been to use the terms '**introvert**' and '**extrovert**' to describe people.

An introvert is someone who is usually shy, quiet and inward looking. Introverts are not always comfortable in social situations and prefer to spend time in their own company. They often prefer to do things alone, such as reading or listening to music.

An extrovert is usually someone who is outgoing and who enjoys talking and mixing with other people. Extroverts often enjoy social situations and prefer to be doing things with other people. They tend not to like to spend much time on their own and get bored easily.

Since sport offers opportunities to participate alone or as part of a team, both introverts and extroverts will find a sport to match their personality type. Extroverts are usually suited to team sports as they are involved with other people and they often enjoy the excitement and thrills of competition. Introverts often enjoy sports where they spend long periods on their own and they do not necessarily need to be involved with other people. Introverts are often attracted to sports such as long distance running, cycling or swimming, whereas extroverts enjoy team sports such as football, rugby, hockey or basketball.

Key terms

Personality – defined as the sum of the characteristics that make a person unique.

Introvert – someone who is shy, quiet and inward looking.

Extrovert – someone who is outgoing, and likes talking and mixing with people.

Type A versus type B personalities

Type A and **type B** personalities were developed as opposites. Type A people are competitive and driven to succeed, whereas type B personalities are calm and laid back. Type A personalities often have a quick temper and get angry easily. Due to their nature, they are prone to developing stress-related illnesses and heart disease in later life. One way of assessing whether an individual is a type A or a type B personality is to ask them to complete a personality questionnaire. An example of such a questionnaire is shown below.

Key terms

Type A personality – these people tend to show a competitive drive and are prone to anger and hostility.

Type B personality – these people are generally laid back and of a calm disposition.

Table 3.1 Example of a personality questionnaire

Statement	Score	Statement
I don't mind leaving things temporarily unfinished	1 2 3 4 5 6 7	I must get things finished once started
I am calm and unhurried about appointments	1 2 3 4 5 6 7	I'm often impatient and never late for appointments
I am not very competitive	1 2 3 4 5 6 7	I am highly competitive
I listen well and let others finish before I speak	1 2 3 4 5 6 7	I tend to anticipate others in conversation and interrupt by finishing their sentences

I don't often feel hurried	1 2 3 4 5 6 7	I'm always in a hurry
I am able to wait calmly	1 2 3 4 5 6 7	I feel uneasy when I have to wait for something
I am happy to take one thing at a time	1 2 3 4 5 6 7	I am always trying to do more than one thing at a time
I tend to speak calmly and deliberately	1 2 3 4 5 6 7	I tend to speak fast and forcefully and use a lot of gestures

Type A personalities would achieve scores in the range 5–7 for each question while type B personalities would score in the range 1–3.

Personality and sports performance

Studied

There are problems in researching personality and how it affects sports performance, as it is difficult to compare the traits of an athlete and a non-athlete. Much of the research in this area is quite old, but research by Schurr, Ashley and Joy (1977) found that there were differences between athletes and non-athletes. Athletes were found to be more outgoing/extroverted, more dependent on other people and less anxious. The same study also found that team athletes were more group dependent, extroverted and anxious than individual sport athletes.

Topic A.4 Methods of measuring personality

Psychologists have attempted to measure personality because it can influence a person's choice of sport and their performance in sport. Two ways of measuring personality are **Eysenck's Personality Inventory** (EPI) and **Profile of Mood States** (POMS).

Figure 3.2a and b Athletes tend to be more extroverted than non-athletes

Key terms

Eysenck's Personality Inventory (EPI) – uses a series of yes/no questions to decide an individual's personality.

Profile of Mood States (POMS) – links mood to sports performance and uses questions relating to mood states to help an individual describe how they feel.

Eysenck's Personality Inventory

Studied ▢

EPI uses a series of yes/no questions to establish whether a person is an introvert or an extrovert and whether they are stable (not affected by feelings) or unstable (affected by feelings). There are 33 questions such as 'Can you let yourself go and enjoy a lively party?' and 'Are you usually quiet and shy when with other people?' Depending on the responses to the questions, Eysenck could then place the person in one of four quarters, as shown below.

Table 3.2 Eysenck's Personality Inventory

Stable introvert	Unstable introvert
Calm, even-tempered, reliable	Anxious, pessimistic, reserved
Stable extrovert	**Unstable extrovert**
Sociable, outgoing, lively, good leader	Touchy, restless, excitable, aggressive

Profile of Mood States (POMS)

Studied ▢

POMS links mood to sports performance and uses a list of mood states to enable people to describe how they feel. An example of a POMS question is shown below:

The following is a list of words describing feelings people have. Using the scale shown below the question, indicate how you are feeling today:

Energetic =

Tense =

Fatigued =

Confused =

Annoyed =

0 = Not at all

1 = A little

2 = Moderately

3 = Quite a bit

4 = Extremely

Observation

Studied ▢

Both the EPI and POMS questionnaires identify a person's personality by analysing the answers they give to a series of questions. However, some psychologists think personality can be identified by observing a person's behaviour and traits. These observations need to be done over a long period of time so that an individual can be studied in a range of situations to see how they behave.

Topic A.5 Views of personality

Researchers have looked at personality from a number of different viewpoints to understand why people behave in the ways that they do. Personality is seen as a predictor of behaviour and so the terms are often used to mean the same thing.

Trait view

Studied

The **trait view** sees personality and thus our behaviour as the result of a series of traits which we can define as 'relatively stable ways of behaving'. If we know a person's traits we can predict how they will behave in certain situations; for example, a person who is competitive on the sports field is likely to be competitive at work as well. However, this view is criticised because it does not always follow that a person will behave the same way in different situations.

> ### Key term
> **Trait view of personality** – says that a person is relatively consistent in the way they behave across a range of situations.

Situational view

Studied

The **situational view** takes the opposite view to trait view. While the trait view says that behaviour is influenced by factors inside a person, the situational view says that behaviour is the result of factors outside a person. The situational view sees the environment or situation as the main factor influencing our behaviour. It explains why some people are shy and quiet until they play sport when they become aggressive and competitive. The situational view is criticised because it is not possible to predict a person's behaviour in any given situation and not everyone will respond by changing their behaviour in a particular situation.

> ### Key term
> **Situational view of personality** – says that a person's behaviour is determined mainly by their environment.

Interactional view

Studied

Most people realise that neither traits nor the situation alone can fully predict our personality and the way we behave. The **interactional view** believes that behaviour is determined by personality traits *and* the situation a person is in, since neither one on its own is strong enough to predict behaviour. Interaction theory looks at traits (relatively consistent ways of behaving) and states (relatively stable ways of behaving), although our behaviour state can change in a particular situation. For example, if a person has trait anxiety they will be anxious in a wide range of situations, whereas if they have state anxiety it means they will be anxious in a specific situation.

So to sum up, when discussing why someone behaves in the way they do we need to consider both their personality traits and their situation.

> ### Key term
> **Interactional view of personality** – considers both the individual's traits and the situation they find themselves in when determining behaviour.

Check your understanding

1. Fill in the blanks in the following sentences
   a. Personality is the sum of _____ that make a person _____ .
   b. Traits are relatively _____ ways of behaving.
2. Are the following statements true (T) or false (F)?
   a. Role-related behaviours describe how we usually behave.
   b. Type A personalities tend to be competitive and driven.
   c. Team athletes are more extroverted and group dependent than individual athletes.
3. Choose the three personality traits that best describe an extrovert personality:
   a. Outgoing
   b. Enjoys own company
   c. Easily bored
   d. Quiet
   e. Reserved
   f. Needs company
4. Match the following views of personality to the correct description.

View of personality	Description
Trait	When examining behaviour, both traits and the situation need to be considered
Situational	Behaviour can be predicted by personality traits
Interactional	Behaviour is determined mainly by the person's environment

In this section we looked at personality and the three depths of personality defined by Martens. We looked at introvert, extrovert, type A and type B personality types and at methods of measuring personality. The key learning points include:

- personality is the sum of characteristics that make us unique
- personality is structured on three levels: psychological core, typical responses and role-related behaviours
- the psychological core is the 'real you' and includes your feelings, attitudes and values
- typical responses are the way we usually respond to situations
- role-related behaviours are the changes we make in behaviour to suit the situation we find ourselves in
- introverts tend to be quiet, shy and inward looking
- extroverts tend to be outgoing and comfortable in other people's company
- type A personalities tend to be competitive and driven, while type B personalities are calm and laid back
- Eysenck's Personality Inventory (EPI) measures personality across four scales – introversion, extroversion, stable and unstable
- Profile of Mood States (POMS) uses a list of mood states to describe how a person feels over a period of time
- the trait view of personality says our personality is stable and consistent across a range of situations
- the situational view of personality says that our personality is the result of our environment or situation
- the interactional view says that when examining personality both traits and the situation need to be considered.

Activities

Activity A.1

Tested ☐

Part 1
Personality traits

Using traits, describe the personalities of the following sports people:

- Jessica Ennis
- Mo Farah
- Usain Bolt
- Victoria Pendleton
- Andy Murray

For each person, state which personality type you think they have: introvert, extrovert, type A or type B.

What effect do you think their personalities have on their success in sport?

Part 2
Situational view of personality

Choose two of the sports people listed above or two of your choice. Based on your own observation of these athletes' performances and interviews explain how much you think their behaviour is influenced by their environment.

Activity A.2

Tested ☐

Measuring personality

Do an online search for personality tests using search terms such as 'personality test', 'type A and type B', Eysenck's Personality Inventory' and 'Profile of Mood States'.

Once you have found two tests complete them yourself and see whether you agree with the results.

Learning aim B: Explore the influence that motivation and self-confidence have on sports performance

Topic B.1 Definition of motivation

Motivation can be defined in different ways. First it is defined as the direction and intensity of effort (Sage, 1977); this means that the direction is the activity that the motivation is aimed at and intensity refers to the strength of the effort made. This makes sense because we put different amounts of effort into different activities depending on such factors as whether we enjoy the activity, whether it is important to us or to others for us to succeed at the activity, or whether succeeding at the activity will result in something else that we want.

A second definition is that motivation is the internal mechanisms and external stimuli that act to arouse and direct behaviour (Sage, 1977). In simple terms, the internal mechanisms are things inside us such as our thoughts and feelings and external stimuli are things outside us such as trophies or medals. This definition leads us to consider two types of motivation that we call **intrinsic** (from internal factors) and **extrinsic** (from external factors).

Topic B.2 Types of motivation

Intrinsic factors that motivate us are the rewards that come from being involved in the activity itself. This would include motives such as enjoyment, satisfaction, fun and excitement. For some people these are the important rewards of playing sport but for other people it is about the extrinsic rewards gained from the activity. Extrinsic rewards that motivate people include trophies, medals, prizes, praise from other people and any financial rewards as well as the desire to win and beat others and the threat of punishment.

Extrinsically motivated people participate in sport to be successful and gain rewards such as money; intrinsically motivated people participate in sport for the enjoyment of the activity itself.

This leads us on to three views of motivation: trait centred, situation centred and interactional.

> ### Key terms
>
> **Motivation** – defined as the direction and intensity of effort. It is also defined as the internal mechanisms and external stimuli that act to arouse and direct behaviour.
>
> **Intrinsic motivation** – comes from internal factors.
>
> **Extrinsic motivation** – comes from external factors.

Topic B.3 Views of motivation

Trait-centred view

Studied ☐

The **trait-centred view** of motivation says that an individual's motivation is the result of their individual characteristics. These are factors such as their personality traits, needs and personal ambitions. If a coach describes an athlete as being a 'winner' or 'very competitive', they are saying that they have these traits as part of their personality and it is these traits that allow them to be successful in their sport. Although this view does make some sense, we are also affected to some extent by our situation, which leads us onto the next view.

Key term

Trait-centred view – believes that a person's personality traits, needs and ambitions are the driving force behind their motivation.

Situation-centred view

Studied ☐

In contrast to the trait-centred view, the **situation-centred view** believes that our situation or environment is the main influence on our motivation. For example, if your PE teacher is enthusiastic and provides exciting activities they will be a positive influence on your motivation. Similarly, if you go into a modern gym with state-of-the-art equipment you will find it more motivating than going into a dark, damp gym with rusty weights. This view would suggest that motivation can be influenced by adapting the situation, either by changing a teacher or coach's behaviour or by changing the environment sports are played in. However, this view is criticised because it does not fully explain motivation. Take the example of someone who continually fails or is told by their coach that they aren't good enough, yet still they come back day after day to play the sport they love. Another example is if you don't enjoy a particular activity, no matter what your coach does or how great your environment is, it is unlikely you will change your motivation.

However, as we saw earlier with personality, most psychologists think that we can really only rely on an approach that considers traits *and* the environment – the **interactional view**.

Key terms

Situation-centred view – believes that the main influence on a person's motivation is their situation or environment.

Interactional view – believes that a person's motivation is due to a combination of both their personality traits and their environment.

Interactional view

Studied ☐

Most psychologists believe that to understand motivation you need to consider traits and the environment and how the two work together. If you get a person with the right personality traits in the right situation with the right support you are likely to have a successful athlete. Successful teams are also the result of getting together a group of people with the right traits and ensuring that they experience a positive environment for maximum performance.

Topic B.4 Definition of achievement motivation

Achievement motivation is described as a person's efforts to master skills, achieve excellence, overcome obstacles and perform better than other people. A person with high achievement motivation will be driven to succeed, keep going despite failures and take pride in their success. A good example of someone with high achievement motivation is Andy Murray who has had to train increasingly harder in order to be successful in an era where three of his fellow tennis players are the best of all time. Despite losing four major finals he finally got the title he craved by winning the US Open in 2012. Achievement motivation is also described as competitiveness.

Key term

Achievement motivation – the efforts an individual makes to perform new skills, achieve excellence, overcome difficulties and perform better than other people.

Topic B.5 Benefits of motivation on sports performance

Motivation is a positive influence on the behaviour of sports performers because they will:

- increase their choice of activity and opponent, for example, they will want to play against opponents of an equal or slightly better standard to test themselves
- increase their efforts to pursue goals, perhaps by training more frequently
- increase their intensity of effort to achieve goals, by working harder during training sessions, for example
- persist despite failure and hard times. Motivated performers will put in more effort when the going gets tough rather than give in.

(Adapted from Weinberg and Gould, 2007)

Topic B.6 Principles of setting goals to increase and direct motivation

An important way to influence motivation is to set individual or team goals. Goals are like our dreams except we put them into words and take action to make them real. Goals increase motivation and provide direction and actions for an individual. The following list shows some examples of goals:

- I want to score 20 goals this season.
- I want to be the champion.
- I want to increase my first serve per cent to 60 per cent.
- I want to improve my golf handicap to 15.
- I want to be able to bench press 70 kg.
- I want to run 30 miles a week.
- I want to train five times a week.

Setting goals seems easy but setting effective goals that work is more difficult. None of the goals stated above would be described as totally effective. To help set effective goals we use the SMARTER principle. This stands for:

Specific

Measurable

Achievable

Realistic

Time-related

Exciting

Recorded

- Specific: a goal must be specific to the outcome you want to achieve. For example, saying you want to improve your performance is not enough as you need to be specific about what parts of your performance you want to improve, such as passing, putting or volleying.
- Measurable: goals must be stated in such a way that they can be measured, which means they must include a figure. For example, saying I want to improve my personal best for 100 m is not measurable, whereas saying I want to improve my time for 100 m to 12.5 seconds is measurable.
- Achievable: goals need to be achievable – they must be difficult enough to be a challenge but not so difficult that they are almost impossible. If a goal is too easy it may be achieved quickly and motivation will then drop; if it is too difficult we become aware we will never achieve it and again motivation drops off.
- Realistic: this is similar to achievable and says that we need to be realistic about what we can achieve given our other responsibilities and commitments. We may want to be an Olympic champion but we have to be realistic about what we will actually achieve. Tom Daley wanted to be the 2012 Olympic diving champion but was realistic because he said it would be difficult to beat the Chinese divers.
- Time-related: all goals need to have a timescale or cut-off date for achieving the goal, so that you can judge your success or failure. You can do this by putting a date on each goal, for example, I want to improve my 100 m personal best by 31 July.
- Exciting: goals should be exciting so that they drive the individual on to success.
- Recorded: it is vital that progress towards the goals and the achievement of goals is recorded, so you can review your progress and what contributed to your success.

In summary, here is an example of a SMARTER goal: 'I want to improve my successful passing percentage to 85 per cent by 30 May'.

Topic B.7 Definition of self-confidence

The importance of **self-confidence** is frequently discussed by athletes, coaches and commentators. Self-confidence is defined as being 'the belief that a desired behaviour or action can be performed'. This action may be winning a header, completing a high jump or recovering from injury before a championship.

Self-confidence can also be described as a personality trait because such a person feels they will be successful whatever situation they find themselves in. However, self-confidence may not always be stable as a sports performer may begin to feel less confident the closer they are to a competition. So, confidence can be a 'trait' in some people and a 'state' in other people.

> ## Key term
>
> **Self-confidence** – the belief that a desired behaviour can be performed.

Topic B.8 Benefits of self-confidence

Self-confidence means believing you will be successful and it replaces any fears or worries you may have about failing.

Self-confidence produces positive emotions such as feeling calm and relaxed and allows the sports performer to perform freely. Confident performers often view any feelings of nerves as an indication that success in a competition is important to them, rather than viewing nerves as being a fear of failure.

Self-confidence helps a sports performer to improve concentration and effort which in turn can lead to improved performance. When a performer feels confident their mind does not focus on negative thoughts and is free to concentrate on the task at hand.

Development of positive game plans – confidence will ensure that a sports performer is 'playing to win' rather than 'playing not to lose'. This means they are happy to take chances or risks rather than being scared about making mistakes. Players with low self-confidence are often happy to settle for performances where they don't make any mistakes.

Topic B.9 Methods to increase self-confidence

Two ways of increasing self-confidence are to use self-talk and imagery.

Self-talk is where you talk to yourself in a positive way and is influenced by the thoughts you are having. It is usually internal, such as when you say to yourself 'I can do it' but it can be external as well, for example, shouting 'come on' to yourself or 'what are you doing?' when you make a mistake. Self-talk can also be used as commands to yourself to do things, such as 'relax', 'stay calm' or 'get your feet in the right place'. Sport psychologists teach athletes to use positive self-talk and avoid saying negative things.

Imagery involves thinking about playing sport and imagining yourself acting confidently or performing successfully. You may also recall times when you were successful and confident when playing sport. While a confident person tends to look relaxed and holds their shoulders back in an upright posture, a person with low self-confidence tends to round their shoulders forward, looking down at the ground. To use imagery well you need to imagine yourself looking confident, behaving in a positive way and being successful in your performance.

Topic B.10 Definition of self-efficacy

Self-efficacy is defined as being an individual's self-confidence in a specific situation. For example, an athlete may feel confident when they are training but this confidence may drain away when they compete.

> **Key term**
>
> **Self-efficacy** – how self-confident an individual is in a specific situation.

Topic B.11 Factors affecting self-efficacy

Bandura (1977) researched self-efficacy and said it was dependent upon a number of factors, as follows:

- Performance accomplishments: these are the athlete's previous experiences of success or failure and have the strongest influence. Success in a previous performance can lead to further success.
- Vicarious experiences: this means watching other people successfully performing the skills that you will perform. Having a skill demonstrated or modelled successfully can inspire you to try harder, for example, if you see one of your class mates successfully performing a skill it gives you the boost to do it yourself.
- Verbal persuasion: teachers, coaches or your peers may persuade you that you can be successful by giving you verbal encouragement, such as 'go on, you can do it'.
- Imaginal experiences: this means imagining performing successfully by seeing yourself doing it in your mind.

Topic B.12 Outcome, performance and process goals

Different types of goals are set for different reasons.

Outcome goals focus on the outcome of a competition, such as winning a race or beating an opponent.

Performance goals focus on achieving a certain performance or standard. For example, scoring two goals or running 800 m in 2.15 minutes are performance goals. Performance goals are preferable to outcome goals because they are not dependent on your opponent's performance. For example, a sports performer could play better than they have done before but not achieve their goal as their opponent played better too.

Process goals focus on the steps (or processes) that are taken to achieve the performance goal. The processes include the training and preparation the sports performer does but also how they play the game. Coaches often say focus on the processes and the performance will follow.

When you set performance or outcome goals you also need to set process goals so that you have steps you can take to achieve your performance/outcome.

Topic B.13 Influence of goal setting on performance

Setting goals works for sports performers because goals:

- direct attention to certain aspects of performance
- move an individual into action (i.e. they mobilise effort)
- make an individual persist at their task (i.e. they prolong persistence)
- help develop new strategies.

Topic B.14 Influence of goal setting on motivation

Setting goals increases motivation for sports performers because goals:

- provide direction for behaviour
- help to maintain focus on the task at hand
- help to work towards improvements in performance.

Check your understanding

1. Fill in the missing words in these definitions:
   a. Motivation is the _____ and _____ of effort.
   b. Achievement motivation describes a person's efforts to master _____ and overcome _____. It is described as _____.
   c. Self-confidence is the _____ that desired action can be _____.
   d. Self-efficacy is self-confidence in a _____ _____.

2. Match the following motivation terms to the correct definition.

Term	Definition
Trait motivation	I am motivated by the environment I find myself in
Situational motivation	I am motivated because sport gives me satisfaction
Intrinsic motivation	The greater the reward the greater my motivation
Extrinsic motivation	Motivation is an important part of my personality

3. The acronym SMARTER is used to remember the principles of goal setting. What do the letters stand for?

4. Match the following factors that influence self-efficacy to the correct description.

Factor	Description
Performance accomplishments	Coach or teacher telling you that you can do it
Vicarious experiences	Based on success or failure in previous competitions
Verbal persuasion	Thinking about being successful and picturing it in your head
Imaginal experiences	Based on watching other people perform the same skills successfully

Summary

In this section we looked at types of motivation, achievement motivation, goal setting, self-confidence and self-efficacy. The key learning points include:

- Motivation is defined as the direction and intensity of effort.
- Motivation is also defined as the internal mechanisms and external stimuli that act to arouse and direct behaviour.
- Intrinsic factors are the rewards that come from being involved in the activity itself.
- Extrinsic rewards include trophies, medals, prizes, praise from other people and financial rewards.
- Achievement motivation is described as a person's efforts to master skills, achieve excellence, overcome obstacles and perform better than other people.
- Goal setting is an important way to influence motivation.
- When setting goals it is important to use the SMARTER principle: Specific, Measurable, Achievable, Realistic, Time-related, Exciting and Recorded.
- Outcome goals focus on the outcome of a competition.
- Performance goals focus on achieving a certain performance or standard.
- Process goals focus on the steps (or processes) that a sports performer takes to achieve a performance goal.
- Self-confidence is defined as being 'the belief that a desired action can be performed'.
- Self-talk is where you talk to yourself in a positive way. It is influenced by the thoughts you are having.
- Imagery means thinking about playing sport and visualising yourself performing successfully in your mind.
- Self-efficacy is defined as being an individual's self-confidence in a specific situation.
- Self-efficacy is influenced by four factors: performance accomplishments, vicarious experiences, verbal persuasion and imaginal experiences.

Activities

Activity B. 1

Tested

Part 1
Motivation

Describe, using examples, the differences between intrinsic and extrinsic motivation.

Part 2
Confidence and motivation

Describe how you would expect a motivated, self-confident athlete to behave in comparison to an unmotivated athlete with low self-confidence.

Activity B.2

Tested

Part 1
Increasing self-confidence

Explain what is meant by self-talk and imagery and give examples of how you could use them to improve your sports performance.

Part 2
Self-efficacy

Using a sport you play yourself as an example, describe each of the four factors that influence self-efficacy.

Activity B.3

Tested

You have been asked to lead a coaching session for children and will be discussing the benefits of motivation and self-confidence with them. Write down some notes for your discussion.

Learning aim C: Know about arousal and anxiety, and the effects they have on sports performance

Topic C.1 Definition of anxiety

Anxiety and **arousal** are two terms that are associated with the feelings experienced by a sports performer before and during a sports competition. Anxiety is defined as the level of worry or nervousness an individual experiences. It is usually seen as a negative emotion because it is not comfortable to feel anxious and it is associated with butterflies in the stomach and sweating palms. Arousal describes how motivated or excited we are by a situation. As our arousal levels increase we become more focused on an activity. Anxiety can be experienced at high levels of arousal too.

Topic C.2 Types of anxiety

Anxiety occurs as a result of the nervous system becoming activated and there are four types of anxiety to consider: state, trait, somatic and cognitive.

- **State anxiety** is a temporary anxiety and occurs as a result of the nervous system becoming activated due to a specific situation.
- **Trait anxiety** is a personality factor where an individual feels tense and apprehensive across many situations due to their nervous system being continually activated. It is characterised by stable, consistent feelings of tension and apprehension.
- **Somatic anxiety** describes the physical effects of anxiety such as an increase in heart rate, breathing rate, muscle tension and butterflies in the stomach.
- **Cognitive anxiety** describes the mental effects of anxiety such as increased feelings of worry, loss of concentration, being quick tempered and feeling less confident.

Topic C.3 How arousal and anxiety affect performance

Changes in arousal and anxiety levels cause changes in performance level. The effects arousal and anxiety have on performance is explained by four theories: drive theory, inverted U hypothesis, catastrophe theory and reversal theory.

Drive theory

Drive theory states that as an individual's arousal levels increase so will their performance (see Figure 3.3). This theory is quite simplistic and only applies to performers who have learnt skills well, since it is likely that a beginner's performance would be worse when their arousal levels rise.

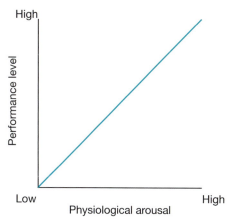

Figure 3.3 Drive theory

Inverted U hypothesis

This theory agrees with drive theory by saying that performance improves as arousal levels increase, but only up to a certain point. After this point, any increases in arousal level will cause a decline in performance. Figure 3.4 shows a shaded area where the arousal level is best suited to the activity and this is called the 'optimal point of arousal' or 'the zone'. This point is different for every individual and each skill performed. For example, strength skills such as weightlifting or pushing a scrum need higher arousal levels than golf putting or kicking a penalty in rugby.

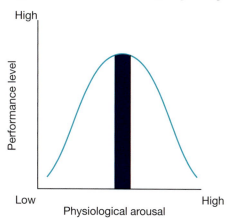

Figure 3.4 Inverted U hypothesis

Catastrophe theory

This theory is similar to inverted U hypothesis, except it states that once arousal level has gone past its ideal point, performance falls off rapidly rather than in a steady way, as shown in Figure 3.5. The point where arousal suddenly drops is called 'the point of catastrophe' and is also known as 'choking'. This can be seen in sport when an athlete's performance suddenly becomes worse and they start making mistakes.

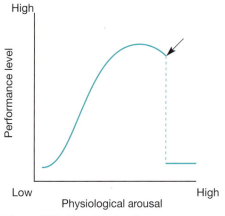

Figure 3.5 Catastrophe theory

Reversal theory

Reversal theory reverses the way people think about arousal and anxiety. It states that if we have high arousal levels and feel anxious before performance it may be because we feel threatened or are scared of failing. However, we can reverse our way of thinking and believe that we feel anxious because we are excited about our performance and that success means a great deal for us. This has the effect of encouraging us and making us more comfortable.

Figure 3.6 Reversal theory: anxiety can have a positive effect on sports performance

UNIT 3 The Mind and Sports Performance

Topic C.4 How anxiety and arousal can be controlled

If a sports performer's arousal and anxiety levels are too high, a sport psychologist can use imagery or relaxation techniques to help lower these levels.

Imagery

Studied ☐

Imagery involves creating pictures in your mind to influence how you feel. For example, a sport psychologist might ask a sports performer to imagine themselves in a relaxing place, such as on a beach, in order to experience feelings of relaxation. Imagery can also be used to mentally rehearse successful performance which can help lower the sports performer's anxiety. Practising imagery during competitions can help to control emotions.

Relaxation techniques

Studied ☐

Muscle tension is a symptom of arousal and can interfere with performance. Relaxation techniques focus on relaxing tense muscles and therefore help to improve performance. Progressive muscular relaxation is a technique where the muscles are tightened and then relaxed in sequence. This method helps to identify which muscles are tight and to relax them. Mind-to-muscle techniques use imagery to relax the mind and this relaxation transfers to the muscles of the body. Breathing techniques are also used because controlling our breathing helps to relax body and mind.

Check your understanding

1. Describe the differences between trait and state anxiety and cognitive and somatic anxiety.
2. Summarise the four arousal-performance theories.

Real world connection

Jodie is a seventeen-year-old heptathlete who works very closely with a sport psychologist, Dr Eddie Sewell. Jodie found that she was getting very nervous before competitions and all the self-confidence that she had in training slowly drained away as the competition approached. She also found that she struggled to be motivated in training for all the seven events in the heptathlon and focused more on those events that she was best at. Dr Sewell helped her to develop a pre-performance routine and built in relaxation and imagery sessions into her training. He spent a lot of time talking to her about the events that she did not enjoy and what could be done to increase her enjoyment of them. Based on these conversations, Dr Sewell set Jodie a series of process goals to help her performance in these events.

Jodie became very interested in sport psychology and asked Dr Sewell about his training: he said that you have to have a degree to become a sport psychologist but studying sport psychology can help you to understand your own performance. Sport psychology can also help you to understand any young athletes that you teach or coach and enable you to offer them advice about how to improve their psychological skills.

Summary

In this section we looked at the definitions of anxiety and arousal, types of anxiety, the arousal-performance relationship and methods to control anxiety. The key learning points include:

- anxiety is defined as the level of worry or nervousness an individual experiences
- anxiety is usually seen as a negative emotion as it is not comfortable and is associated with butterflies in the stomach and sweating palms
- arousal describes how motivated or excited we are by a situation
- trait anxiety is a personality factor where an individual feels tense and apprehensive across many situations due to their nervous system being continually activated
- state anxiety is situation-specific and is defined as temporary feelings of tension and apprehension due to activation of the nervous system in that situation
- somatic anxiety describes the physical effects of anxiety, such as increases in heart rate, breathing rate, muscle tension and butterflies in the stomach
- cognitive anxiety describes the mental effects of anxiety, such as increased feelings of worry, loss of concentration, being quick tempered and feeling less confident
- drive theory says that as arousal levels increase so will performance
- inverted U hypothesis says that as arousal levels increase performance will improve, up to an optimal point of arousal
- catastrophe theory is similar to the inverted U hypothesis but says that once the optimal point of arousal has been reached, any further increases will cause a dramatic decline in performance
- reversal theory says that how we interpret arousal will affect our feelings and performance.

Activities

Activity C.1

Tested

Think of a time when you were anxious about playing sport and describe your feelings at the time. Divide your feelings into those that belong to cognitive anxiety and those that belong to somatic anxiety.

Activity C.2

Tested

Examine each of the four theories that describe the effect of arousal and anxiety on performance and then summarise the main points of each. Using examples from your own sporting performance, describe how each theory can explain your performances. Then write down one strength and one weakness for each theory.

Unit 3 Model assignment

This assignment will assess the following learning aims:

A Investigate personality and its effect on sports performance

B Explore the influence that motivation and self-confidence have on sports performance

C Know about arousal and anxiety, and the effects they have on sports performance

Scenario

You have been given a work experience placement as an assistant to a sport psychologist at a professional club. While you are not qualified to work directly with the athletes, the sport psychologist has asked you to prepare some resources that can be used to educate the athletes.

Task 1

Produce a handbook that uses sporting examples to describe personality, three different views of personality and methods that can be used to measure personality. You need to explain the three different views of personality and how personality can affect sports performance. You also need to analyse three different views of personality and how personality can affect sports performance.

Task 2

Produce a handbook that uses sporting examples to describe the types and views of motivation and the benefits that motivation and self-confidence have on sports performance. You need to discuss the benefits that motivation and self-confidence have on sports performance. You also need to analyse the benefits that motivation and self-confidence have on sports performance.

Using sporting examples summarise methods that can be used to increase self-confidence in sport.

Use sporting examples to describe the factors that influence self-efficacy in sport.

Task 3

Design an A3 poster that describes goal setting, the different types of goal that can be set and how goal setting can influence sports performance and motivation. You need to discuss how goal setting can influence motivation and the roles of the different types of goals that can be set.

Task 4

Create a series of PowerPoint slides for a sport psychologist to use. The slides should use sporting examples to describe different types of anxiety.

Using four theories, describe the effect that arousal and anxiety have on sports performance and the control of arousal and anxiety. Use the four theories to assess the effect that arousal and anxiety have on sports performance and the control of arousal and anxiety. You need to evaluate imagery and relaxation techniques as methods of controlling arousal and anxiety and improving sports performance.

Unit 4

The Sports Performer in Action

This chapter explores the effects of both short- and long-term exercise on the body. The short-term effects of exercise on the musculoskeletal, cardiovascular and respiratory systems will be explored, followed by the long-term effects of exercise and how the various body systems adapt to training.

You will also look at the different energy systems of the body and the sports that use these systems to supply energy. Lastly, the impact of drugs on sport and sports performance and the effect of drugs on society will be examined.

Learning aims

By the end of this unit you will:

✓ know about the short-term responses and long-term adaptations of the body systems to exercise

✓ know about the different energy systems used during sports performance.

Assessment criteria

Assessment and grading criteria

To achieve a **PASS** grade the evidence must show that the learner is able to:	To achieve a **MERIT** grade the evidence must show that, in addition to the pass criteria, the learner is able to:	To achieve a **DISTINCTION** grade the evidence must show that, in addition to the pass and merit criteria, the learner is able to:
P1 Describe ways in which the musculoskeletal system responds to short-term exercise	**M1** Explain responses of the musculoskeletal system to short-term exercise	**D1** Using three different sports activities, compare and contrast how the musculoskeletal and cardiorespiratory systems respond and adapt to exercise
P2 Describe ways in which the cardiorespiratory system responds to short-term exercise	**M2** Explain responses of the cardiorespiratory system to short-term exercise	
P3 Summarise, using relevant examples, long-term adaptations of the musculoskeletal system to exercise	**M3** Explain long-term adaptations of the musculoskeletal system to exercise	
P4 Summarise, using relevant examples, long-term adaptations of the cardiorespiratory system to exercise	**M4** Explain long-term adaptations of the cardiorespiratory system to exercise	
P5 Describe the function of the three energy systems in the production and release of energy for sports performance	**M5** Using two selected sports, explain how the body uses both the anaerobic and aerobic energy systems	**D2** Compare and contrast how the energy systems are used in sports with different demands

Learning aim A: Know about the short-term responses and long-term adaptations of the body systems to exercise

Topic A.1 Short-term effects of exercise on the musculoskeletal system

The musculoskeletal system consists of the skeletal system and the muscular system.

Before taking part in exercise, we know that we should warm up our body to prepare it for the different types of movements and activities that we are about to take part in. This process of warming up helps our musculoskeletal system to get ready for exercise and also makes us less likely to injure this system.

During a warm up we usually increase our heart rate and carry out mobilisation activities. The increase in heart rate occurs because blood is pumping around the body at a faster rate which then has the effect of warming up the muscles. When muscles become warmer they become more pliable (meaning they are able to change shape more easily). Imagine a piece of Plasticine®. When it is cold and you pull it apart, it is likely to break and split into two pieces. However, if you warm it in your hands and then pull it apart, it will start to stretch rather than break – this is because it has become more pliable. This same principle applies to muscles – if a muscle is cold and then suddenly stretched it is more likely to tear, where as if it is warmed up, it is more likely to stretch and not tear.

The process of mobilisation is used to increase joint mobility. Joint mobility means the joints become lubricated by the release of additional synovial fluid. As this fluid becomes warm, it helps the joint to become more efficient. To achieve joint mobility, joints need to move through their full range of movement. Movement should start off small and slowly become bigger until a full range of movement is achieved. The joints that need to be mobilised are shoulders, elbows, spine, hips, knees and ankles.

Resistance exercises such as lifting weights are deliberately intended to cause tears in some of the muscle fibres. These micro tears create very minimal damage and the 'damage' stimulates the muscle to rebuild itself so that over time it will become slightly bigger and stronger.

High impact exercises encourage the body to produce new bone formation.

Exercise also increases metabolic activity as the muscles use energy in order to make them contract and produce movements.

Topic A.2 Short-term effects of exercise on the cardiorespiratory system

The cardiorespiratory system consists of the heart, the blood vessels through which the heart pumps blood around the body, and the lungs. During exercise, a number of changes occur in this system to ensure that the muscles receive the required amounts of oxygen and nutrients.

Heart rate

Studied ☐

Once you start exercising, your body releases adrenaline which increases your heart rate. Your heart rate increases because your heart must work harder to pump oxygenated blood around the body. In a trained athlete, heart rate can increase by up to three times within one minute of starting exercise.

Increased heart rate along with increased stroke volume results in increased cardiac output, so that more oxygenated blood is sent to the working muscles.

Blood pressure

Studied ☐

Blood pressure is caused by the heart pumping the blood around the body under pressure. It does this by contracting and forcing blood into the blood vessels. Two values are given when a person has their blood pressure taken: the systolic value (when the heart is contracting) and the diastolic value (when the heart is relaxing). A typical blood pressure for the average adult male is 120/80. The higher value is the systolic value and the lower is the diastolic value. Blood pressure is measured in milligrams of mercury (mmHg).

An increase in the heart rate as a result of exercise will lead to an increase in blood pressure as the cardiovascular system works to deliver more oxygen and glucose to the muscles. During exercise, the systolic pressure rises while the diastolic pressure remains unchanged. A typical blood pressure reading for a person at the onset of exercise would be around 140/85.

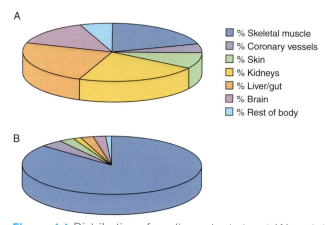

Figure 4.1 Distribution of cardiac output at rest (A) and during exercise (B)

Redistribution of blood flow

Studied ☐

Blood flows through the body through arteries, arterioles, capillaries, veins and venules, although not all of these blood vessels are in use at the same time. Blood is directed to where it is needed most and is redistributed by the **vasoconstriction** (narrowing) of those arterioles supplying inactive parts of the body and the **vasodilation** (opening) of those arterioles supplying the skeletal muscles with more blood and nutrients. For example, after a person has eaten some food they need to digest it, so more blood will be directed to their stomach.

When a person is exercising or taking part in sport, blood is directed to the muscles that are working harder. For example, if a person is running, blood will be directed to flow around their leg muscles to supply the muscles with oxygen and nutrients, enabling them to function. In the case of a tennis player, more blood will be directed to the arm that is holding the racket because that arm is doing more work than the other arm.

> ### Key terms
> **Vasoconstriction** – the narrowing of the arterioles.
>
> **Vasodilation** – the opening of the arterioles.

Skin reddening and production of sweat

Studied ☐

Exercise leads to an increase in the metabolic activity of the muscles which in turn produces heat. The body tries to reduce its temperature by sweating because the evaporation of sweat from the body has a cooling effect.

Blood is also directed to flow through blood vessels that are close to the skin's surface to help cool the body down, resulting in skin reddening.

Increased breathing rate

Studied ☐

The amount of air we breathe in and out per minute is called **pulmonary ventilation** and can be worked out using the following equation:

Pulmonary ventilation = Frequency x Tidal volume

Frequency is the number of breaths per minute.

Tidal volume is the volume of air inhaled and exhaled during one breath.

At rest, average breathing rate is around 12 breaths per minute. The average tidal volume is 0.5 litres (but will vary depending upon age, gender and size of a person).

> ### Key term
> **Pulmonary ventilation** – the amount of air inhaled and exhaled in one minute.

Therefore, the average pulmonary ventilation at rest is:

Pulmonary ventilation = 12 x 0.5 = 6 litres

When exercise begins, the breathing rate increases because the body needs to supply more oxygen to the working muscles and remove the increased amounts of carbon dioxide which occur as a result of muscular activity. This increased oxygen demand is met by breathing at a faster rate and inhaling and exhaling more air during each breath, leading to an increase in **tidal volume** (see Figure 4.2). The volume of air inhaled and exhaled by the lungs can be measured by a piece of apparatus called a **spirometer**.

There is also an increase in the build up in lactic acid in the blood as the body produces some energy anaerobically.

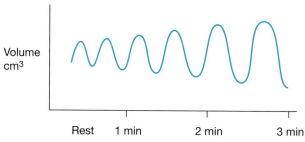

Figure 4.2 Increasing tidal volume

> ## Key terms
>
> **Tidal volume** – the amount of air inhaled and exhaled in one breath.
>
> **Spirometer** – a piece of apparatus that measures the volume of air inhaled and exhaled by the lungs.

Topic A.3 Long-term adaptations of the musculoskeletal system

Chronic exercise means that a person has been participating in regular exercise for long periods of time (a minimum of eight weeks). This regular participation affects the body in a number of ways and makes it more able to cope with the stresses of the exercise. This results in the person being able to exercise at higher intensities and/or for longer periods of time – a process known as **adaptation**.

Key term

Adaptation – how the body can, over a period of time, increase its ability to cope with exercise at higher intensities and/or longer periods of time.

Figure 4.3 Usain Bolt's body has undergone adaptation as a result of his training regime

If you exercise using some sort of resistance, for example weights, dyna band or your own body weight during press-ups, it will put stress upon the skeletal muscle. As described in Topic 1.1, this results in parts of the muscle tearing and breaking. The more stress, the more the muscle breaks down. After resting and eating the right foods, your body will start to repair itself and will mend the muscle tissue, making it bigger and stronger than before. If you continue this process, the muscle tissue will keep getting bigger, resulting in an increase in muscle size called **hypertrophy** (see Figure 4.4). Resistance exercise also increases the strength of muscle tendons and ligaments, making them less likely to be injured.

Key term

Hypertrophy – an increase in muscle size.

Figure 4.4 Muscles get larger through resistance training

Endurance training results in increased capillaries in the muscle which means there is greater blood flow through the muscle, enabling it to use more of the oxygen being delivered by the blood. Endurance training will also increase the number of mitochondria in the muscles. Mitochondria produce energy through **aerobic** respiration, so the more mitochondria there are the more energy can be produced. These adaptations result in an increased maximum oxygen uptake (VO_2 max) being obtained, before excessive amounts of lactic acid are produced to stop the person from exercising.

Your skeleton responds to aerobic **weight-bearing exercise** or resistance exercise by becoming stronger and more able to withstand impact, which means you are less likely to break a bone. This occurs because the stimulation of exercise means the mineral content (calcium in particular) of bones is increased (bone density), which makes bones harder and stronger and makes a person less prone to **osteoporosis**.

Exercise also has an effect on joints by increasing the thickness of the hyaline cartilage at the ends of the bones and increasing the production of synovial fluid. Joints become stronger, more stable and less prone to injury. Strength training increases the strength of muscle tendons, which again makes them less prone to injury. Exercise also means the connective tissues such as ligaments and tendons which hold our bones together are able to stretch to a greater degree, preventing injury.

Long-term exercise also results in an improvement in posture. **Posture** is the way a person stands and holds their body. Many people have a slouched body posture where their shoulders are forwards, stomach is relaxed and the upper back is arched. This can lead to health problems such as back ache, back pain, migraines and an increased risk of a slipped disc. A good posture is where the shoulders are back, the back is straight and the head is looking forwards. This can occur by strengthening the shoulder, back and neck muscle groups, by taking part in a variety of sports and/or resistance training.

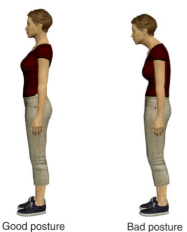

Good posture   Bad posture

Figure 4.5 Good and bad posture

Topic A.4 Long-term adaptations of the cardiorespiratory system

Increase in heart size and strength

Participation in endurance exercise or sport results in changes to an athlete's cardiorespiratory system because of the increase in the delivery of oxygen to the working muscles. An increase in the size of the heart muscle occurs in the same way as for the skeletal muscles – the more we exercise our muscles, the larger or more toned they become. For example, if you were to dissect the heart of a top endurance athlete, you would find that the walls of the left ventricle were markedly thicker than those of a person who did not perform endurance exercise (see Figure 4.6). This increase in the size of the heart is called **cardiac hypertrophy**.

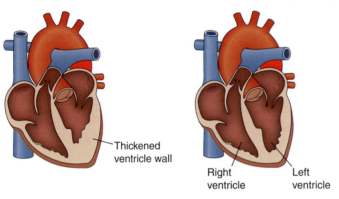

(a) Endurance athlete's heart   (b) Normal heart

Thickened ventricle wall

Right ventricle   Left ventricle

Figure 4.6 An endurance-trained athlete's heart (a) compared to a non-endurance trained athlete's heart (b)

> **Key term**
>
> **Cardiac hypertrophy** – the heart wall becomes thicker and stronger as a result of endurance exercise.

Increase in stroke volume and decrease in resting heart rate

An increase in the size of the heart results in an increase in **stroke volume**, which is the amount of blood that the heart can pump out per beat. As the heart wall becomes bigger, it can pump more blood per beat as the thicker wall can contract more forcibly. As the stroke volume is increased, the heart no longer needs to beat as often to get the same amount of blood around the body. This results in a decrease in resting

> **Key term**
>
> **Stroke volume** – the amount of blood pumped out of the heart per beat.

heart rate (**bradycardia**). This will also reduce the risk of a person from suffering from high blood pressure (**hypertension**).

An average male adult's resting heart rate is 70 bpm (beats per minute). However, former British cyclist Chris Boardman, who won three stages of the Tour De France during his career, had a resting heart rate of 38 bpm at his peak.

Adaptation to endurance training also increases the number of an athlete's capillaries, allowing more blood to travel through them. This process, called **capillarisation**, also helps with the removal of oxygen from the blood which is used to make energy in aerobic respiration.

Key terms

Bradycardia – a decrease in resting heart rate.

Hypertension – high blood pressure.

Capillarisation – an increase in the number of capillaries in the body as a result of endurance training.

Increased lung efficiency and vital capacity

Studied ☐

The function of the lungs is to take oxygen into the body and to help remove waste products associated with muscle metabolism such as carbon dioxide. Training reduces the resting respiratory rate and the breathing rate during sub-maximal exercise. Endurance training can also provide a small increase in lung volume because as **vital capacity** increases, so does **tidal volume** during maximal exercise. The increased strength of the respiratory muscles is partly responsible for this as it aids lung inflation.

Key terms

Vital capacity – the amount of air that can be forcibly expelled from the lungs after breathing in as a deeply as possible.

Tidal volume – the amount of air inhaled and exhaled with each breath.

Increased gaseous exchange

Studied ☐

Endurance training also increases the capillarisation around the alveoli in the lungs. This helps to increase the rate of gas exchange in the lungs and, therefore the amount of oxygen entering the blood and the amount of carbon dioxide leaving the blood. These adaptations result in increased maximal oxygen consumption (VO_2 max) in the athlete.

Check your understanding

1. Fill in the blank spaces in the following sentences using the correct word from the boxes below.

   a. The average breathing rate for a person at rest is _____ breaths per minute.

   b. The _____ can be used to measure the range of movement in some joints.

   c. _____ is released before and during exercise to increase the heart rate.

   d. The technical term for breaths per minute is _____.

   e. _____ is released into the joints during a warm up to help increase their range of movement.

   f. An adult's average resting blood pressure is _____.

   g. The amount of air breathed in and out in one breath is called _____.

   h. A _____ can be used to measure tidal volume.

   i. During resistance exercises, _____ occur in muscle tissue.

   j. During exercise blood is directed to _____.

adrenaline	pulmonary ventilation	spirometer	120/80	tidal volume
synovial fluid	12	micro tears	sit and reach test	skeletal muscle

2. Place a tick in the appropriate column to show whether each statement is true or false.

Statement	True	False
Long-term exercise makes the heart muscle smaller		
Long-term exercise increases the vital capacity of the lungs		
Long-term exercise increases a person's resting heart rate		
Long-term exercise results in the decreased production of synovial fluid		
Long-term exercise results in an increase in thickness of hyaline cartilage		
Long-term exercise makes a person's bones more likely to break if they should fall over		
Swimming is an example of weight-bearing exercise		
The resting heart rate of an average male is 120 bpm		
Hypertrophy is the name given to the increase in lung size which occurs as a result of long-term exercise		
Stroke volume is the amount of blood forced through the heart with each beat		

Summary

In this section we looked at the short-term responses and long-term adaptations of the musculoskeletal and cardiorespiratory systems to exercise. The key learning points include:

- exercise causes an increase in synovial fluid which aids joint lubrication and nourishment
- exercise leads to an increased range of movement in the joints because of an increase in blood flow and muscle temperature
- exercise creates micro tears in muscle fibres which cause the muscle to rebuild itself and become bigger and stronger
- high impact exercise encourages new bone formation and increased metabolic activity
- exercise causes an increased heart rate because the heart works harder to pump oxygenated blood around the body and an increased breathing rate in order to supply more oxygen to working muscles and remove carbon dioxide
- exercise creates an increase in body temperature which leads to sweat production and skin reddening
- blood flow can be redistributed to those areas of the body where muscles are working hard via the vasoconstriction of arterioles supplying inactive parts of the body and the vasodilation of arterioles supplying the skeletal muscles with more blood and nutrients
- exercise leads to an increased build-up of lactic acid in the blood
- the long-term effects of exercise include an increase in bone density, stronger connective tissues that are more resistant to injury, an increase in the stability of joints and thickening of the hyaline cartilage
- exercise leads to a decreased risk of osteoporosis and an improvement in posture
- long-term changes to the cardiorespiratory system include a lower resting heart rate, an increase in heart size, strength and stroke volume and a decreased risk of high blood pressure
- long-term exercise makes the body more efficient at delivering oxygen and removing waste products and improves lung efficiency and gaseous exchange.

Activity

You are working in a health and fitness centre and your manager is keen to try to make the centre users more aware of what happens to their body when they exercise.

Part 1

Effects of short-term exercise

Produce a leaflet for centre users that describes and explains the responses of the musculoskeletal system and the cardiorespiratory system to short-term exercise.

Part 2

Long-term adaptations of the body systems

Prepare a poster with illustrations and text that summarises and explains, using relevant examples, long-term adaptations of the musculoskeletal and cardiorespiratory systems to exercise.

Learning aim B: Know about the different energy systems used during sports performance

The purpose of an energy system is to produce **adenosine triphosphate (ATP)**. ATP is a molecule that makes our muscles contract and therefore allows us to take part in exercise. ATP is not stored in large amounts in skeletal muscle and will only supply energy for around 4 seconds, so it has to be made constantly in order for our muscles to continue contracting. There are three energy systems that the body uses to make ATP:

1. **anaerobic** energy system
2. ATP-CP alactic acid anaerobic system
3. glycolysis/lactic acid anaerobic system
4. aerobic energy system.

The energy system used by the body to make energy depends on the speed at which the body needs that energy. For example, fast, explosive sports need energy to be supplied very quickly and so the anaerobic energy system would produce the energy needed. A long walk, however, would not need such a fast production of ATP, so the body would use the aerobic system to make produce energy.

Topic B.1 The anaerobic energy system

The term anaerobic means not using oxygen. This system supplies energy very quickly. Sports that use this system are very high intensity and explosive sports where the activity only lasts for a few seconds, such as during a shot put throw, sprinting or weightlifting.

There are two types of anaerobic energy systems:

1. the ATP-CP/alactic acid anaerobic system
2. the glycolysis/lactic acid anaerobic system.

Topic B.2 ATP-CP/alactic acid anaerobic system

The ATP-CP/alactic acid anaerobic system supplies ATP much quicker than any other energy system. It is used for rapid, high-intensity contractions, such as in sprinting or jumping.

This system uses **creatine phosphate (CP)**, which is a stored molecule, to produce energy. CP is made up of a phosphate and a creatine molecule. When the bond between the phosphate and the creatine is broken, energy is released which is then used to make ATP.

> **Key terms**
>
> **Adenosine triphosphate (ATP)** – the molecule that produces energy in all living things.
>
> **Anaerobic** – does not require oxygen.

> **Key term**
>
> **Creatine phosphate (CP)** – a molecule stored in the body which, when broken down, releases energy that is used to create ATP.

Stores of CP that are used to make ATP are used for rapid, high-intensity contractions, such as during javelin throws, but the stores only last for a short while. Stored ATP and CP provide enough energy for around 4 to 20 seconds of activity.

Aerobic processes are then required to restore the CP molecule so that it is ready for the next set of rapid, high intensity movements.

When this system runs out of ATP-PC stores, glycolysis takes place to provide energy to the body.

Topic B.3 Glycolysis/lactic acid anaerobic system

Once the CP stores have run out, the body uses the lactic acid anaerobic system. This is also known as anaerobic glycolysis (see Figure 4.7), which literally means the breakdown of glucose in the absence of oxygen. Glucose is provided from stores of glycogen in the liver and muscles. When the glucose is broken down it is converted into a substance called pyruvate. When there is no oxygen present, pyruvate is converted into the waste product lactic acid. Energy is supplied by ATP, CP and muscle glycogen for around 20 to 45 seconds and then by muscle glycogen alone for between 45 and 240 seconds. This system produces ATP very quickly, but not as quickly as the ATP-CP system.

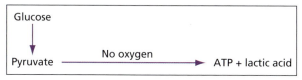

Figure 4.7 Anaerobic glycolysis

The glycolysis/lactic acid energy system produces the majority of ATP for moderate to high intensity sports such as running 400 m, 800 m and 1500 m distances.

When this system is no longer able to maintain the body's energy requirements, the aerobic system beings to produce energy.

Topic B.4 The aerobic energy system – using oxygen

Aerobic literally means with oxygen and the aerobic energy system uses oxygen as a means of making energy (re-synthesising ATP). It provides energy for longer periods of exercise or activity which are at a low to moderate exercise intensity, for example, long-distance events such as marathon running, long-distance swimming and long-distance cycling. Sustained energy also relies on this system.

The aerobic energy system uses a series of reactions, the first being aerobic glycolysis which occurs when oxygen is available to break down glucose. As in the anaerobic energy system, glucose is broken down into pyruvate. Because oxygen is present, pyruvate is not turned into lactic acid but continues to be broken down through a series of chemical reactions in mitochondria. The majority of ATP is produced in the mitochondria organelles, so they are very important for aerobic energy production.

Muscle glycogen and fatty acids supply the energy for the aerobic energy system and can supply energy for long periods of time.

Check your understanding

1. Place a tick in the appropriate column to show whether each statement is true or false.

Statement	True	False
The ATP-CP/alactic acid anaerobic system requires oxygen		
The aerobic energy system would be used to provide energy for a 100 m sprint		
An example of a sport that uses the lactic acid energy system is a 400 m race		
A person competing in an iron man triathlon will mainly use the aerobic energy system to supply their energy		
The ATP-CP/alactic acid anaerobic system produces lactic acid		
The energy system used to make energy is determined by the speed at which the body needs that energy		
Anaerobic means with oxygen		
Lactic acid is a waste product produced by the glycolysis anaerobic system		

Real world connection

Janine studied GCSE and A Level PE and went on to take a range of exercise instruction qualifications. She now works as a personal trainer for people of different ages who have a range of goals. Having first established each client's goals and carried out health screening tests, Janine works out an individual training programme for them. In many instances, her clients have not taken part in exercise for some time so she has to make them aware that their acute responses to exercise are perfectly normal and tell them why their body is reacting in the way that it is! Janine discusses with her clients the reasons why she has included each type of exercise and the training adaptations that should occur, so that they understand the sort of benefits they may attain after training for eight weeks. Many clients want to improve their overall fitness for health reasons, while others wish to train for a specific sports event, so it is important that Janine knows which of the long-term adaptations will result from the training programme in order to meet her clients' needs.

Summary

In this section we looked at the different energy systems used during sports performance. The key learning points include:

- anaerobic energy systems do not use oxygen and supply energy in short bursts for high intensity sports
- the ATP-CP/alactic acid anaerobic system relies on stored ATP to supply energy for up to 4 seconds
- creatine phosphate (CP) helps restore ATP and energy supplied by ATP and CP together lasts between 4 and 20 seconds
- when the ATP-CP/alactic acid anaerobic system runs out of ATP-PC stores, glycolysis occurs
- the glycolysis/lactic acid anaerobic system makes ATP from glucose stored in the liver and muscles and the energy that is supplied lasts 20 to 45 seconds, while energy that is supplied by muscle glycogen lasts 45 to 240 seconds
- lactic acid is produced as a waste product from the glycolysis/lactic acid system and when this system is unable to maintain energy requirements the aerobic system starts to produce energy
- the aerobic energy system uses oxygen and produces energy for long periods of exercise such as long-distance running, long distance swimming and long-distance cycling
- the aerobic energy system produces energy supplied by muscle glycogen and fatty acids and lasts 240 to 600 seconds and it is the main energy system for supplying energy for low to moderate intensity exercise.

Activity

You are working with an athletics coach at your local athletics club. In order to try to understand how energy is produced for the different types of athletics, the coach has asked you to carry out some research into the body's energy systems.

Part 1
Function of the three energy systems

Prepare a written report that describes the function of the each of the three energy systems:

- the ATP-CP/alactic acid anaerobic system
- the glycolysis/lactic acid anaerobic system
- the aerobic energy system.

You should include details of how each system produces and releases energy for different sporting performances.

Part 2
Anaerobic and aerobic energy systems

Select two athletics events and explain how the body uses both the anaerobic and the aerobic energy system to supply energy for both of your selected athletic events.

Part 3
Comparing energy systems

Consider a range of track and field athletics events that have different energy demands. Compare and contrast how the energy systems are used in these varying athletic events.

Unit 4 Model assignment

This part of the assignment will assess the following learning aim:

A know about the short-term responses and long-term adaptations of the body systems to exercise

> ## Scenario
>
> You are on workplacement at a secondary school and are assisting the PE department teaching PE lessons.
>
> The year 8 children are learning about how their body responds to exercise and you have been asked to produce some support materials to help these children to understand more about the short-term and long-term effects of exercise.

Task 1

Produce a poster with illustrations and written text that describes and explains how the body initially responds to taking part in exercise.

In your poster you should include the responses of the

- musculoskeletal system and
- cardiorespiratory system

Task 2

Prepare a leaflet that can be handed out to the year 8 children that describes and explains how the body responds to training over a long period of time. Include in your leaflet the adaptations of the:

- musculoskeletal system
- cardiorespiratory system.

Task 3

Select three different types of sports activities.

For these sports write a report that explores the similarities and differences of how the musculoskeletal system and cardiorespiratory system respond:

● in the short term to these different activities and,
● how they can produce adaptations to each of these systems through long-term participation.

This part of the assignment will assess the following learning aim:

B know about the different energy systems used during sports performance

Scenario

You are on workplacement at a secondary school and are assisting the PE department with teaching PE lessons.

The year 9 children are doing athletics in their PE lessons. They have noticed that the class have preferences for different events, some prefer the long distance running, some are better sprinters or throwers, whereas a few prefer the 400 m run. Their teacher has told them that different energy systems supply the energy for each of these different events.

Task 1

Prepare a written report that can be given to the year 9 children which helps to describe and explain to them the three different energy systems and how they release energy for athletics performance.

Include in your report information about two different sports and explain how the body uses both the anaerobic and the aerobic energy systems to supply energy.

Also, compare and contrast how the energy systems are used in a range of different athletic events including the 100 m sprint, javelin throw, 400 m run and 1500 m run.

Unit 5

Training for Personal Fitness

Maintaining an effective personal fitness training programme is an important part of sports performance and leading a healthy lifestyle. However, designing an effective training programme is a skill that needs to be learnt as everyone has different goals and needs. This chapter covers the skills and knowledge that you need to be able to design a personal fitness training programme.

Learning aims

By the end of this unit you will:

✓ design a personal fitness training programme

✓ know about exercise adherence factors and strategies for continued training success

✓ implement a self-designed personal fitness training programme to achieve own goals and objectives

✓ review a personal fitness training programme.

Assessment criteria

Assessment and grading criteria		
To achieve a **PASS** grade the evidence must show that the learner is able to:	To achieve a **MERIT** grade the evidence must show that the learner is able to:	To achieve a **DISTINCTION** grade the evidence must show that the learner is able to:
P1 Summarise personal information for designing a fitness training programme	**M1** Assess personal information for fitness training programme design	**D1** Justify the training programme design, explaining links to personal information
P2 Independently design a safe six-week personal fitness training programme	**M2** Design a safe six-week personal fitness training programme, showing creativity in the design	
P3 Describe the principles of training and their application to the personal fitness training programme design		
P4 Describe four personal exercise adherence factors and four strategies for training success		
P5 Safely implement a six week personal fitness training programme, maintaining a training diary	**M3** Safely implement a successful six-week personal fitness training programme, maintaining a training diary summarising outcomes for each session	**D2** Safely implement a successful six-week personal fitness training programme, maintaining a training diary to evaluate performance and progress
P6 Review the six-week personal fitness training programme, describing strengths and areas for improvement	**M4** Explain strengths of the training programme and areas for improvement, providing recommendations for future training and performance	**D3** Justify recommendations for future training and performance

Learning aim A: Design a personal fitness training programme

Topic A.1 Personal information to aid training programme design

Personal goals

All fitness training programmes need to start with identifying **goals** as they inform everything that goes into the training programme. Goals are what you want to achieve or the gains that you want to obtain from the programme. Your goals should take into account your own fitness requirements which are based on the sport you play, the fitness gains that you want to make and any injuries or medical conditions that you may have.

When setting goals you need to use the SMARTER principles of goal setting to ensure they are effective:

Specific – means that the goal relates to the types of fitness that need to improve. To get fit is a poor goal because it is not specific, whereas to improve muscle tone is a better goal.

Measurable – the goal must be stated in figures so you can measure whether it has been achieved. 'I want to reduce body fat' is a poor goal but 'I want to reduce body fat by 3%' is much better because you can now measure it.

Achievable – the goal must be possible to achieve or it will not be motivational.

Realistic – the goal must be realistic for an individual and take into account factors which may prevent the goal being achieved.

Time-related – there must be a time scale for the goal achievement because a deadline is needed to review whether the training programme has been successful.

Exciting – the goal and its rewards must be exciting for the individual.

Recorded – writing goals down increases their power to influence.

You should set performance goals for each of the components of fitness that you need to improve. Before you set your goals you should undergo fitness tests to measure your current position for each of the components of fitness. These tests can be repeated at regular intervals to show how

> **Key term**
>
> **Goals** – the achievements or gains that a person wants to achieve.

you are progressing toward your goal. Here are some examples of SMARTER goals:

- I will improve my sit and reach score by 5 cm in one month's time.
- I will improve my beep test score by 3 levels in three months.
- I will improve my 1RM bench press by 15 per cent in six months.

Outcome, performance and process goals were discussed in Unit 3 and these goals can be set over different time scales. In this unit we will look at short-, medium- and long-term goals.

- **Short-term goals** are set over a short period of time, ranging from one day to one month; they can also be set for a single session.
- **Medium-term goals** are set from one month to six months and fill the gap between short-term and long-term goals.
- **Long-term goals** relate to periods of six to twelve months. They are usually set to cover a season and what the individual wants to achieve by the end of that time.

Long-term goals are usually outcome or performance goals and cover the outcomes that you want to achieve over the season, while short- and medium-term goals are often process goals. These goals give support towards the achievement of the long-term goals.

Aims and objectives

Studied

Aims are the details of what an athlete would like to achieve and will tie in with their goals, while **objectives** describe the actions that the individual will take to achieve their aims.

> ## Key terms
>
> **Aims** – these are linked to the sports performer's goals and are the specific details of what they wish to achieve.
>
> **Objectives** – the actions a sports performer must take in order to obtain their aims.

Questionnaires

Studied

The key to designing an effective training programme is to gather as much information as possible on an individual. This is done through the use of a comprehensive questionnaire which usually covers the following: medical history, activity history, goals and outcomes required, lifestyle factors, nutritional status and any other factors that will affect fitness. The medical history part of the questionnaire is included for health screening reasons to ensure that the physical activity is going to be safe for the sports performer. It covers existing medical conditions and injuries and is intended to highlight those people who should seek medical advice before taking part in physical activity.

> ## Key terms
>
> **Short-term goals** – set over a short period of time, ranging from one day to one month or even a single session.
>
> **Medium-term goals** – set for a period of one to six months.
>
> **Long-term goals** – relate to periods of six to twelve months or cover a season.

Attitudes and personal motivation

The success of the training programme is dependent on the attitude of the individual to their training and their likes and dislikes of the different activities within it. Identifying what motivates an individual will also help you to set goals.

Topic A.2 The basic principles of training (FITT)

When designing a training programme the principles of training must be considered to ensure that the programme will be effective. We use the acronym FITT to remember the principles of training:

Frequency is how often the sports performer will train each week.

Intensity is how hard the sports performer will work. It is usually expressed as a percentage of maximum intensity.

Time will indicate how long the sports performer will train for each session

Type shows the type of training method used to improve a specific component of personal fitness and/or sports performance.

Topic A.3 Further principles of training and how they are applied to training methods

This section describes the principles of training that must be considered, together with the personal information gained from the questionnaire, when designing a training programme.

Intensity

Intensity describes how hard the individual will train. The intensity of cardiovascular training is described in relation to maximum heart rate (HR max) while resistance training is described as a percentage of an individual's 1 rep max (1RM).

Training zones are calculated as a percentage of heart rate max. Heart rate max is generally calculated as 220 minus age in years, so for example, a 15-year-old sports performer would have a HR max of 205 beats per minute (bpm). It is important to note that this is an estimation and some people have a much lower or higher HR max.

Training zones are calculated as a percentage of HR max and to improve cardiovascular fitness you need to work at 60–85 per cent of HR max. Therefore, the training zone for a 15-year-old would be 60–85 per cent of 205:

Lower limit: 60% of 205 = 123 bpm

Upper limit 85% of 205 = 174 bpm

The 15-year-old sports performer's training zone would therefore be 123–174 bpm in order to achieve cardiovascular fitness gains.

The Borg Rating of Perceived Exertion (RPE) scale (see Table 5.1) can be used to estimate exertion and it is useful to combine the two methods when deciding whether the intensity of training is appropriate.

Table 5.1 Borg Rating of Perceived Exertion scale

6	Rest
7	Extremely light
8	
9	Very light
10	
11	Light
12	
13	Somewhat hard
14	
15	Hard
16	
17	Very hard
18	
19	Very, very hard
20	Exhaustion

Borg designed his scale to roughly match heart rate, so an RPE of 10 would be equivalent to a heart rate of 100 bpm and an RPE of 20 would be equivalent to 200 bpm. This scale needs to be explained to anyone who uses it as it can be difficult to estimate what an RPE of 13 would feel like. It has also been adapted to a 10-point scale to make it more user-friendly (see Table 5.2).

Table 5.2 10-point RPE scale

1	Extremely light
2	Very light
3	Moderate
4	
5	Somewhat hard
6	
7	Hard
8	Very hard
9	Extremely hard
10	Maximal exertion

Progressive overload

Studied

Progressive overload means that you keep working the body harder than it is used to. It is important because in order to make progress, training needs to be demanding enough to make the body adapt. Overload can be produced by increasing frequency, time and intensity of exercise or reducing recovery time. However, these methods should not all be used at the same time as the increase in workload will be too much for the body. Overload will differ for each person, depending on their fitness. For a sedentary person overload may be walking for five minutes, while for a marathon runner it may be running for 2–3 hours.

Specificity

Studied

Specificity means that training needs to be specific to the sport or physical activity that a person is involved in. To make a programme specific you need to assess the demands of each sport and train to meet these demands. For example, long distance running is not valuable to footballers as they need to train using different distances and different speeds to mimic the type of running involved in playing football.

Individual differences/needs

Studied

This is similar to specificity as the programme should be designed to meet personal training goals and individual needs. These goals are identified through the health screening questionnaire that is done as part of the planning process.

Variation

Studied

The programme must include a variety of activities and exercises to ensure the sports performer remains interested in their training programme. Variety also ensures that the body is overloaded in different ways and produces more adaptations.

Rest and recovery

Studied

Fitness levels do not increase when we are training. In fact, as we train we do damage to our muscles and it causes our fitness levels to temporarily drop slightly. However, as we rest and recover our muscles, tendons and ligaments are replaced and we become stronger and fitter. Rest, recovery and eating properly are vital for this adaptation to occur.

Adaptation

Studied ☐

Adaptation to training occurs when the body's systems change to cope with the extra demands placed on them. These extra demands are the result of the body's systems being overloaded. Adaptation occurs during the recovery period after training and the time taken for adaptation will depend on how intense the training has been. Aerobic training sessions such as running take around 24–48 hours for full recovery, while recovery from resistance training sessions can take 2–4 days.

Reversibility

Studied ☐

If training stops or the training intensity is not sufficient to cause overload and thus adaptation then any training effects are reversed – a process known as reversibility. Reversibility is also known as the 'use it or lose it' principle because if a fitness gain is not used then it is lost as reversal occurs.

Topic A.4 Programme design

Flexibility

Studied ☐

Stretching increases flexibility and should be part of any fitness programme.

Static stretching

Static stretching is when a muscle is stretched in a steady, controlled manner and then held in a static or still position. A static stretch can be a maintenance stretch or a developmental stretch. A maintenance stretch is held for about 10 seconds and is used to stretch a muscle back to its pre-exercise length. A developmental stretch is held for 10 seconds and then the muscle is stretched further to develop the length of the muscle.

Figure 5.1
Quadriceps standing

Figure 5.2 Shoulder strangle

Ballistic stretching

This type of stretching is a 'bouncing' stretch as the muscle is forced beyond its point of stretch by a bouncing movement. It is a high risk method of stretching but it may be used in specific sports such as gymnastics. It must never be used on people who are training for health and fitness reasons only.

Resistance training

Studied ☐

Resistance training means using any form of resistance to place an increased load on a muscle or muscle group. Resistance can be applied through any of the following:

- free weights
- resistance machines
- cable machines
- medicine balls
- resistance bands

P2

M2

D1

Aerobic endurance training

Studied ☐

Continuous training

This is also called 'steady-state' training and involves an individual maintaining a steady pace for a long period of time. To be effective it needs to be done for a period of over 20 minutes. It is useful for developing a strong base of aerobic fitness, but will not develop speed or strength.

Interval training

This type of training is described as 'a structured period of work followed by a structured period of rest'. In other words, an athlete runs quickly for a period of time and then rests at a much lower intensity before speeding up again. This type of training has the benefit of improving speed as well as aerobic fitness. Some examples of interval training sessions are:

- 4 sets of 5 minutes at 70 per cent effort with 2 minutes' rest in between each set
- 6 sets of 45 seconds at 90 per cent effort with 90 seconds' rest in between each set
- 6 sets of 50 metres at 100 per cent effort with 1 minutes' rest in between each set

The intervals need to be designed so that they are specific to the demands of the particular sport.

Fartlek

Studied ☐

Fartlek is a Swedish term for 'speed play' and it involves an athlete running at a range of different speeds for a period of 20 to 30 minutes. This type of training is excellent for replicating the demands of a sport such as football, rugby or hockey, where different running speeds are required at different times. It can also be useful for cycling or rowing training.

Selection of appropriate activities for warm-up

Studied ☐

The warm-up consists of light aerobic activity to prepare the body for the exercise to follow. The warm-up exercises should raise the heart rate and warm up the muscles and could, for example, involve 5–10 minutes on a treadmill, rower or exercise bike with the intensity rising every minute.

Selection of appropriate activities for cool down

Studied ☐

The cool down should lower the heart rate, remove lactic acid and stop the blood collecting in the legs (venous pooling). The cool down consists of around 5 minutes of aerobic exercise to lower pulse. This time the intensity is reduced every minute. This is followed by static stretching consisting of 6–8 stretches of all the muscles worked in the main session.

Creative design

When you design a training programme you need to be creative to ensure that the individual enjoys their training sessions and is motivated to keep on training. This is done by considering any barriers to training and including interesting exercises that vary in style in order to maintain the individual's commitment and motivation to their training programme and to prevent them becoming bored.

Check your understanding

1. Fill in the blanks in the following sentences.
   a. Short-term goals are set for periods between one _____ and one _____ or they may cover a _____ session. Medium-term goals will cover a period of _____ to _____ months.
   b. Long-term goals usually cover a period of _____ _____ or a _____ .
   c. Long-term goals are usually _____ goals while short-term goals are _____ goals as they contribute to the achievement of long-term goals.

2. State five items that should be included in a pre-exercise questionnaire.

3. Match the principles of training to the correct description.

Principle	Description
Type	The time length of each session
Frequency	Doing more than the body is used to
Reversibility	The number of training sessions per week, month or year
Specificity	How hard you work in each training session
Time	Targeting the component of fitness you wish to improve
Intensity	If you do not use a fitness gain you will lose it
Overload	Choosing muscular endurance, strength or flexibility

In this section we looked at the information that is needed to design a personal fitness training programme including short- and long-term goals, medical, lifestyle and physical activity history and the principles of training. The key learning points include:

- always use the SMARTER principles of goal setting to ensure goals are effective
- short-term goals are set over a period of time ranging one day to one month; they can also be set for a single session
- medium-term goals are set from one to six months and fill the gap between short- and long-term goals
- long-term goals relate to periods of six to twelve months but they are usually set to cover a season and what the individual wants to achieve in that time
- aims are the details of what an athlete would like to achieve
- objectives describe the actions that the individual will take to achieve their aims
- frequency means how often the athlete will train each week
- intensity is how hard the athlete will work and is usually expressed as a percentage of maximum intensity
- time will indicate how long they will train for each session
- type refers to the type of training method used to improve a specific component of personal fitness and/or sports performance
- intensity describes how hard the individual will train
- progressive overload means that the body is continually worked harder than it is used to
- specificity means that training must be specific to the sport or physical activity that the performer is involved in
- adaptation to training occurs when the body's systems change to cope with the extra demands placed on them
- reversibility says that if training stops or the training intensity is not sufficient to cause overload and thus adaptation then any training effects are reversed.

Activities

Activity A.1

Tested

Design a questionnaire that covers medical history, lifestyle, physical activity history and short- and long-term goals. Fill in the questionnaire yourself and summarise the most important information. Assess what implications this information has for designing your training programme and what it enables you to do and not do.

Activity A.2

Tested

Using the information you gathered in Activity 1, design your own training programme. Complete the first week of training and then using the principles of training (FITT) develop the next five weeks to show how your training will develop and how progressive overload will be continually applied. Justify the way you have designed your training programme and the time, type and intensity of the activities you have chosen and explain how they link to the personal information contained in your questionnaire.

Activity A.3

Tested

Fill in the table to describe the principles of training and how you have applied them in your training programme.

Principle of training	Description	How it is used in your training programme
Frequency		
Intensity		
Time		
Type		
Progressive overload		
Specificity		
Rest and recovery		
Variation		

Learning aim B: Know about exercise adherence factors and strategies for continued training success

Topic B.1 Factors influencing exercise adherence

A big issue in physical activity is the number of people who start training programmes but then give them up after a short period of time. There are many reasons for this and research presented in Weinberg and Gould (2007: 419) showed the main barriers stated by people who were not currently taking exercise:

Major barriers (and the percentage of people who stated them)

- Lack of time (69%)
- Lack of energy (59%)
- Lack of motivation (52%)

Moderate barriers (and the percentage of people who stated them)

- Excessive cost (37%)
- Illness or injury (36%)
- Lack of facilities (30%)
- Feeling uncomfortable (29%)
- Lack of skill (29%)

Topic B.2 Strategies to overcome barriers to adherence

Adherence means keeping to or sticking to the exercise sessions that you have started. For example, if you have committed to taking exercise three times a week then adherence is keeping to that promise. **Strategies** are techniques that are used to achieve an aim.

> ### Key terms
>
> **Adherence** – keeping to or sticking to the exercise sessions that you have started.
>
> **Strategies** – techniques that are used to achieve an aim.

Benefits of exercise

Studied ☐

To help people maintain their motivation it is important that they understand the benefits of their personal training programme. These benefits include:

- improved sports performance
- improving and maintaining health
- improving self-esteem
- weight management or changing appearance
- managing or controlling stress
- enjoyment and socialising.

Implementing enjoyable activities

Studied ☐

It is vital that people choose activities that they enjoy because they will not be able to maintain something they don't like. Think about trying to eat an item of food that you don't like – you may do it for a day or two but you will start to dread having to do it and will eventually do anything you can to avoid it! As a sports trainer, it is important to remember that some people do not enjoy the activities available in a gym, so you may need to think of an alternative that they will prefer. Even if you know that an activity will benefit someone, it is not a good enough reason to make them do it if they would rather not.

Goal setting

Studied ☐

Setting goals is an effective way of keeping an individual motivated and to make sure the goals are effective they need to be SMARTER, as described earlier in Topic A.1.

Support and reinforcement

Studied ☐

It is beneficial to have a support group around an individual to keep them motivated. At a gym a trainer or instructor often supports the people who train there and may even ring them or send them a text if they miss an exercise sessions. Other people in the gym or those doing the same activity can support you, as can your friends and family.

Rewards for achieving goals

Studied ☐

It is common for gyms to offer rewards for people who attend frequently; this may be something as simple as a t-shirt or water bottle or maybe even a massage. People like to be recognised for the efforts they put in. You can even give yourself a reward of something special if you achieve your goals.

Check your understanding

1. State five barriers that people say prevent them from exercising regularly.

2. Fill in the blank spaces in the following sentences about the benefits of exercise.

   a. People are motivated to exercise as it brings benefits such as improvements to _____ performance and improvements to _____.

   b. Exercise can improve self _____ and help with _____ management and appearance.

3. Write a short description for each of the strategies to improve adherence shown in the table below.

Strategy	Description
Goal setting	
Making activities enjoyable	
Support and reinforcement	
Rewards for achieving goals	

Summary

In this section we looked at the factors that may act as barriers to prevent someone taking part in physical activity and strategies that can be used to overcome these barriers. The key learning points include:

- lack of time, energy and motivation are the major barriers to sports participation that are identified by people
- adherence means keeping to or sticking to the exercise sessions that you have started
- to help people maintain their motivation it is important that they understand the benefits of their personal training programme
- it is vital that people choose activities that they enjoy because they will not be able to maintain something they don't like
- setting goals is an effective way of keeping an individual motivated
- developing a support group around an individual and offering rewards for the successful completion of goals can help keep an individual motivated.

Activity

Part 1

Choose four personal exercise adherence factors and describe why they influence adherence. Choose four strategies for ensuring adherence to the training programme and describe how they would work to ensure adherence.

Topic C.1 Safely implement a personal fitness training programme

When undertaking your self-designed training programme you must show full commitment to each session and ensure that you are wearing the appropriate clothing and using the equipment safely. You should obtain the agreement of your coach/trainer if you have to miss a session and show an awareness of the importance of commitment. When you complete each training session you must record details in a training diary.

Topic C.2 Training diary

The training diary is the method that you use to record details of each session. For each session you need to record the following information:

- date, time, location and session duration
- aims and objectives for the session
- resources required (weights, machines, mats, medicine balls)
- details of training undertaken, programme details (FITT) and intensity of training (using % HR max and RPE)
- the principles of progressive overload and details of how this has been achieved in the course of the programme
- personal performance and achievements.

Topic C.3 Measures for success

You need to record information immediately after the training session so that you don't forget it, including:

- motivation for training – how you felt before, during and after the session. You can rate your feeling in terms of how much energy you had for the session (1 for very low up to 5 for very high) and how enthusiastic you felt about the session (1 to 5)
- how the programme was adapted during the session
- achievement of personal goals, aims and objectives
- any barriers you faced and how you overcame them.

By recording this information you build up valuable information which you can use to review your training programme.

Learning aim D: Review a personal fitness training programme

Topic D.1 Review a personal fitness training programme

Training should be reviewed after every training session, but it is also useful to review a session before it starts by checking each exercise in the programme and its intensity level. The reason for doing this is because if previous sessions have been adjusted or gone particularly well, you may need to make some changes to the programme before you start. Questions you can ask yourself at the end of a session include:

- Was the programme suitable in terms of its structure, i.e. did it meet my aims and goals?
- What were my physical, psychological and health-related achievements during the session?
- What did I enjoy and what did I not enjoy?
- Were there any periods of boredom or where motivation was lacking?
- How could the training session be improved – do I need to make changes to activities or goals?

Information from a review can be used to modify the programme to ensure that it achieves your personal goals. Once the review has taken place you can divide the information into two categories:

- strengths – areas where goals, aims and objectives were met
- areas for improvement – areas where they were not met.

Some of the benefits of reviewing the training programme include:

- changes can be made to future sessions to ensure they are enjoyable, safe and effective
- making changes means you will stay interested and motivated
- ensuring you keep progressing through progressive overload
- any goals that become too easy or hard can be adapted or changed
- becoming more aware of what is and what is not effective.

Once the training period has come to an end you can assess whether your goals have been achieved through fitness testing or by studying your performance. This information can then be used to plan future training programmes and to identify any further training methods or strategies you need to use or any psychological skills you need to develop.

Check your understanding

1. State four pieces of information you should record after a training session.
2. Explain three reasons why you should review each session after you have completed it.

Real world connection

William is a fitness instructor and he believes that designing training programmes is one of the most important aspects of his job. William says:

'People come to me with very clear reasons as to why they want to start taking exercise. Sometimes they have had bad experiences of exercise which they found boring and not motivational. I have to really listen to them and find out what they want to achieve and what they like doing and not doing. Then I design them a training programme and set them some challenging goals to achieve. Above all, I make sure that I remain enthusiastic and keep them motivated during their training sessions so they look forward to coming back. The training programme must be specific to their needs because then they will achieve their goals and will keep coming back to me.'

Summary

In this section we looked at the information that must be recorded after each training session, how the success of each session could be measured and how the training programme can be reviewed. The key learning points include:

- the training diary is used to record details of each training session
- information from the review can be divided into two categories: strengths, which are the areas where the programme has achieved its stated goals, aims and objectives and areas for improvement, where it has not
- when you review your session ask yourself questions about what went well and what could be improved
- the information from a review can be used to modify the training programme to ensure that it achieves your personal goals.

Activities

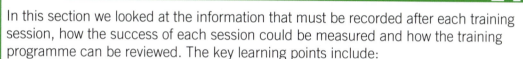

Activity C.1

Tested

Before you begin your personal training programme prepare sheets for your log book that can be used to maintain your training diary, summarise the outcomes of each session and evaluate your performance and progress towards your goals.

Activity C.2

Tested

Once you have completed your six-week training programme conduct a review of the six weeks and your success in achieving your goals. Describe your strengths and areas for improvement, offer and justify recommendations for future training and performance.

Unit 5 Model assignment

This assignment will assess the following learning aims:

A design a personal fitness training programme

B know about exercise adherence factors and strategies for continued training success

C implement a self-designed personal fitness training programme to achieve own goals and objectives

D review a personal fitness training programme

Scenario

You are working as an assistant to a sports coach at a sports club of your choice. The coach wants you to design training programmes for the players but first you need to convince the players that you have the skills and knowledge to write personal training programmes. The coach asks you to develop a six-week personal fitness training programme for yourself and then to complete the training programme to assess its effectiveness.

Task 1

Summarise the personal information that you have collected to enable you to design your fitness training programme. You need to assess the information to identify the main items that will impact on the design of your training programme.

Independently design a safe six-week personal fitness training programme. You need to show that you have been creative in the design of your training programme. You also need to justify why you have chosen the activities in the training programme and explain the links between the personal information you gathered and the content of the training programme.

Describe the principles of training and show how you have applied them to the design of your personal training programme.

Task 2

Describe four personal factors that may affect your adherence to the exercise programme and for each factor describe a strategy to help you to stick to your training programme.

Task 3

Safely complete the six-week personal training programme and record details of each session in your training diary. You will need to summarise the outcomes of each training session and evaluate your performance and progress in your training.

Once you have completed the six-week training programme, review the programme and describe the strengths and areas of weakness of the programme. You will need to explain the strengths and areas for improvement of the programme and make recommendations for future training and performance. You must justify the recommendations you have made for future training and performance.

Unit 6

Leading Sports Activities

Sports leaders play a vital role in developing skills, improving performance levels and providing motivation to sports performers This chapter concentrates on the factors required to lead a range of sports activities and provides young sports leaders with the basic skills that will help them teach and coach participants in sport.

Learning aims

By the end of this unit you will:

✓ know the attributes associated with successful sports leadership

✓ undertake the planning and leading of sports activities

✓ review the planning and leading of sports activities

Assessment criteria

P1
P2
P3
P4
P5
M1
M2
M3
M4
M5
D1
D2

Assessment and grading criteria		
To achieve a **PASS** grade the evidence must show that the learner is able to:	To achieve a **MERIT** grade the evidence must show that the learner is able to:	To achieve a **DISTINCTION** grade the evidence must show that the learner is able to:
P1 Describe, using relevant examples, the attributes required for, and responsibilities of, sports leadership	**M1** Explain the attributes required for, and responsibilities of, sports leadership	
P2 Describe the attributes of two selected successful sports leaders	**M2** Evaluate the attributes of two successful sports leaders	**D1** Compare and contrast the attributes of two successful sports leaders
P3 Plan two selected sports activities	**M3** Justify the choice of activities within the sports activity plan	
P4 Independently lead a sports activity session	**M4** Lead a successful sports activity session	
P5 Review the planning and leading of the sports activity session, describing strengths and areas for improvement, and targets for future development as a sports leader	**M5** Explain targets for future development as a sports leader, including a personal development plan	**D2** Justify targets for future development as a sports leader and activities within the personal development plan

Learning aim A: Know the attributes associated with successful sports leadership

Topic A.1 Sports leaders

Sports leaders play a vital role in developing skills, improving performance levels and providing motivation to sports performers. The growth in popularity of sport and leisure activities has meant that more people are needed to run a variety of different sports sessions, such as after school clubs and voluntary sports clubs. Examples of the different types of sports leaders are:

- sports coaches
- fitness instructors
- school/college coaches
- local club coaches
- national club coaches
- amateur coaches.

Figure 6.1 A sports leader coaching swimmers

Topic A.2 Attributes

Skills associated with successful sports leaders

Studied ☐

A sports leader must have a range of skills and qualities to be successful and these are described below.

Communication skills

Communication is the process of successfully sharing information with other people and is one of the most important skills for a sports leader to have. However, the art of good communication can be a difficult skill to learn. There are many ways of communicating within a sporting environment, but for communication to be successful you must know that the message sent has been understood.

A sports leader can communicate to a group in the following ways:

- **verbal communication**: this involves speaking to a person or group. You should always try to speak clearly to help the participants understand what it is you are telling them. Try to be concise and avoid any jargon that may cause confusion. You should also try to be constructive and positive in your comments, as being negative or critical can affect motivation

- **non-verbal communication**: this involves communicating to a person or team without speaking and is useful in situations where it can be difficult to be heard, such as during a sports event. Examples of non-verbal communication include body language, gestures, hand signals and facial expressions. Next time you are watching a sporting event, look out for the coach or manager on the side lines – throughout the game they will probably be making various gestures to their team to help them to play better or congratulate them on doing well
- by listening: this is a vital part of the communication process but its importance is often forgotten. A good sports leader will listen to their group when appropriate and act on the information they receive
- by demonstrating: this is a method of communication that helps participants learn new skills. It is important to keep demonstrations simple and to ensure they are technically correct, so that participants do not pick up incorrect techniques
- by assisting: this is where a sports leader helps a participant to perform a sports skill correctly. This method may also include some of the techniques described above to help the participant understand how they should perform the skill.

> **Key term**
> **Non-verbal communication** – includes body language, gestures, hand signals and facial expressions.

Organisation of equipment

As a sports leader you must consider what facilities are available when planning and organising your session. Once you know this you can start to organise the sports equipment that you will need.

Before running a sports session, you need to consider the following:

- who you are leading
- where the session is taking place
- how many participants you will have
- health and safety considerations.

You must also check that any equipment to be used is in a safe, working condition and that it is returned in the same condition in which it was lent out.

Knowledge

To successfully lead a sports activity session requires knowledge in many areas and as a sports leader you will develop this knowledge over time. Taking part in lots of sports activities run by different people and showing a willingness to learn new things will give you a better understanding of delivering sports sessions. A sports leader also needs a good understanding of health and safety factors associated with sports. This includes an understanding of emergency procedures, an awareness of the facilities being used and basic first aid knowledge.

As a sports leader you must also have good knowledge of the skills, techniques, rules and tactics of the sport that you are leading. You also need to know how to use and demonstrate any specialist equipment that may be required for the sport.

You will also need to have good knowledge of the individual requirements and needs of the participants you are leading. You must be able to plan appropriate activities to address each participant's individual requirements, including, for example, whether they have learning difficulties, high levels of ability, an injury or a disability.

Advanced skills

Studied ☐

Advanced skills refer to such things as structuring activities to ensure participants get the maximum benefit from the sports session, setting targets, use of language during a sports session and evaluation following a sports session.

Activity structure

When planning sessions effective sports leaders are aware of how to use the time effectively. They will make sure as many participants are as active as possible at any one time, maximise learning and ensure health and safety. Each of these elements will influence the structure of the activities. The sports leader must ensure that there is fast transition between different parts of the session so that time is not wasted. Clear and simple instructions should be given to the participants and the activities themselves should match the aims of the session. Drills and practices should be organised in such a way that they reduce the risk of harm to the participants while also ensuring that the maximum number of participants are as active as possible to reduce the possibility of boredom and participants becoming distracted.

Target setting

Setting targets and individual goals will help participants to improve their own sports performance and also maintain motivation. A sports leader will understand the appropriate targets for each individual sports performer and ensure they set realistic and attainable goals. Targets can be set relating to many different areas of sporting performance, including improving fitness, learning new techniques or improving knowledge of rules or tactics. A sports leader needs to have clear targets for each session and these should contribute to longer-term targets. Targets can be:

- short term – set over a short period of time, such as one session up to a maximum period of one month
- medium term – these fill the gap between short- and long-term targets and are for a period of two to four months. They provide progressive support towards achievement of the long-term target
- long term – these relate to periods of six to twelve months or longer, and can be a goal such as being ready for a half marathon race.

Use of language

The language and vocabulary used by a sports leader plays a key role in communication. Language must be appropriate for the group that the leader is working with and the vocabulary used must be appropriate to the age of the group. For example, the language and vocabulary used to address a group of young children should be fairly basic and easy to understand, whereas more complex terminology can be used to address a group of adults. Most sports will have some technical jargon but this should not be used when working with beginners to the sport or young children as they will not be able to understand what is being said. Positive language should be used to encourage and motivate participants. A sports leader should never use bad language as this is inappropriate, whatever the age of the participants, but especially when working with young children.

Figure 6.2

Evaluation

A good sports leader will take time to evaluate their performance as well as that of their participants. Evaluating your own sessions will help you improve them in the future. Consider what worked well, what could be improved and how you can make your session more enjoyable. You should always try to gain feedback from the participants to find out what they thought of the session too, rather than simply relying on your own ideas and opinions.

Qualities of a sports leader

Studied ☐

Appearance

The personal appearance of a sports leader is very important. Sports leaders must remember that they are setting the standard for the participants that they lead. By dressing in the appropriate attire and having good personal hygiene, you will gain the respect of the group, some of whom may see you as a role model. Looking smart and having good personal hygiene can also make you feel more confident when delivering your session. What you wear should differentiate you from the rest of the group so that you can be easily spotted.

Enthusiasm

Being enthusiastic and positive in everything you do is an important quality for a sports leader. Using positive language will encourage and motivate participants, while demonstrating genuine passion for the sport will also help with motivation, as a group's outlook on things often mirrors that of the leader. Participants within the group will feel comfortable and confident and more likely to approach an enthusiastic and positive sports leader. When communicating or analysing performance, it is important that you maintain an enthusiastic approach. Any weaknesses should be discussed constructively so that the group understands what it is they need to work on. A good sports leader must be optimistic even when things are looking gloomy, because an unenthusiastic leader will find that participants view their sessions as less enjoyable and they may become bored and disruptive or decide not to come to further sessions.

Confidence

A confident sports leader makes fewer mistakes, becomes less frustrated and maintains focus. Mistakes are unavoidable but if you are a confident leader you will be able to deal with them and learn from them. Displaying self-assurance will result in participants having more confidence and trust in your abilities. A display of confidence shows the group that you are capable and competent in leading activities.

Additional qualities

Leadership styles

Different sports leaders use different leadership styles, as described below.

Autocratic leadership: this is sometimes known as the command style and is where the person leading the group makes all of the decisions and imposes them on the group, who respond by doing what they are told. The leader concentrates more on the outcome, rather than the group. It is a method that is often used when dealing with large groups or in circumstances where there may be potential hazards.

Democratic leadership: this is different from the autocratic style as the leader involves the group and asks for their opinions when making the decisions. This enables the group to take more responsibility for their actions, although the leader has the final say.

> **Key terms**
>
> **Autocratic leadership** – the leader makes all decisions.
>
> **Democratic leadership** – the leader involves the group in making decisions, but ultimately has the final word.

Laissez-faire leadership: this style of leadership allows the group to make all of the decisions required. The group has the freedom to do what they like, but for this to work effectively, the group must be highly motivated as the leader does not provide any direction.

> ## Key term
> **Laissez-faire leadership** – the leader passes on the responsibility for decision making to the group.

Motivation

A good sports leader will be self-motivated and work for a sense of achievement and satisfaction – this is called intrinsic motivation. Leaders may also be extrinsically motivated by money or prizes. Good motivation will enable the leader to plan effectively, ensure good organisation and deliver fun and exciting sessions.

Humour

Good humour on the part of the leader will make sessions more fun for the participants. Humour can be used to:

- raise the morale of the group
- help participants learn in a relaxed environment
- defuse tension in a group.

Humour can promote creativity and encourage a more playful atmosphere and is often used to break up boring or difficult routines or to allow the participants to cope with demanding training sessions. Humour must be used appropriately though; laughing at a participant if they make a mistake is not appropriate and can have a negative impact on their performance.

Personality

Personality refers to all the traits and characteristics that make up a person. Sports leaders will have a range of different personality traits, some of which are well suited to sports leadership, such as empathy and confidence.

You should also know the personalities of your participants as this will help you to understand what motivates different people and how they learn.

Topic A.3 Responsibilities

The responsibilities of a sports leader can be divided into core responsibilities, which relate to conduct, health and safety and equality, and their wider responsibilities, which relate to areas such as insurance, legal obligations, ethics and rules/regulations.

Core responsibilities

Professional conduct

Sports leaders must always conduct themselves in a professional manner. Professional **conduct** means demonstrating proper personal and professional behaviour at all times, having the correct qualifications and experience, dressing appropriately, respecting all athletes, officials and opponents, promoting fair play and honesty and using suitable language at all times. As mentioned earlier in the unit, many participants will view the leader as a role model so they must behave appropriately at all times.

> **Key term**
>
> **Conduct** – how we behave and act.

Health and safety

As a sports leader you are responsible for the health and safety of all participants. You must provide a safe environment for people to undertake sport in and minimise the risk of any potential injuries. You should conduct a risk assessment and ensure that equipment is safe and working correctly to reduce the risk of potential injuries and be aware of the emergency procedures for the facilities you are working in. You must also know all of the rules and regulations of the sport you are leading and ensure that these are applied fairly and consistently.

Equality

The Equal Opportunities Act (2010) makes it illegal to discriminate against anyone based on their beliefs, attitudes or characteristics. A good leader will ensure that equal opportunities are given to all participants without prejudice, for example, girls and boys must be given the same level of support and guidance, people with disabilities should be supported appropriately and people from different races should be given the same opportunities. As sports leader you must make sure your sessions are accessible to all people, as far as is practically possible.

Wider responsibilities

Insurance

Sports leaders are required to have appropriate personal insurance cover to participate in and lead sports activities. If someone is injured in a session then you may be deemed to be liable and could be considered negligent if you have not given due care to the planning and implementation of your activity session. It is the responsibility of the sports leader to ensure all aspects of health and safety have been covered. An insurance policy provides protection for you in case something does go wrong despite having taken all the required health and safety precautions.

Child protection

Society today requires sports leaders to have a good understanding of what child protection is. Over the past decade the number of children who have reported experiencing forms of abuse has risen drastically. It is important that the sport leader does not put children at risk and knows how to spot any potential signs of abuse. You should also do your best to ensure that young people can have fun and enjoy their participation, while in a safe environment. All sports leaders must undergo an enhanced **Criminal Records Bureau** (CRB) check, which involves checking a person's criminal record to ensure that they have not had any criminal convictions that would make them unsuitable to work with children.

Legal obligations

Sports leaders have a legal duty of care for the health and safety of others who may be affected by their actions. You are said to have a duty of care when it is 'reasonably foreseeable' that your actions may cause harm. If the standard of care is not of an 'accepted standard', the sports leader may be considered negligent and can be held liable.

Negligence means failing to meet the standard duty of care. It may be that someone was careless or did not do everything necessary prior to or during an activity, for example, failing to carry out a risk assessment before an activity session which resulted in a participant being injured. A person found to be negligent could be prosecuted.

A higher duty of care is required when a person is supervising children. This means that the sports leader must be prepared for children to be less careful than adults would be in a similar situation and to take appropriate action to cover this.

A number of laws have been passed by the UK government that are designed to ensure the health and safety of young people, for example the Children Act (1989), Protection of Children Act (1999) and the Care Standards Act (2000). You must be aware of these laws and take steps to ensure you follow the requirements of this legislation. The NSPCC has published standards for safeguarding and protecting children in sport. These documents are useful in understanding the different requirements as they are based on good practice, legislation and research. They can be downloaded from www.nspcc.org.uk

Key terms

Criminal Records Bureau (CRB) check – an investigation into a person's background to make sure they are safe to work with children.

Negligence – failure to meet the standard duty of care.

Ethics and values

Ethics refers to fair, honest and responsible actions and behaviour and it is important for a sports leader to promote these qualities. **Values** are thoughts and beliefs that are important to us. In sport, values would include fair play, mutual respect and sportsmanship. A sports leader should encourage these values and discourage any antisocial behaviour.

Key terms

Ethics – are actions and behaviour that are fair, honest and responsible.

Values – thoughts and beliefs that are important to us.

Check your understanding

1. Draw a spider diagram to show the attributes and responsibilities of a sports leader.
2. Describe why a leader should have insurance.
3. What is a CRB check is and why it is carried out?
4. What is meant by professional conduct?

Summary

In this section we looked at the attributes and responsibilities associated with successful sports leadership. Their attributes include:

- **Skills:** communication skills, organisation of equipment, knowledge
- **Advanced skills:** activity structure, target setting, appropriate and correct use of language, evaluation of a session
- **Qualities:** smart and professional appearance, enthusiasm, confidence
- **Additional qualities:** leadership style, motivation, humour, personality

The responsibilities of sports leaders include core responsibilities, which are professional conduct, making sure they abide by health and safety guidelines and equality so that all participants are treated fairly.

Wider responsibilities include getting correct insurance where required, child protection to make sure children are safe (including legal obligations such as ensuring all those working with children have a CRB check), ethics and values and rules and regulations.

Activity

Part 1

Prepare a leaflet that describes and explains the attributes and responsibilities required of a sports leader. You should include relevant examples of sports leaders that you know or have watched leading sports teams.

Part 2

Describe, evaluate and compare and contrast the attributes of two successful sports leaders – these may be people that have led you in sports activities or leaders that have led other sports teams.

Learning aim B: Undertake the planning and leading of sports activities

Topic B.1 Sports activities

There are lots of different types of sports activities that a sports leader can plan and run. Some examples include:

- individual sports – tennis, badminton, cycling, swimming
- team sports – netball, football, hockey, volleyball, basketball, rounders, cricket
- fitness activities – aerobics, circuits, spinning, aqua aerobics, jogging.

Figure 6.3 There are many types of sports activities

Topic B.2 Components of a sports activity session

A sports activity session has three main components:

1. warm-up
2. main component
3. cool down.

Warm-up

A warm-up has three main objectives:

1. to raise the heart rate
2. to increase the temperature of the body
3. to mobilise the major joints of the body.

The aim of the warm-up is to slowly raise the body temperature by moving all the major muscle groups in a steady, rhythmical way. The effect of this is an increase in blood flow to the muscles, bringing with it oxygen to produce energy. Increased blood flow also means the muscles will become more elastic and less likely to become injured. It is important to make sure that the skill-related activities in the warm-up are related in some way to the planned activities, for example a game of tag rugby would be a good warm-up for a session that focuses on passing and receiving the ball. This gives the warm-up 'specificity' and acts as a rehearsal for the sport to follow.

A typical warm-up involves the following components:

- Pulse raiser: this involves a cardiovascular-type activity to promote rhythmical movements of the large muscle groups. The pulse raiser should gradually increase in intensity as time goes on. A warm-up for a run may involve one minute walking, one minute brisk walking, one minute jogging, one minute running and then one minute fast running. A pulse raiser typically lasts for around five minutes but may go on for ten minutes. At the end of the warm-up the heart rate should be just below the heart rate that will be achieved during the main session.
- Joint mobility: this is used to enable the joints to become lubricated by releasing more synovial fluid onto the joints and then warming it up so that the joint becomes more efficient. It involves moving joints through their full range of movement. The movements start off small and slowly become larger until a full range of movement is achieved. The joints that need to be mobilised are shoulders, elbows, spine, hips, knees and ankles.
- Muscle stretching: this involves stretching the muscles through their full range of movement. Dynamic stretching is usually carried out in a warm-up as this keeps the heart rate high. To perform dynamic stretching, the participant needs to copy the movements in the session they will perform and repeat the movements in a steady and controlled fashion.

Main component

Studied ☐

The main component will vary, depending on the type and the aims of the session. For a fitness session the main component would be fitness work. The aim would be to focus on one or two components of fitness and work on those using an accepted method of fitness training, such as circuit training, interval training or resistance work.

When leading sport-related activities the main component may include some or all of the following:

- skill introduction: whatever the main aims of the session are this element is designed to introduce the skill. It may involve a simple drill where the basic technique is practised in a fixed or artificial situation, for example passing a ball to a partner.
- development: as the session progresses the drills should become increasingly challenging in order to make them more game specific. The development of these skills is called 'progression'. Progressions are achieved by introducing more complex situations, for example, passing a moving ball or passing to keep the ball away from an opponent.
- conditioned game: this is designed to reinforce the elements that were practised in the drills. A conditioned game will have certain rules that help the participants put into practice the skills they have developed in the session so far, for example, one-touch passing.
- final activity: this could be an unconditioned game or it may be used to practise other elements such as tactical play or set pieces.

Cool-down

Studied ☐

A cool-down is performed following exercise to bring the body back to its pre-exercise state. The aim of the cool-down is to:

- return the heart rate to normal
- rid the body of any waste products which built up during exercise
- return muscles to their original pre-exercise length.

The aim of the cool-down is the opposite of the warm-up in that the pulse will lower slowly and waste products such as carbon dioxide and lactic acid will be removed from the muscles. As the muscles worked during the main session, they continually shortened to produce force and will have ended up in a shortened position. They must therefore be stretched out so they do not remain shortened.

The cool-down consists of:

- lowering the heart rate: a cardiovascular-based activity is used which gradually decreases in intensity to cause a drop in heart rate
- stretching: muscles are stretched and held for around ten seconds. All the muscles which have been worked in the main session need to be stretched.

Topic B.3 Plan

Planning a session means looking at every detail of the activity and considering every eventuality. The time spent planning may be time-consuming, but it will help ensure that you get the best out of your sessions. Planning involves thinking about the session in terms of participants, aims and objectives, resources and health and safety considerations.

Remember: Proper Planning Prevents Poor Performance!

Participants

Studied ☐

During planning, you will need to consider:

- the age of the participants that the session is being planned for
- the number of participants
- the ability of the participants
- the gender of the group
- specific needs of the group or individuals in the group
- any medical concerns – for example participants with asthma may need medication during the session.

The age of sports participants is a very important factor as a session that is appropriate for a group of 18 year olds will not be suitable for a group of 8 year olds. The younger the age group, the simpler the activity needs to be. You will also need to take into account the fact that you will need a higher number of helpers when working with younger children, whereas older participants, such as teenagers or adults, won't require so many helpers.

The number of participants will also dictate what sort of physical activity session you plan. You should always try to make sure that all the participants are actively involved in the session for the majority of the time: participants that have to sit and watch are more likely to become bored, which often leads to misbehaviour.

The ability of the participants will also need to be factored into your planning. Leading an activity for a group of beginners is completely different from organising a session for more advanced performers. When planning your sports activity session you might also consider what the group has done prior to your session or what is planned for any following sessions.

The gender of the group should be taken into account. Some activities such as netball tend to be played only by females, whereas rugby tends to be a more male-dominated sport. If the participants are both male and female then it is usually better to choose an activity that can appeal to both and does not involve contact, such as volleyball or badminton.

Before you run a session it is important to know of any medical or special needs that participants may have. A good way for a leader to know the medical background of the participants is to get them to complete a

Physical Activity Readiness Questionnaire (PAR-Q) before taking part in exercise. A PAR-Q looks at an individual's medical history and highlights any major factors that could stop them from participating. Some examples of the questions that might appear on a PAR-Q are shown below.

1. Have you ever been told by a doctor that you have a heart condition or have you been recommended to undertake only medically supervised physical activity?
2. Do you suffer from chest pain brought on by physical activity?
3. Have you developed chest pain in the past month?
4. Do you sometimes lose consciousness or fall over as a result of dizziness?
5. Do you have a bone or joint problem that could be aggravated by the proposed physical activity?
6. Has a doctor ever recommended medication for your blood pressure or a heart condition?
7. Are you aware through your own experience, or a doctor's advice, of any other physical reason why you should not exercise without medical supervision?
8. Have you had any operations?
9. Have you suffered any injuries?
10. Do you suffer or have you suffered from back pain?
11. Are you pregnant?
12. Have you recently given birth?

If the person answers YES to one or more questions they should be instructed to speak to their doctor before beginning an exercise programme or taking part in sports activity sessions.

Aims and objectives

Studied ☐

One of the first things to consider when planning your activity session is to think about what you want your participants to get out of the activity session. It is important to set aims and objectives – what you want the participants to be able to do at the end of the session – for example, the main aim of the session could be for participants to successfully perform a smash shot in badminton.

Resources

Studied ☐

Planning and organising what equipment you will require for your activity should be done before the session. Time spent putting goals up or pumping up balls during the activity itself uses up the participants' time and means they are sitting around not taking part in sport, which in turn can lead to boredom or messing around. So, planning resources and checking them before the start of the session will help it to run more smoothly.

You should also consider what facilities you will need to use for your session, particularly if they need to be booked in advance, as it is your responsibility as sports leader to ensure the session has all the resources needed. When planning your session make sure you have enough material and activities to last for the length of the session. It is a good idea to have more activities planned than you think you will need, as this will ensure you do not run out of things to do during the session.

Health and safety considerations

Studied ☐

A risk assessment should have been written before the activity session takes place (see Unit 10, pages 280–81 for an example of a risk assessment form and details of how to write a risk assessment). An informed consent form (see below) is completed by a sports participant to ensure they are aware of what is involved in the activity session and any risks there may be. It should also inform them they can stop taking part in the session at any point. Once a participant has read the consent form they should sign it to show that they have given their consent to participate in the session and are aware of any risks which are involved. A person under the age of 18 will need to have a parent or guardian sign the form to give consent to the child taking part in the activity.

Medical information and consent form (Under 18) *(Please complete in Block Capitals)*			
Activity/Event and date:			
Name:			
Address:			
Name and address of Next of Kin:		**Name and contact address of Doctor:**	
Telephone:		**Telephone:**	
Any medical disabilities, treatment, regular medication or allergies to declare (e.g. asthma, hay fever or diabetes, etc):			
Special dietary requirements?			
I acknowledge receipt of and understand the details of all of the information about the activity/event and consent to the participation of:			
I will make sure that my son/daughter understands the information given about his/her safety and the safety of the group, and that any rules and instructions given by staff are adhered to.			
I will inform the leader of any changes to my son's/daughter's health or fitness before the start of the activity.			
I am in agreement that those in charge may give permission for the participant mentioned above to receive medical/dental treatment in an emergency.			
Signed (parent/guardian):		**Date:**	
Give relationship to participant if not parent:			
I understand that for my own safety, and the safety of the group, I will undertake to obey the rules and instructions of members of staff.			
Signed (Under 18):		**Date:**	

Figure 6.4 An example of a medical consent form

Session plan

A session plan contains all of the information that needs to be considered when planning an activity session, as well as a time schedule for each activity that is planned. This can then be referred to by the sports leader before and during the activity session. An example of a session plan template is shown below.

Session Plan				
Activity:			Date:	
Duration:		Number of participants:		
Ability:		Age:		
Equipment required:				
Aims and goals of session:				
Timings	**Session content**		**Teaching Points**	
10 mins	Warm up			
30 mins	Main component Skill introduction Drill Conditioned game			
5 mins	Cool-down			
Evaluation of session:				

Table 6.1 Example of a session plan template

Topic B.4 Lead

When delivering your session you need to ensure your participants understand what it is you are trying to cover. You can do this by first explaining and demonstrating the skills they are required to undertake. Keep your demonstration simple and make sure it is carried out correctly. Some participants will need additional support when learning new skills, so remember to move around the group and look out for their different needs.

Progressing the session is essential to keep participants motivated and prevent them from losing interest. Spending too much time on one activity can cause participants to switch off. Progression also gives encouragement to performers as they can see their own achievements.

Sometimes you may need to adapt the session if things are not going to plan or if changes are necessary due to factors that are out of your control. For example, you may be leading a rugby activity session outside but the weather changes and there is a thunderstorm. If available, you could then move to the indoor facilities in a sports hall. You would need to adapt the game to touch rugby rather than having players tackle each other as they would be more likely to injure themselves falling on a hard sports hall floor compared with a grass rugby field.

Core and wider responsibilities should also be included when leading a sports session to make sure that the partipants are safe and treated fairly.

Topic B.5 Measures of success

In this section we have looked at the different measures of success for a sports leader. These include

- making sure that the planned components have all been covered
- meeting the set aims and objectives of the session
- making sure the session was organised
- making sure that all participants were safe.

Check your understanding

1. Fill in the blank spaces in the sentences below by choosing the correct word from the boxes.

   a. _____ will need to have more helpers in an activity session.
   b. A _____ should take place at the end of an activity session.
   c. Netball is more often played by _____ participants.
   d. A PAR-Q can be completed to find out about the _____ of sports participants.
   e. A sports leader should always ensure a _____ is delivered correctly and clearly.
   f. A _____ should be written out before any activity session.
   g. The _____ should take place at the start of an activity session.
   h. The _____ are what the sports leader wants their participants to be able to do by the end of the session.
   i. The _____ is the part of the activity session where participants get to put the skills learnt into a game context.
   j. A sports leader may need to _____ a session plan if things are not going as expected.

warm-up	young children	demonstration	aims	cool down
medical needs	female	session plan	game play	adapt

Summary

In this section we looked at planning and leading sports activities. The key learning points include:

- different types of sports activities include individual sports, team sports and fitness activities
- the components of a sports activity session are a warm-up, the main component and a cool down
- it is important to plan an activity session and consideration must be given to the participants, the aims and objectives, resources available and health and safety
- a sports leader must be able to demonstrate an awareness of both their core and wider responsibilities
- a sports leader can measure whether their sports session has been successful by assessing whether it has covered the planned components, met the set aims and objectives, been well organised and safe.

Activity

Part 1

Prepare two session plans for two selected sports activities. Write a report which justifies your choice of activities in your session plans for both sports.

Part 2

Independently and successfully lead one of the sports activity sessions that you have planned.

If possible, try to video yourself leading the activity session so that you can see how you lead the session and get ideas on how you can improve your leadership skills.

Learning aim C: Review the planning and leading of sports activities

Topic C.1 Review

It is always a good idea to review your part in both the planning and leadership of a sport session as soon after the event as possible. You will need to consider your own effectiveness and assess the strengths and weaknesses of the session. This will allow you to make improvements to future sessions that you are involved in.

Feedback for review

You should seek feedback from a range of people, including observers, participants and your teacher. Ask them specifically what you did well and what could be improved. Feedback from the participants will give you an idea of how much they enjoyed the activity session and what sorts of things they liked and disliked. Feedback from a supervisor who has experience in leading sports activities and understands the roles and responsibilities of leading a sports activity session can provide useful guidance and tips to help to improve your leadership skills. Self-analysis of how well you performed and how you can improve your sports leadership skills is important too.

Methods of feedback

You can obtain feedback from participants by simply asking them 'How was the activity session for you?' or you could ask them to complete a more detailed questionnaire where they are asked to comment on the different aspects of the session content.

Your supervisor could complete a learner observation record where they detail areas of the activity session that were led well and areas where there is room for improvement.

Another method of gaining feedback is to video-tape yourself while you lead a session. You can then analyse how you deliver the session, for example, what sort of communication skills you use and how they are received by the participants.

Strengths and areas for improvement

Information about strengths and weaknesses provides us with a template for improvement. A sports leader should learn something new from every session that they lead. When considering strengths and areas for improvement, ask yourself the following questions:

1. Was enough planning undertaken before the event?
2. Was the organisation on the day sufficient?
3. Were there any health and safety concerns?
4. What personal skills and qualities did I develop through running the event?
5. Were the aims and objectives of the event met?

You should also note down what considerations you would take into account if you were to organise another sports event. This method should be used when setting targets for improving your planning, skills and qualities as a sports leader.

Topic C.2 Targets for development

SMARTER targets

Studied ☐

When you have identified areas for development, it is good practice to apply SMARTER targets.

For example, if you identified improving your teaching to a group of beginners, your target might look like this:

- Specific – make sure your area for development is specific to a certain area of your leadership skills – it may be that you want to improve your knowledge of a certain sport so you could go on a coaching course.
- Measurable – the target has to be measured, this may be the completion of a coaching course to improve your skills in coaching a certain sports skill.
- Achievable – make sure you are capable of executing a skill well enough to demonstrate it clearly to a group of beginners
- Realistic – can the goal be achieved and are there any barriers to it being achieved?
- Time-related – review the situation in one month to check that you have enrolled on a coaching course and you are on target to complete it
- Exciting – the target must be exciting to you so that you are motivated to complete it – this could mean ensuring that you make sure you enrol onto a coaching course for a sport that you already know you enjoy
- Recorded – by making records of your targets and showing that you have completed them it helps to encourage future target setting as you know you are able to achieve them and want to continue improving your skills and abilities

Development plan

Once you have identified what the key areas for development are, you can begin to develop an action or development plan. The development plan is a set of targets that will help you achieve your ultimate aim of improving as a leader.

Some examples of action points that you might find on a development plan are shown below.

- Aims and objectives – for example, plan before a session in order to meet the needs of all participants.
- SMARTER targets.
- Activities and opportunities that will help you to achieve your targets – for example, undertake training to improve my understanding of how different people learn, working on non-verbal communication (NVC) by practising a set of skills in a small group and using my voice as little as possible. You could also include observation of a leader or coach who is excellent at NVC.
- Possible barriers that may stop you from meeting the aims of your development plan – for example, costs of courses may be too expensive, the courses may be held a long way from your home so they may be difficult to get to.

Check your understanding

1. Describe three methods of obtaining feedback after leading an activity session.
2. What does SMARTER stand for?
3. Describe why a review should be carried out after an activity session.
4. Devise a development plan to help with your sports leadership skills.

Real world connection

Anita is in her second year at university. When she was at school she took a number of sports leadership and coaching qualifications and worked part time in a leisure centre as a leisure assistant and lifeguard. During the university summer holidays, which last three months, Anita earns money to fund her time at university. She has managed to find work each summer as a senior summer play scheme sports leader. In this role she has to plan activity sessions for children of different ages from 3 to 16 years of age. She uses the skills and experience that she gained from her leadership awards and coaching qualificatioins to plan and run sessions that are appropriate to the different age groups. Anita is careful to ensure that all sessions are fun, improve sporting performance where appropriate and are safe for all participants.

Summary

In this section we looked at how to review the planning and leadership of a sports activity session. The key learning points include:

- feedback can be obtained via questionnaires, observation records, direct verbal feedback and video footage
- obtaining Information about strengths and weaknesses helps a sports leader to improve
- targets for development should always be SMARTER
- a development plan should include aims and objectives, goals, SMARTER targets, activities and opportunities and possible barriers

Activity

Part 1

Write a review of the activity sessions you prepared for the learning aim B Activity, which describes your strengths and areas for improvement.

Part 2

Prepare a personal development plan in which you describe, explain and justify your targets for future development to help you to improve your sports leadership skills and abilities.

Unit 6 Model assignment

This assignment will assess the following learning aims:

A know the attributes associated with successful sports leadership

B undertake the planning and leading of sports activities

C review the planning and leading of sports activities

Scenario

You have been asked to prepare a portfolio of evidence in preparation for a forthcoming employer's visit. The employer is called Coaches4U and they are looking for potential staff to undertake paid work during weekends and school holidays. Based on each student's portfolio of evidence for planning, delivery and evaluation, Coaches4U will select a small number of students to join their organisation.

Task 1

Prepare a PowerPoint presentation that describes the attributes required for, and responsibilities of, sports leadership, using relevant examples. You also need to explain the attributes required for, and responsibilities of, sports leadership.

In your PowerPoint presentation describe the attributes of two successful sports leaders (these do not have to be famous sports leaders). You need to evaluate the strengths and weaknesses of the two sports leaders you have chosen and say why you think each of them is effective in their role. You should relate your examples to the attributes and responsibilities you have already described. Compare and contrast the attributes of the two successful sports leaders.

Task 2

Choose two sports activities that you feel competent in delivering to a group. Devise a session plan for one session in each sport that includes information on participants, equipment, timings, environment, health and safety and session aims. Within this plan should be correct sequencing of the session, progression, coaching points and details of the warm-up, main content and cool down.

Give reasons why you have chosen the activities within your plan, linking your ideas to the participants, the aims of the session, organisation and health and safety.

Lead the session independently and obtain feedback from your tutor. The session needs to be successful. This can be measured by how well you covered the planned components, met the aims and objectives of the session, ensured the safety of the participants and organised the session.

Task 3

Review your own performance as a sports leader in the planning and leading of sports activities. State what areas you feel you are good at (your strengths) and what areas you need to improve and develop further in order to be a better sports leader. Use this information to plan targets for your future development as a sports leader.

Explain your targets and use these to create a personal development plan. Make sure you use SMARTER targets for improvement and identify the activities and opportunities you could access to help you improve. You should also discuss any barriers to your improvement.

Justify your targets for future development as a sports leader and give reasons why the targets and activities in your personal development plan will help you to improve your planning and leadership of sports activities.

Unit 7

Anatomy and Physiology for Sports Performance

The human body is an amazing piece of equipment that allows us to perform hundreds of functions effortlessly. Our systems of bones, joints, connective tissue and muscles allow us to move in all directions and in different ways. Our airways, lungs, heart, blood vessels and blood allow oxygen to be transported around the body and deliver oxygen to tissues so that we can produce the energy that we need to fuel movement.

When we play sport we rely heavily on our skeletal and muscular systems to produce the skills needed to perform our specific sports and our cardiorespiratory system to continue to supply the oxygen to produce the energy that we need. In this chapter we will investigate the structure and functions of these systems.

Learning aims

By the end of this unit you will:

✓ know about the structure and function of the musculoskeletal system

✓ know about the structure and function of the cardiorespiratory system.

Assessment guidance

This unit is externally assessed using an onscreen test.

Learning aim A: Know about the structure and function of the musculoskeletal system

Topic A.1 Voluntary muscles

The muscles attached to the skeleton are called 'skeletal' muscles and they are voluntary. Figure 7.1 shows the major skeletal muscles and their location.

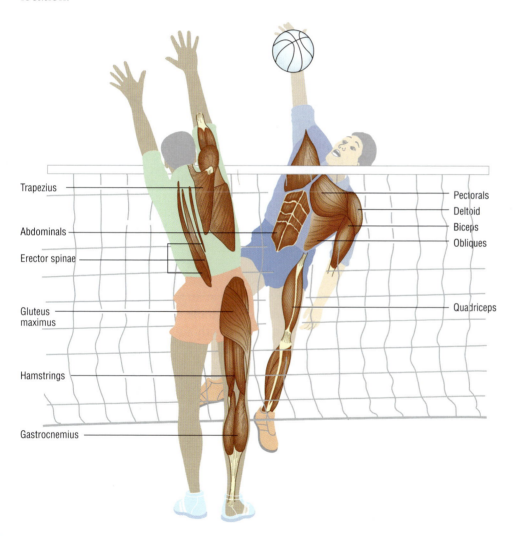

Figure 7.1 Major skeletal muscles

Topic A.2 Types of muscles

There are three types of muscle tissue: voluntary, involuntary and heart.

Voluntary muscle

Studied ☐

Voluntary muscles are also known as skeletal muscles (as they are attached to the skeleton) and striated (which means 'striped' because they have a striped appearance). They are responsible for body movement and allow you to take part in sports. If you 'work out' you will obtain good muscle tone and shape and it is these skeletal muscles you are training.

They are called voluntary muscles because you consciously control what they do. For example, if you want to kick a ball, you have to think about it and this makes your skeletal muscles contract to allow the movement to happen.

Involuntary muscles

Studied ☐

Involuntary muscles are also known as smooth or visceral muscles as they are smooth in appearance. You cannot consciously control this type of muscle; your brain and body tell them what to do without you even having to think about it. They contract in a slow, rhythmical manner as they squeeze and relax, for example, squeezing food through the intestines. Smooth muscle can be found all over your body, for example in your large and small intestine, your stomach and your arteries and veins.

Heart muscle

Studied ☐

Heart muscle is also known as cardiac muscle and is only found in the heart. Heart muscle is also an involuntary muscle as it contracts without you consciously having to control it. Heart muscle consists of specialised fibres that produce rapid and sustained contractions. This means that the fibres keep contracting without tiring because if they did then your body would not get the oxygen it needs to keep you alive.

> ### Key terms
>
> **Voluntary muscles** – muscles that are attached to the skeleton and are responsible for body movement under conscious control.
>
> **Involuntary muscles** – contract in a slow rhythmical way and are found in internal organs.
>
> **Heart muscle** – contracts in a rapid and sustained way under unconscious control.

Topic A.3 Voluntary muscle movements

The voluntary muscles of the skeleton work in pairs to produce movements. The pairs are often on opposite sides of the body, such as the biceps and triceps that are on the front and back of the upper arm. To bend the elbow, such as during a biceps curl, the biceps will contract to produce the movement and the triceps will relax to allow the movement to happen.

The muscle that produces the movement is called the 'agonist' or the 'prime mover' meaning 'first mover' and the muscle that relaxes to allow the movement to occur is called the 'antagonist'. Two muscles working together are called an 'antagonistic pair' and there are many **antagonistic muscle** pairs in the body:

- biceps and triceps
- quadriceps and hamstrings
- rectus abdominis (abdominals) and erector spinae
- pectoralis major (pectorals) and trapezius.

The agonist/antagonist relationship will change depending on which muscle is actively working.

> **Key term**
> **Antagonistic muscles** – pairs of muscles that work together to produce joint movement.

Topic A.4 Types of contraction

The main types of muscle contraction are concentric contraction, eccentric contraction and isometric contraction.

Concentric contraction

Studied ☐

A **concentric contraction** occurs when the muscle gets shorter in length and develops tension as it contracts. During a concentric contraction the muscle fibres slide over each other and the muscle becomes thicker. Examples of concentric muscle contractions are pushing a barbell upwards on a bench press or flexing the knee in preparation for kicking a ball.

> **Key term**
> **Concentric contractions** – occur when a muscle shortens to develop tension.

Figure 7.2 Knee flexion produces a concentric contraction of the hamstrings

157

Eccentric contraction

In an **eccentric contraction** the muscle increases in length while producing tension. For example, in the lowering phase of a bicep curl, the biceps are working eccentrically to control the lowering of the weight. If a muscle did not contract eccentrically on the downward phase gravity would work to quickly to return the weight towards the ground.

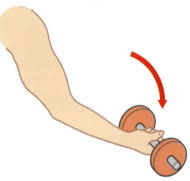

Key term
Eccentric contractions – occur when a muscle lengthens to develop tension.

Figure 7.3 An eccentric contraction of the biceps controls the downward phase of the biceps curl

Isometric contraction

In an **isometric contraction** the muscle contracts but stays the same length – it does not shorten or lengthen. An isometric contraction will not produce movement but will hold a body part in position, for example, a gymnast holding the Iron Cross on the rings. Isometric contractions hold parts of the body in position or stabilise joints during movements.

Key term
Isometric contractions – occur when the muscle develops tension but does not shorten or lengthen.

Figure 7.4 Isometric contractions in the arms and shoulders hold the gymnast in position

Topic A.5 Muscle movements and sports performance

Identifying agonist and antagonist muscles during sports performance

Studied ☐

During sports movements muscles will be acting as agonists and antagonists and be changing roles depending upon the forces they have to work against. Muscles have to overcome forces to kick balls, throw javelins or cricket balls or jump against gravity to shoot a basket. To produce force a muscle will act as an **agonist** and produce a concentric contraction in specific muscle groups while other muscles act as **antagonists** and relax to allow the agonist to produce force. Other muscles will work to hold joints in place and they will be contracting isometrically as they neither shorten nor lengthen. These muscles are called the **fixators**. In Figure 7.5 you can see how muscles act as agonist, antagonist and fixator.

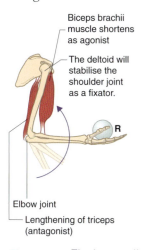

Biceps brachii muscle shortens as agonist

The deltoid will stabilise the shoulder joint as a fixator.

R

Elbow joint

Lengthening of triceps (antagonist)

Figure 7.5 Flexion at elbow with agonist labelled

> ### Key terms
>
> **Agonist** – a muscle that produces a force by producing a concentric contraction.
>
> **Antagonist** – a muscle that relaxes to allow the agonist muscle to produce force.
>
> **Fixator** – a muscle that contracts isometrically to stabilise the agonist so it can act effectively. Neither shortens or lengthens during contraction.

During sport muscles have to produce forces of different strength. For example, if you are running for a long distance you will produce low amounts of force over a long period of time, but if you perform a sprint start you produce high amounts of force over a short period of time. The body is able to do both these activities well because it has two different types of muscle fibre: slow twitch fibres (type I) and fast twitch fibres (type II).

Slow twitch fibres

Studied ☐

These are also called type I fibres. They contract slowly to produce low intensity forces and are slow to become tired (slow to fatigue). They are used for prolonged activity from 3 minutes to 3 hours, such as rowing or swimming for long periods of time. **Slow twitch type I fibres** are red in colour because they have a good blood supply as they need oxygen to produce energy. They are described as having a 'high aerobic capacity' where 'aerobic' means 'with oxygen' as they can use oxygen to produce energy and can keep producing energy as long as they have a supply of oxygen and glucose as a source of energy.

> ## Key term
>
> **Slow twitch fibres (type I)** – contract slowly to produce forces of low intensity and are slow to fatigue.

Fast twitch fibres

Studied ☐

These are also called type II fibres. They produce high intensity forces and become tired quickly (fast to fatigue). They are used for activities for a few seconds up to 2–3 minutes. Fast twitch fibres are white or grey in colour because they have a very poor blood supply and do not need oxygen to produce energy. They are described as 'anaerobic' which means that they produce energy 'without oxygen'. Type II fibres are roughly twice as large as type I fibres and contract twice as quickly.

There are two types of type II fibres – **fast twitch type IIa** and **fast twitch type IIb**.

Type IIa fibres are fast contracting (but not as fast as type IIb) and produce medium force. They are described as being fairly resistant to fatigue because despite being mainly fast twitch they have an aerobic capacity as well. They can keep contracting for longer than type IIb fibres and are used for middle distance running events and swimming events of 200–400 m.

Type IIb fibres are fast contracting and produce high forces. However, they tire quickly as they soon run out of energy and lactic acid builds up. They are used for high intensity anaerobic events such as 100 m sprinting and 200 m canoe sprint. They are also used for activities that require explosive power such as shot put or jumping to make a block in volleyball.

> ## Key terms
>
> **Fast twitch fibres (type IIa)** – contract quickly to produce medium force and can keep contracting for longer periods of time than type IIb fibres.
>
> **Fast twitch fibres (type IIb)** – fast contracting to produce high force but become tired quickly.

Recruitment of muscle fibres

Studied ☐

Muscle fibres have to be activated by the nervous system to make them contract. The brain sends a nervous impulse to a muscle via a nerve and this causes it to contract and produce force. The number of muscle fibres that are needed to contract (or be recruited) depends upon the size of the load or its intensity. Simply put, the heavier the load the more muscle fibres need to be recruited to move the load. At low intensities the slow twitch muscle fibres can produce enough force to move the load, but if the load becomes heavier (i.e. there is an increase in intensity) then more muscle fibres need to be recruited and this is when the fast twitch fibres start to work. Once we have to produce a force that is close to the maximum force we can produce, our type IIb fibres are recruited too.

Muscle fibres are recruited in a ramp-like effect as shown in Figure 7.6 because the number rises as the intensity rises and type IIa and b are recruited at moderate and high intensities.

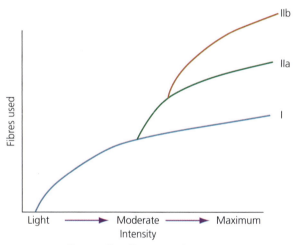

Figure 7.6 Ramp-like fibre recruitment

Topic A.6 Bones of the skeleton

Major bones

Studied ☐

You are born with around 350 bones. However, as you grow, some of your bones join together to form one bone. Once you become an adult your skeleton will consist of 206 bones. Some of the major bones are described below.

- Cranium: this is the skull that protects the brain.
- Sternum: this is the flat bone located in the middle of the chest. The sternum is made up of different parts: the top part is called the manubrium, followed by the body and on the bottom of the sternum is the xiphoid process that points down and makes the sternum look like a dagger.
- Ribs: adults have 12 pairs of ribs. The ribs are flat bones that are joined to the sternum and the vertebral column to form a protective cage around the heart and lungs. There are three different types of ribs:

  - 7 true ribs that are attached to the vertebrae at the back and to the sternum at the front
  - 3 false ribs that are attached to the vertebrae at the back but attached to the rib above by **cartilage**
  - 2 floating ribs only attached to the vertebrae at the back.

- Clavicle (collar bone): this bone connects the upper arm to the trunk of the body. One end is connected to the sternum (breast bone) and the other is connected to the scapula (shoulder blade).
- Scapula (shoulder blade): this bone is situated on the back of the body.
- Arm: this consists of three bones: the humerus (upper arm), the radius and the ulna (lower arm).
- Vertebral column: this is made up of 35 individual bones stacked on top of each other. There are five areas to the vertebral column, each with different numbers of bones:

  - cervical – 7 bones that make up the neck
  - thoracic – 12 bones that attach to the ribs
  - lumbar – 5 bones of the lower back
  - sacrum – 5 bones fused together in the pelvic area
  - coccyx – 4 bones fused together in the pelvic area.

- Pelvis (hips): the pelvis protects and supports the lower internal organs, including the bladder, the reproductive organs and also, in pregnant women, the developing foetus.
- Leg: the leg consists of four bones: the femur (thigh bone), tibia (shin bone), fibula (lower leg) and patella (kneecap).

> **Key term**
> **Cartilage** – cushions joints and acts as a shock absorber.

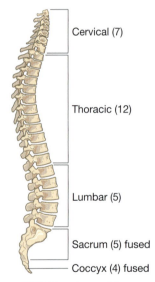

Cervical (7)

Thoracic (12)

Lumbar (5)

Sacrum (5) fused

Coccyx (4) fused

Figure 7.7 Structure of the vertebral column

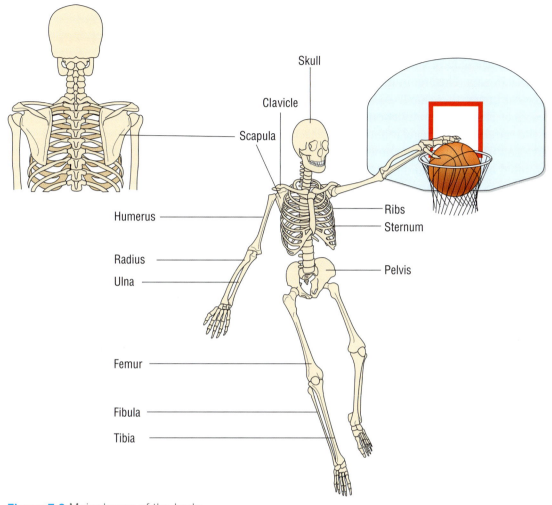

Figure 7.8 Major bones of the body

Axial and appendicular skeleton

Studied ☐

The human skeleton is divided into two parts: the axial and appendicular skeleton.

- The axial skeleton includes the cranium, vertebral column, sternum and ribs.
- The appendicular skeleton includes the clavicle, scapula, humerus, ulna and radius, pelvis, femur, patella, tibia and fibula.

Different types of bones

Studied ☐

The bones of the body fall into five categories based on their shape:

- long bones: these are long in shape and each end is covered in articular cartilage. They are designed to produce large body movements. Examples of long bones include the femur, humerus, radius and tibia

- short bones: these are cube-shaped and are designed for strength and tiny movements. Examples include the bones in the body of the hand (carpals) and foot (tarsals)
- flat bones: these have a large surface area and are designed to protect internal organs. The cranium, pelvis and sternum are all flat bones
- irregular bones: these are irregular in shapes that are difficult to describe. They perform functions specific to their shape. All the bones of the vertebrae are irregular and they protect the spinal cord and have points for muscle attachments
- sesamoid bones: sesamoid means 'seed-like' and these bones are like seeds in a pod. They are often oval in shape and enclosed in a tendon. For example, the patella is a sesamoid bone that is enclosed in the patella tendon.

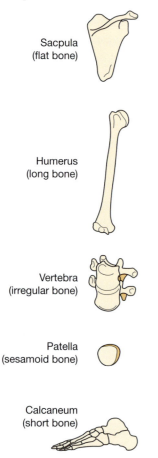

Sacpula
(flat bone)

Humerus
(long bone)

Vertebra
(irregular bone)

Patella
(sesamoid bone)

Calcaneum
(short bone)

Figure 7.9 Five types of bone

Topic A.7 Functions of the skeletal system

The skeleton performs six main functions: shape, support, movement, protection, blood production and mineral storage.

- **Protection:** Internal organs are delicate in comparison to bones and muscles, and would be unable to withstand the many everyday stresses we place on our body unless they were protected by the skeleton. Various parts of the skeleton protect different vital organs, for example the ribs and sternum protect the heart and lungs, the brain is protected by the skull, the vertebral column protects the spinal cord and in pregnant females the pelvis protects the developing foetus.
- **Shape:** The shape of our body is produced by our skeleton, muscles and fat. Our skeleton forms a frame under the skin to which muscles attach and within which internal organs can sit.
- **Support:** The skeleton forms a framework to support the body.
- **Muscle attachment and movement:** The skeleton is made up of bones that are connected by joints that allow different degrees of movement. Muscles are then attached to these bones which pull on them and produce movement.
- **Blood production:** Red bone marrow makes red and white blood cells. The centres of some bones in the skeleton contain red bone marrow and are therefore the site of blood production. The main bones that are responsible for blood production are the sternum, vertebral column and the pelvic girdle.
- **Storage of minerals:** The bones in the skeleton store minerals, including phosphorus, sodium, potassium and calcium, which is the main and most important mineral. The calcium in our bones is largely responsible for ensuring they remain hard and are able to withstand impact, i.e. they do not break when we fall over. As our bones are continually being broken down and replaced, we require a constant supply of calcium to ensure the 'new' bones are tough and durable.

Topic A.8 Classification of joints

Joints are formed at any point where two bones meet. There are three categories of joints, based on the amount of movement they have available.

Key term

Joints – formed wherever two bones meet.

Figure 7.10 Synovial joints in action

Fixed (immoveable joints)

Studied ☐

As the name suggests, fixed or immoveable joints allow no movement. These types of joints can be found in the skull and sacrum.

Slightly moveable or cartilaginous joints

Studied ☐

These joints allow small amounts of movement and are linked by cartilage. They can be found between the vertebrae in your spine and also between the ribs and the sternum.

Freely moveable or synovial joints

These joints allow varying degrees of movement. Six types of freely moveable joints are found in different parts of the body: hinge, ball and socket, pivot, condyloid, saddle and gliding.

- Hinge joint: these can be found in your elbows and knees and they allow you to bend and then straighten your arms and legs in one direction only.
- Ball and socket joint: these types of joint can be found at your shoulders and hips and allow movement in every direction. A ball and socket joint is made up of a round end of one bone that fits into a small cup-like area of another bone. Examples include the hip joint and shoulder joint.
- Pivot joint: this joint can be found in the cervical vertebrae in your neck. It only allows rotational movement, for example, it allows you to move your head from side to side as if you were saying 'no'.
- Condyloid joint: this type of joint can be found at the wrist. It allows movement in two planes because it allows you to bend and straighten the joint and move it from side to side.
- Saddle joint: this type of joint is only found in the carpo-metacarpal joint in your thumbs. It allows the joint to move in two planes – backwards and forwards and from side to side.
- Gliding joint: this type of joint occurs between the surfaces of two flat bones, for example, in the intertarsal joints in the feet and the intertarsal joints of the hands. Gliding joints allow very limited movement in a range of directions.

Topic A.9 Types of cartilage

Cartilage is soft connective tissue that mainly works to cushion joints or give shape to an organ. There are three types of cartilage: fibrocartilage, hyaline cartilage and elastic cartilage.

Fibrocartilage

Fibrocartilage consists of thick chunks of cartilage that are tough and act as shock absorbers. It contains collagen fibres and is found in the knee between the femur and the tibia and between the bones of the vertebrae.

Hyaline cartilage

This is found on the ends of bone and it helps to produce smooth movement at joints as well as helping to cushion joints, absorb shock and reduce wear and tear in joints.

Elastic cartilage

This type of cartilage is flexible tissue that gives support and shape to organs, such as the ears and the nose.

Topic A.10 Synovial joint structure

Figure 7.11 shows the structure of a synovial joint.

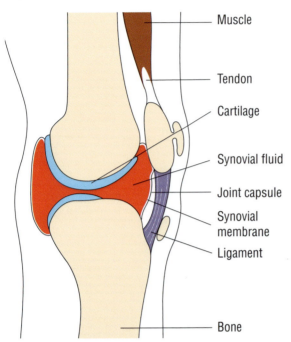

Figure 7.11 Structure of a synovial joint

The synovial joint is made up of a number of different parts:

- joint synovial capsule encases the joint and contains the synovial membrane and fibrous capsule
- bursae are tiny fluid-filled sacs between the tendon and the bone that help to reduce friction
- bone ends are coated with hyaline cartilage to ensure smooth movement between bones
- synovial membrane acts as a lining to the joint capsule and produces synovial fluid
- synovial fluid fills the joint capsule and acts to lubricate and nourish the joint
- tendons attach muscle to bone that are made of tough, strong collagen
- ligaments are tough connective tissue made from collagen that join bone to bone and prevent any unwanted joint movement.

Topic A.11 Joint movement

Flexion – bending the joint. This occurs at the knee when you prepare to kick a football.

Flexion

Figure 7.12 Flexion

Extension

Figure 7.13 Extension

Extension – straightening the joint. Extension occurs at the elbow when shooting in netball.

Adduction – movement towards the body. It occurs at the shoulder when you are in the pulling phase of the breast stroke.

Abduction – movement away from the body. This occurs at the hip during a star jump, for example.

Circumduction – combination in sequence of movements; flexion, extension, abduction, adduction. The limb moves in a circle. This occurs at the shoulder joint during an overarm bowl in cricket.

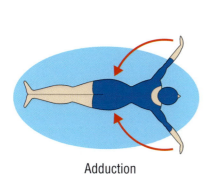

Adduction

Figure 7.14 Adduction

Abduction

Figure 7.15 Abduction

Circumduction

Figure 7.16 Circumduction

Rotation – the limb moves in a circular movement towards the middle of the body. This occurs in the hip while performing a drive shot in golf.

Rotation

Figure 7.17 Rotation

Plantarflexion – occurs at the ankle and means pushing the foot downwards, such as when you point your toe.

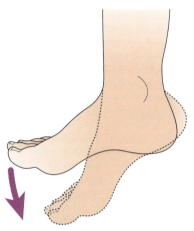

Figure 7.18 Plantarflexion

Dorsiflexion – happens at the ankle and means pulling the foot upwards, such as when you stretch your calf.

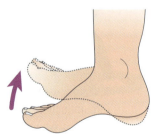

Figure 7.19 Dorsiflexion

Elevation – happens at the shoulder girdle which is made up of a joint between the scapula and clavicle. It means pulling your shoulders upwards like when you are shrugging.

Depression – occurs at the shoulder girdle which is made up of a joint between the scapula and clavicle. It means pushing your shoulders downwards.

Topic A.12 Joint movement and muscle group contractions related to sports performance

An important skill for sports students is to be able to analyse sporting movements by identifying the joints moving and the muscles that are producing those movements. If you are able to do this then you can think about exercises that may reproduce these movements in training and stretches that can be used to stretch muscles that have been worked. Table 7.1 looks at a range of actions and identifies the muscles that produce these actions and the joints that these muscles cross.

Table 7.1 Muscles and joints and their actions

Muscle	Joints crossed	Action when contracting concentrically
Triceps	Elbow	Elbow extension
Biceps	Elbow	Elbow flexion
Quadriceps	Knee	Knee extension
	Hip	Hip flexion
Hamstrings	Knee	Knee flexion
	Hip	Hip extension
Deltoids	Shoulder	Shoulder abduction
		Shoulder flexion
		Shoulder extension
Gluteus maximus	Hip	Hip extension
Gastrocnemius	Ankle	Ankle plantarflexion
	Knee	Knee flexion
Abdominals	Spine/vertebrae	Flexion of spine
		Lateral flexion
		Rotation of spine
Obliques	Intervertebral joints of the spine (lumbar and thoracic vertebrae)	Flexion of spine
		Lateral flexion of spine
	Hip	Trunk rotation
		Compression of abdomen
Pectorals	Shoulder	Shoulder adduction
		Horizontal flexion of shoulder
Trapezius	Shoulder girdle	Shoulder elevation
		Neck extension
Latissimus dorsi	Shoulder	Shoulder adduction
Soleus	Ankle	Ankle plantarflexion
Erector spinae	Spine/vertebrae	Extension of spine

Check your understanding

1. Match the muscles to their correct location in the body.

Muscle	Location
Latissimus dorsi	Shoulder
Hamstrings	Lower leg
Deltoids	Chest
Gastrocnemius	Back
Pectorals	Back of upper leg

2. Are the following statements true or false?
   a. Voluntary muscle is striped in appearance.
   b. Voluntary muscle is found in the intestines.
   c. Voluntary muscle is responsible for movement.
   d. Heart muscle contracts in a slow, rhythmical way.
   e. Involuntary muscle is smooth in appearance.

3. Fill in the blank spaces to complete the paragraph about types of muscle contraction.

   During a concentric muscle contraction the muscle gets _____ in length as it develops tension and the two ends of the muscle get _____ and the muscle becomes _____. In an eccentric contraction the muscle _____ in length as it develops tension to _____ movement. An isometric contraction is where a muscle contracts but its length _____ _____ _____ and it is used to stabilise _____.

4. Fill in the gaps in the table below about slow and fast twitch muscle fibres.

Feature	Slow twitch (type I)	Fast twitch (type IIa)	Fast twitch (type IIb)
Colour		Greyish	
Speed of contraction			Fast
Force of contraction	Low		
Fatigue	Slow to fatigue		
Aerobic or anaerobic		Anaerobic but some aerobic capacity	

5. Select the correct answer to the following questions.
   i) How many bones does an adult have?
      a. 202
      b. 204
      c. 206
      d. 208
   ii) What is the name of the flat bone across the chest?
      a. Clavicle
      b. Sternum
      c. Scapula
      d. Humerus

iii) Which two bones make up the lower leg?
- **a.** Femur and patella
- **b.** Ulna and radius
- **c.** Clavicle and scapula
- **d.** Tibia and fibula

iv) The bones of the vertebrae fit into which category of bone:
- **a.** Irregular
- **b.** Flat
- **c.** Short
- **d.** Sesamoid

v) Which of the following is *not* a function of the skeleton?
- **a.** Production of energy
- **b.** Storage of minerals
- **c.** Production of blood
- **d.** Attachment of muscles

6. Identify the types of cartilage from the descriptions below.

Description of cartilage	Type of cartilage
This cartilage is found on the ends of bone and helps to produce smooth movements between bones	
This cartilage comes in thick chunks and acts as a shock absorber	
This cartilage gives shape to organs such as the ears	

7. Match the following movements to their descriptions.

Movement	Description
Flexion	Movement away from the body
Extension	Moving a joint around in a circle
Adduction	Straightening a joint
Abduction	Movement towards the body
Circumduction	Bending a joint

In this section we looked at the major muscles of the body, different types of muscles, how they contract and how this produces movements in sport. We then looked at the bones of the skeleton, the functions of the skeleton, how joints are classified and structured and the names of joint movements. The key learning points include:

- the muscles attached to the skeleton are called 'skeletal' muscle and they are voluntary
- involuntary muscles are also known as smooth muscle as they are smooth in appearance and under unconscious control
- heart muscle is also known as cardiac muscle and is only found in the heart
- the voluntary muscles of the skeleton work in pairs to produce movements
- two muscles working together are called an 'antagonistic pair'
- a concentric contraction occurs when a muscle gets shorter in length and develops tension as it contracts.
- an eccentric contraction is one where the muscle increases in length while producing tension
- an isometric contraction is one where the muscle contracts but stays the same length
- slow twitch fibres are also called type I fibres and they contract slowly to produce low intensity forces and are slow to fatigue
- fast twitch fibres are also called type II fibres and they will produce high intensity forces and are fast to fatigue
- the adult skeleton consists of 206 bones
- the bones of the body fall into five categories based on their shape: long, short, flat, irregular and sesamoid
- there are six main functions that the skeleton performs: shape, support, movement, protection, blood production and mineral storage
- joints are formed at any point where two bones meet
- joints belong to one of three categories based on the amount of movement they have available: fixed, slightly moveable and freely moveable
- cartilage is soft connective tissue that mainly works to cushion joints or give shape to an organ.

Activities

Activity A.1

Part 1

Using the list of muscles shown below, label the muscle groups on the volleyball players in the picture.

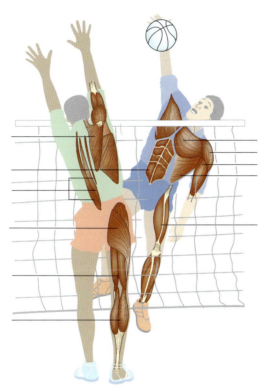

Hamstrings	Gastrocnemius	Biceps
Obliques	Latissimus dorsi	Erector spinae
Trapezius	Deltoid	Pectorals
Abdominals	Quadriceps	Gluteus maximus

Part 2

Identify the three different types of muscle in the body and give examples of where you would find them.

Part 3

Explain, using sporting examples, what is meant by concentric, eccentric and isometric contractions.

Activity A.2

Part 1

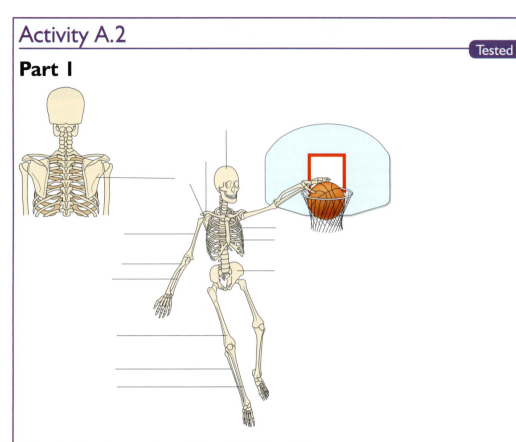

Using the list of bones shown below, label the skeleton.

Cranium	Ulna	Femur
Tibia	Fibula	Clavicle
Radius	Sternum	Scapula
Ribs	Pelvis	Humerus

Part 2

The skeleton has six functions. Complete the table below by naming and describing the different functions.

Function	Description
Shape	Along with muscle and fat the skeleton gives the body shape

Part 3

There are five types of bones in the skeleton. Complete the table below to describe the different types of bone and their function.

Type of bone	Function of this type of bone
Long bone	Allows large movements to be produced

Activity A.3

Tested ☐

Part 1

Name and describe the three types of joints in the skeleton and give examples of where you would find each one.

Part 2

Complete the table below to check your knowledge of synovial joints. The first line has been completed for you.

Name of synovial joint	Description of joint	Example of where you would find this type of joint
Hinge	This joint is like a hinge on a door and only allows movement in one direction	Elbow and knee

Activity A.4

Part 1

Fill out the following table that brings together what you have learnt about the muscular and skeletal systems. The first line has been completed for you.

Name of joint	Type of joint	Muscle crossing this joint	Types of movement at this joint
Hip	Ball and socket	Quadriceps Hamstrings Gluteus maximus Obliques	Flexion Extension Abduction Adduction
Elbow			
Shoulder			
Shoulder girdle			
Knee			
Ankle			
Vertebrae/spine			

Topic B.1 Structure of the cardiovascular system

The cardiovascular system is also known as the circulatory system and is made up of the heart and all the blood vessels that take blood to and from all parts of the body. The heart is the central organ of the cardiovascular system.

Atria and ventricles

Studied ☐

The inside of the heart is hollow and is made up of four different hollow areas called chambers. The top two chambers are called atria and the bottom two are called ventricles. The atria receive blood from the body and the ventricles are responsible for pumping the blood out of the heart. The heart is divided into two sides, the right and the left side, by a wall of muscle called the septum.

Valves of the heart

Studied ☐

There are four valves in the heart and their job is to ensure blood flows in the right direction. Table 7.2 describes the valves and their position.

Table 7.2 Valves of the heart

Name of valve	Position
Tricuspid valve	Found between the right atrium and right ventricle
Bicuspid	Found between the left atrium and left ventricle
Semilunar valve (aortic)	Found between the left ventricle and the aorta
Semilunar valve (pulmonary)	Found between the pulmonary artery and right ventricle

The heart as a double pump

Studied ☐

The heart is called a 'double pump' because both sides of the heart act as pumps. The right-hand side pumps blood to the lungs to be oxygenated and the left-hand side pumps blood around the body to distribute oxygen.

Blood flow through the heart: right-hand side

1. When the heart is relaxed, deoxygenated blood from the body enters the heart via the vena cava.
2. Blood enters the right atrium.

3. The right atrium contracts (tightens) and pushes blood down through the tricuspid valve and into the right ventricle.
4. The right ventricle contracts, the tricuspid valve closes and blood is pushed up and out of the heart through the semilunar valve and into the pulmonary artery which takes the blood to the lungs.
5. The heart relaxes and the semilunar valves close to prevent blood flowing back into the heart.

Blood flow through the heart: left-hand side

1. When the heart is relaxed, oxygenated blood from the lungs enters via the pulmonary vein.
2. Blood enters the left atrium.
3. The left atrium contracts (tightens) and pushes blood down through the bicuspid valve and into the left ventricle.
4. The left ventricle contracts and the bicuspid valve closes. Blood is then pushed up and out of the heart through the semilunar valve and into the aorta which takes blood to the rest of the body.
5. The heart relaxes and the semilunar valves close to prevent blood flowing back into the heart.

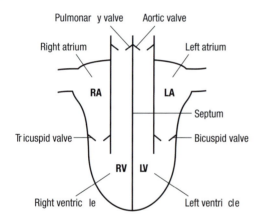

Figure 7.20 Structure of the heart

Coronary arteries

The **coronary arteries** supply the heart muscle itself with blood and oxygen. They sit on top of the heart like a crown and they branch off the aorta which is the major artery that leaves the heart. The heart itself is the first organ to receive a fresh supply of blood with fresh oxygen because if it does not receive oxygen it will not be able to produce energy to enable it to contract. The heart is very clever and makes sure it looks after itself above any other organ!

Key term
Coronary arteries – arteries that supply the heart muscle itself with blood and oxygen.

Types of blood vessels

In order to make its journey around the body, blood is carried through five different types of blood vessels – arteries, arterioles, capillaries, veins and venules.

- **Arteries:** Arteries have thick, muscular walls. They carry blood which has been pumped out of the heart and which is therefore under high pressure. Consequently, these blood vessels need to be elastic in order to be able to expand and they have a thick wall to prevent them from bursting when blood under high pressure is pumped into them. Arteries mostly carry oxygenated blood; the only exception being the pulmonary artery that carries de-oxygenated blood away from the heart to the lungs. An artery is defined as a blood vessel that carries blood *away* from the heart.
- **Arterioles:** Arterioles are smaller versions of arteries that the arteries divide into.
- **Capillaries:** It is in the capillaries that the action really happens! As already stated, the purpose of blood flowing around the body is to deliver oxygen and nutrients to all the body cells and take away waste products. It is in the capillaries that this exchange takes place, so capillaries are designed to allow maximum transfer of oxygen and nutrients to the body cells. They have extremely thin walls – only one cell thick – which allow the oxygen and nutrients to pass through to the body cells relatively easily. Capillaries allow blood to pass through only in 'single file', one red or white blood cell at a time. This means that there is more time for the body cells to take up the oxygen and nutrients they need and 'unload' their waste products into the blood.
- **Veins:** Veins are blood vessels that carry blood under low pressure back to the heart. They have thin walls, are non-elastic and contain one-way valves which prevent blood flowing in the wrong direction and aid venous return (return of blood to the heart). Veins mostly carry de-oxygenated blood from the body back to the heart, except for the pulmonary vein which carries oxygenated blood from the lungs to the heart. The definition of a vein is a blood vessel that carries blood *towards* the heart.
- **Venules:** Venules are smaller than veins and they feed into the larger veins. Capillaries feed blood into the venules that in turn feed blood into the veins.

Topic B.2 Functions of the cardiovascular system

Circulation of oxygen

All body cells need a steady and constant supply of oxygen and this is supplied by blood. Once the oxygen has been delivered to organs and muscles it can then be used to produce energy for movement and to meet the body's needs.

Circulation of carbon dioxide

Carbon dioxide is a waste product of energy production and respiration and the body needs to get rid of it. The cardiovascular system removes carbon dioxide from the muscles and other tissues and transports it to the lungs where it is breathed out.

Provides cells with nutrients

Cells need oxygen, glucose, fats, vitamins and minerals to survive and repair and the blood carries these nutrients to them.

Transport hormones to cells

Hormones carry messages to cells and organs to tell them what to do. For example, the hormone insulin tells cells to allow glucose to enter. The blood carries hormones around the body.

Protects the body against disease and infection

White blood cells act to fight against infection.

Stops bleeding after injury by clotting

The blood contains platelets that move to the site of a wound and these cause the blood to clot and seal the wound against further bleeding and infection.

Regulates body temperature

During exercise, the blood vessels open up to allow excess heat to dissipate out of the body and this is why we go red during exercise as the blood rises to the skin's surface. The body continually works to maintain an internal temperature of around 37°C. Both the skin and body fat insulate the body against heat loss. Any changes in body temperature are sensed by the brain and the body then reacts to maintain temperature – a process known as **thermoregulation**.

If the internal temperature rises the body will respond in the following ways:

- vasodilation will occur which means that the blood vessels under the skin will dilate (open up) and increase blood flow to capillaries under the skin. This causes heat to be lost through the skin
- sweat glands will produce sweat that evaporates on the surface of the skin bringing with it a cooling effect.

If internal temperature drops the body will respond by:

- vasoconstriction of blood vessels which means that they will close or become constricted to reduce the flow of blood to the skin's surface and to keep the heat in the muscles
- directing blood away from the skin's surface towards the centre of the body to reduce heat loss
- shivering because this creates muscle contractions that produce heat.

Key term

Thermoregulation – refers to the way the body works to maintain an internal temperature of around 37°C.

Topic B.3 Structure of the respiratory system

The respiratory system (see Figure 7.21) is responsible for transporting the oxygen from the air we breathe around our body. We use this oxygen in combination with the food we have eaten to produce energy that allows our heart to keep beating and pumping blood around the body. This allows us to move and take part in many different types of activities, including sports.

We have two lungs in our body, which sit against the back of the ribs and move when the ribs move. Pleural membranes cover the outside of the lungs and are lubricated by pleural fluid that helps the lungs to stick to the ribs.

The respiratory system is made up of a system of tubes and muscles that allows us to breathe air in from the surrounding atmosphere and take it down into our lungs.

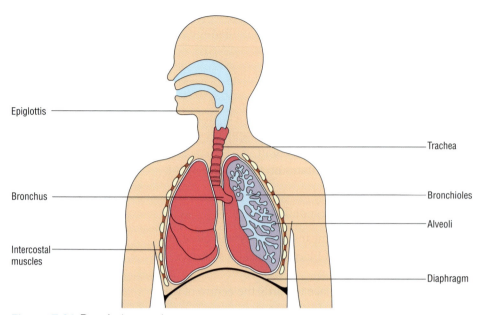

Epiglottis

Trachea

Bronchus

Bronchioles

Alveoli

Intercostal
muscles

Diaphragm

Figure 7.21 Respiratory system

As the air enters the body through the nose and mouth it passes through several structures:

- Nasal cavity: this is where the air is warmed, cleaned by being filtered by the cilia (tiny hairs) and moistened by mucus.
- Epiglottis: this is at the top of the trachea and is a flap of cartilage that covers the pipe to the stomach when we breathe in. It also covers the pipe to the lungs when we swallow food.
- Trachea: this is the windpipe that delivers the air to the lungs. It contains rings of hyaline cartilage which stop it from collapsing.
- Bronchus or bronchi: there are two bronchi, one to each lung, that take the air into the right and left lung.
- Bronchioles: in the lungs the bronchi split into hundreds of smaller tubes called bronchioles (little bronchi).
- Alveoli: these are tiny air sacs at the end of the bronchioles where the oxygen from the air enters the bloodstream.

The respiratory system uses two types of muscles which work to move air into and out of the lungs: the diaphragm and the intercostal muscles.

The diaphragm is a sheet of muscle which runs along the bottom of the lungs. The intercostal muscles are found between the ribs.

Topic B.4 Functions of the respiratory system

Mechanics of breathing

Breathing is the term given to inhaling air into the lungs (inspiration) and then exhaling it (expiration).

Breathing in (inspiration)

When breathing in the diaphragm contracts and moves downwards. This results in an increase in the size of the ribcage and air is forced into the lungs. The intercostal muscles that run between the ribs contract to move the ribs upwards and outwards and increase the size of the ribcage. As a result of this the volume or size of the ribcage increases and the pressure decreases; this causes the air to rush into the lungs.

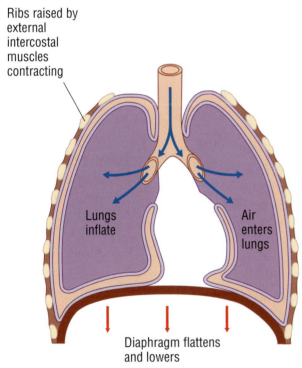

Ribs raised by external intercostal muscles contracting

Lungs inflate

Air enters lungs

Diaphragm flattens and lowers

Figure 7.22 Inhalation, diaphragm and intercostal muscles

Breathing out (expiration)

When breathing out the diaphragm relaxes and returns upwards to a domed position. The ribcage gets smaller, which results in an increase in air pressure within the lungs so that air is breathed out of the lungs.

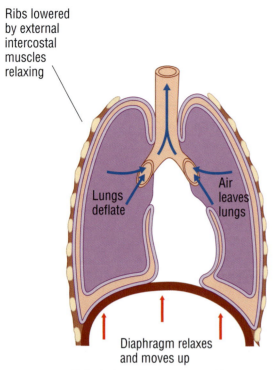

Ribs lowered by external intercostal muscles relaxing

Lungs deflate

Air leaves lungs

Diaphragm relaxes and moves up

Figure 7.23 Exhalation, diaphragm and intercostal muscles

Gaseous exchange

Gaseous exchange is the exchange of gasses (oxygen and carbon dioxide) that happens in the lungs by a process of **diffusion**. Diffusion means moving from an area of high concentration to an area of low concentration. An example of diffusion with which you are probably familiar with is when someone wears strong perfume or aftershave. Its smell moves from their body (a high concentration) to around the room (a low concentration) so that everyone can smell it.

The oxygen in the air that has been breathed into the lungs (alveoli) replaces the carbon dioxide that is present in the blood in the capillaries surrounding the lungs. Oxygen diffuses from the alveoli in the lungs to the blood, while carbon dioxide diffuses from the blood into the lungs to be breathed out.

> **Key term**
>
> **Diffusion** – moving from an area of high concentration to an area of low concentration.

Real world connection

Nicola is a coach for a women's football team and a player herself. She studied sport at school and went on to study sport at college. After college she took sports coaching awards and trained to be a fitness instructor so she could learn even more about how to train people. Nicola says:

'Every course I have done to do with sport and fitness has always started with anatomy and physiology and so I am glad I took the time at school to learn about bones, muscles and the heart and lungs. I need this knowledge because I use it on a daily basis when deciding what training needs to be done and what exercises to choose. To me, anatomy and physiology is the cornerstone of understanding sports performance and is something that you can never know too much about. When I first studied it at school I thought I had learnt it all but I have since discovered that I continue to learn every day by reading about it and talking to other coaches and athletes.'

Topic B.5 Functions of the cardiorespiratory system

The cardiovascular and respiratory system work together as the cardiorespiratory system to create a system that the whole of the body relies on to keep it alive.

In summary the functions of the cardiorespiratory system are:

- supplying oxygen to the body – muscles and other tissue
- producing blood flow through the heart, lungs and the rest of the body
- taking up of oxygen in all tissues of the body with the aim of producing energy
- getting rid of carbon dioxide – a waste product of energy production – from the body.

Check your understanding

1. Are the following statements true or false?
   a. The cardiovascular system is made up of the heart and lungs.
   b. The heart has two sides divided by the septum.
   c. The bottom chambers of the heart are called ventricles.
   d. The tricuspid valve is found between the right atrium and the right ventricle.
   e. The bicuspid valve is found between the left ventricle and aorta.

2. Fill in the blank spaces to complete the paragraph about blood flow through the heart.
   Deoxygenated blood enters the heart on the _____ _____ side via the _____ _____ and enters the _____ _____. The blood is pushed through the _____ valve to the _____ _____ which contracts to send blood through the semilunar valve into the _____ _____ and to the lungs. Blood is oxygenated in the lungs and then returns via the _____ _____ into the left _____ which contracts to push the blood into the left _____ where it leaves the heart via the _____ to be taken around the body.

3. Put the five blood vessels in the correct order that the blood would flow through them once they have left the heart.
   Venules Capillaries Arteries Veins Arterioles

4. Select the correct answer to the following questions.
   i) Which of the following is a feature of an artery?
      a. Carries blood under low pressure
      b. Carries mostly de-oxygenated blood
      c. Has thick, muscular walls
      d. Carries blood towards the heart

ii) Which of the following is a feature of a vein?
   a. Carries blood away from the heart
   b. Has thick, muscular walls
   c. Carries blood under high pressure
   d. Carries mostly de-oxygenated blood

iii) Which of the following is *not* a function of the cardiovascular system?
   a. Production of nervous impulses
   b. Stops bleeding after injury
   c. Provides cells with nutrients
   d. Transports hormones to cells

iv) At which point of the respiratory system does gaseous exchange occur?
   a. Bronchioles
   b. Alveoli
   c. Bronchi
   d. Trachea

Summary

In this section we looked at the structure and functions of the cardiorespiratory system and how the cardiovascular and respiratory systems work together to take oxygen around the body and carbon dioxide away to be breathed out. The key learning points include:

- the cardiovascular system is made up of the heart and the blood vessels that take blood to and from all parts of the body
- the heart is divided into two sides, the right and the left side, by a wall of muscle called the septum
- the coronary arteries are the arteries that supply the heart muscle itself with blood and oxygen
- in order to make its journey around the body, blood is carried through five different types of blood vessels: arteries, arterioles, capillaries, veins and venules
- arteries have thick, muscular walls and carry blood which has been pumped out of the heart
- veins are blood vessels that carry blood under low pressure back to the heart
- thermoregulation is how the body works to maintain an internal temperature of around 37°C
- the respiratory system is responsible for the intake of oxygen from the air
- the right lung is slightly larger as the left lung has a space for the heart
- air entering the body passes through several structures: nasal cavity, epiglottis, trachea, bronchi, bronchioles and alveoli
- the functions of the cardiorespiratory system are to supply oxygen to the body, produce blood flow through the body, take up of oxygen in the body to produce energy and rid the body rid of carbon dioxide.

Activity B.1

Part 1

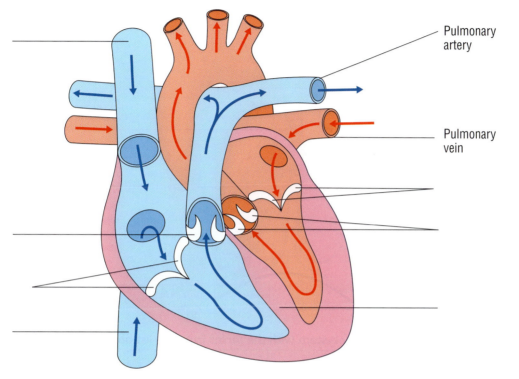

Pulmonary
artery

Pulmonary
vein

Label the diagram of the heart with the terms from the list below.

Right ventricle	Septum	Left ventricle	Bicuspid valve	Vena cava
Tricuspid valve	Right atrium	Aorta	Semi-lunar valve	Left atrium

Part 2

Complete the table to test your knowledge of blood vessels. An example has been completed for you.

Blood vessel	Description of structure	Function of blood vessel
Arteries		
Arterioles	Are smaller versions of arteries and have muscular walls	To carry oxygenated blood to the tissues of the body
Capillaries		
Veins		
Venules		

Part 3

Produce an information sheet that describes the functions of the cardiovascular system.

Activity B.2

Part 1

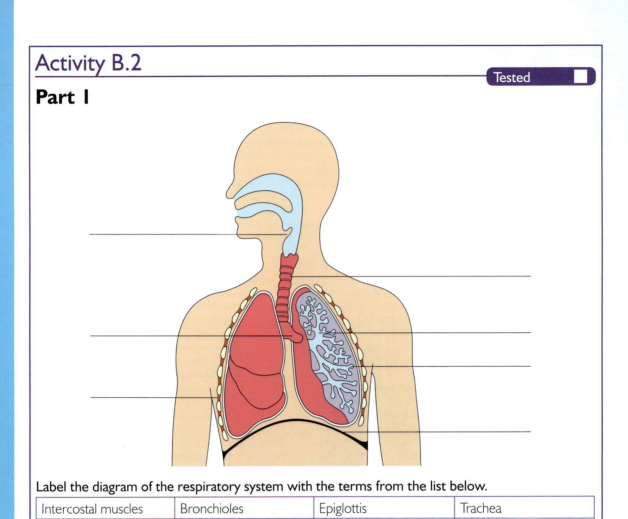

Label the diagram of the respiratory system with the terms from the list below.

Intercostal muscles	Bronchioles	Epiglottis	Trachea
Diaphragm	Alveoli	Bronchus	

Part 2

Describe the journey that air goes on through the six structures of the respiratory system.

Part 3

Produce an information sheet that describes the mechanics of breathing.

Unit 8

Promotion and Sponsorship in Sport

In this unit you will investigate promotion and sponsorship in sport before having a chance to promote or sponsor your own event. Not so long ago, sponsorship in sport existed on a far more modest scale. Now, due largely to the media revolution that makes all elite sporting events available across the globe, promotion and sponsorship in sport are big business that have shaped, and are still shaping, the way sport is played and watched today.

Learning aims

By the end of this unit you will:

✓ investigate issues involved in promoting sport

✓ explore sponsorship in sports promotion

✓ plan the promotion of a sports event or scenario.

Assessment criteria

Assessment and grading criteria

To achieve a **PASS** grade the evidence must show that the learner is able to:	To achieve a **MERIT** grade the evidence must show that the learner is able to:	To achieve a **DISTINCTION** grade the evidence must show that the learner is able to:
P1 Describe four different reasons for the promotion of sport	**M1** Assess the role of the media in the promotion of two selected sporting events	
P2 Explain the role of the media in the promotion of sport		
P3 Explain the effects the promotion of a selected sporting event has on participants and spectators		
P4 Describe public, private, regional, national, international and global sources of sponsorship available, including procedures involved in securing sponsorship	**M2** For two selected sports individuals, teams or events, summarise information on their sponsorship	
P5 Describe the range of different ethical issues which can arise from sponsorship of a selected sports individual, team or event	**M3** Explain ethical issues which can arise from sponsorship of a selected sports individual, team or event	**D1** Compare and contrast the impact of sponsorship on two selected sports individuals, teams or events
P6 Independently create a plan to promote a selected sports event or scenario, describing strengths and areas for improvement	**M4** Explain strengths of the plan and areas for improvement, providing recommendations for future promotion	**D2** Justify recommendations for future promotion of a selected sports event or scenario

Topic A.1 Reasons for the promotion of sport

The promotion of sport by the UK government has changed in recent years. In 2002 the government published a document called *Game Plan*. This supported sport at elite, competitive and recreational levels as well as wider forms of physical activity. It did so because it was felt that sport and physical activity would provide a wide range of benefits in communities in terms of things like health, education, promoting stronger communities and social inclusion. This was summed up in the government's catchphrase of the time: 'sport for good'.

From 2008 the government's policy changed. A new policy called *Playing to Win* also supported elite, grassroots and recreational sport, but stated that sport should now be promoted, not just because of the wider benefits to health, behaviour and education, but because of the value of sport itself. The key phrase now was 'sport for sports sake'.

Health benefits of sport and physical activity

`Studied` ☐

The National Health Service describes exercise as 'the miracle cure we've always had, but we've neglected to take our recommended dose for too long'. Of course, the advice that we should exercise regularly is not new. Indeed, many of the benefits of exercise have been known for a long time. However, over the last twenty to thirty years the amount of scientific evidence has grown to indicate that participation in regular exercise provides a huge array of health benefits, including:

- up to a 35 per cent lower risk of coronary heart disease and stroke
- up to a 50 per cent lower risk of type 2 diabetes
- up to a 50 per cent lower risk of colon cancer
- up to a 20 per cent lower risk of breast cancer
- up to a 30 per cent lower risk of early death
- up to an 83 per cent lower risk of osteoarthritis
- up to a 68 per cent lower risk of hip fracture
- a 30 per cent lower risk of falls (among older adults).

No wonder it's called a 'miracle cure'! Furthermore, being overweight or obese are important risk factors in a variety of illnesses and conditions. Regular participation in exercise, along with an appropriate diet, can reduce or control weight and therefore reduce the risks of ill health associated with obesity. It is estimated that an increase of five points on the body mass index scale (see Unit 1, Learning aim C, Topic C.1) is associated with a 40 per cent increase in the risk of coronary heart disease. Weight control can also help individuals to achieve greater feelings of wellbeing about themselves which may in turn help their general health.

In addition, regular activity can lead to a reduction of anxiety, promote social contact and increase confidence and self-esteem. It is estimated that regular exercise may provide:

- up to a 30 per cent lower risk of depression
- up to a 30 per cent lower risk of dementia.

The government has recently changed its recommendations on the amount of exercise necessary for health. The Chief Medical Officers' report of July 2011 issued new guidelines covering the amount of activity for different age groups:

- Pre-school children: 180 minutes spread throughout each day.
- Children (5–18 years): between 60 minutes and several hours every day (include vigorous intensity activities at least three days a week).
- Adults (18–65 years): 150 minutes (2.5 hours) per week in 'mini' bouts of more than 10 minutes or 75 minutes of vigorous activity spread across the week, or a combination of these moderate and vigorous activity levels.
- Adults (over 65 years): 150 minutes (2.5 hours) per week in bouts of 10 minutes or more of moderate intensity activity daily spread across a week. One way of doing this is to do 30 minutes on at least 5 days a week.

It is also recommended that people of all ages should minimise the amount of time spent being sedentary (sitting) for extended periods, thus cycling to school, college or work and using the stairs rather than the lift are to be encouraged!

If exercise were a pill, it would be one of the most cost-effective drugs ever invented.

(Source: www.nhs.uk)

Studied ☐ PI

Economic benefits of sport and physical activity

People who play sport or keep active already contribute to a reduction in health costs by helping themselves to stay healthier. Indeed, Sport England estimates that with 'one million more people across the country playing sport each week, it would save the taxpayer £22.5bn in health and associated costs'. Coronary heart disease costs the UK £9 billion a year. Therefore, if participation rates could be increased sport has the potential to generate huge further savings in health expenditure.

Sport is also very important to the economy and many sports organisations contribute to the economy in the tax they pay. In 2008 a report conducted by Sheffield Hallam University found that consumer spending on sport in England amounted to £17.384 billion, equivalent to 2.3 per cent of total expenditure. Also 441,000 people had sports-related jobs in England, this accounted for 1.8 per cent of the workforce in England.

Quality of life

Studied ☐

Sport improves the quality of life of individuals and communities in many ways:

- It allows people to gain satisfaction through self-improvement and the achievement of goals, such as completing a half marathon, doing a personal best or reaching a cup final.
- It allows people to undertake something they enjoy that can become an important part of their life.
- Sport has educational benefits and helps to teach things like discipline, respect for others and the ability to focus on targets and teamwork that can lead to an improved quality of life.
- Sport is often a social activity where people meet and make friends, have fun and develop lifelong personal and social skills.

Real world connection

The FA Skills Programme is sponsored by Tesco and aims to reach 4.7 million 5–11 year olds by 2014. However, it doesn't just focus on football skills but instead aims to help develop:

> 'physical, technical, psychological and social elements, helping children to develop more than just their football skills – we'll help them to gain confidence, build self-esteem, learn to work as a team and improve their decision making.'

(Source: The FA.com (www.thefa.com))

Sport and social inclusion, crime and antisocial behaviour

Studied ☐

In some areas of the country there are high levels of unemployment, deprivation and crime. This is particularly the case in some run-down inner city areas and this can lead to a situation of **social exclusion** which in turn can lead to antisocial behaviour and crime. Sport is thought to be a powerful tool in combating these problems.

> ### Key term
> **Social exclusion** – this occurs when people or areas suffer from a combination of linked problems such as unemployment, poor skills, low incomes, poor housing, high crime environments, bad health, poverty and family breakdown.

Real world connection

The Kickz programme began in London in 2006 and now involves 42 Premier and Football League clubs. It is run in partnership with other organisations such as the Police. Its aim is to:

'build safer, stronger, more respectful communities through the development of young peoples' potential.'

(Source: www.premierleague.com)

One of the 42 clubs is Manchester United where The Manchester United Foundation runs a variety of schemes in the community. On days when the Kickz scheme was running it was reported that:

- Antisocial behaviour was down in Salford by 16.4 per cent and in Trafford by 28.4 per cent.
- Violence against the Person was down in Salford by 42.9 per cent and in Trafford by 47.7 per cent.
- Overall crime was down 25.4 per cent in Salford and 41 per cent in Trafford on scheme days.
- Antisocial behaviour in East Wythenshawe was down by over 25 per cent since the start of the evening community cohesion project.

(Source: Manchester United Foundation Annual Report 2012)

Sport and active citizenship

Studied ☐

By simply playing in a local sports team you are engaging in **active citizenship** and contributing to your community. That is because by playing you are helping your team to keep going and that in itself is of value to your neighbourhood. However, sport contributes far more than this in terms of helping active citizenship. Many people give up their time to be club officers, performing roles such as club secretary, club treasurer or team captain. Others help by working through their governing bodies at grass roots level by organising tournaments, leagues and fixtures or by keeping the local association going. Many people spend their weekends as referees, umpires or officials. There are around 5.8 million volunteers supporting sport and it is estimated that the FA alone has 250,000 volunteers supporting grass roots football. One clear expression of active citizenship was the 70,000 volunteers, known as Games Makers, that helped the London 2012 Olympic and Paralympic Games to be such a success.

> ### Key term
> **Active citizenship** – taking an active and positive part in the community.

Sport and local and national identify

Studied ☐

Sport is important in creating and reinforcing local and national identity. This is because when a representative team plays it brings a country together against a common opposition. National identity can be enhanced by promoting sport through having a national representative team, by hosting a mega-event or by achieving international success.

National representative team

The role of representative sports teams in promoting and helping to shape national identity has been appreciated for over 100 years. Since the 1908 Olympics in London, athletes have been required to compete in the Olympic Games only through their recognised National Olympic Committees. This in turn has meant that many countries or athletes have been unable to compete under their own flag until their country achieved independence. Organisations such as FIFA followed this model when their World Cup began in 1930.

For newly independent nations it is an important expression of nationhood to have a national team in as many sports as possible. For this reason each country that becomes independent tries to place itself on the international sporting stage as soon as possible after independence, for example:

- the Czech Republic and Slovakia play separately since the split of Czechoslovakia
- until recently the Soviet Union competed as one nation in the Olympics and the FIFA World Cup. Now, apart from Russia, the following former nations of the Soviet Union compete: Armenia, Azerbaijan, Belarus, Estonia, Georgia, Kazakhstan, Kyrgyzstan, Latvia, Lithuania, Moldova, Tajikistan, Turkmenistan, Ukraine and Uzbekistan
- Yugoslavia formerly competed as one nation but there are now six in-dependent countries competing: Bosnia-Herzegovina, Croatia, Mace-donia, Montenegro, Serbia and Slovenia. On the other hand, Kosovo has not played in the football World Cup because it is not considered by FIFA to be sufficiently recognised as an independent country.

Sport is also important in expressing regional identity. For example, Catalonia FC cannot compete in the European Championships or the FIFA World Cup because the region is part of Spain. However, a Catalonian team has existed since 1904 and still represents the region by playing one or two friendlies per year against international opposition. It includes such famous Spain and Barcelona players as Carlos Puyol, Xavi Hernández, Víctor Valdés, Cesc Fàbregas and Gerard Piqué. Catalan identity is also expressed through FC Barcelona where the motto 'more than a club' represents the strong links with Catalan identity.

Figure 8.1 Gerard Piqué playing for Catalonia versus Tunisia

Hosting a mega-event

Hosting a mega-event like the Olympic Games or the FIFA World Cup is another powerful method of a nation projecting itself to the world. That is why governments often back bids to try to win the right to host major events. The UK will host the 2017 World Athletic Championships at the Olympic Stadium in Stratford, but the attempt supported by Prime Minister David Cameron, Prince William and David Beckham for England to win the right to host the 2018 FIFA World Cup was unsuccessful as Russia won the bid.

Achieving international success

International success in sport is also seen as a symbol of national success. Many countries now back their national squads by funding elite training programmes. In order to achieve success nations will target resources into those sports that it is thought will best deliver success. For the 2012 London Olympics, around half of the total elite funding for Team GB was focused on just five targeted sports: athletics, cycling, rowing, sailing and swimming.

Winning also promotes local identity. For example, football teams that win major honours such as the UEFA Champions League or the Premier League title are given civic receptions in their home town by the local council. Successful Olympians are sometimes honoured too:

- Mansfield District Council named a local swimming baths as the 'Rebecca Adlington Pool' after the success of their local swimmer in the Beijing Olympics.
- A statue of Sir Steve Redgrave has been erected in his home town of Marlow.
- There is a statue of the famous athlete, Steve Ovett, in Brighton.

Organisations promoting healthy living and sport campaigns

Studied ☐

The roles of national organisations promoting healthy living have been modified in recent years. Sport England promotes sports participation in the community and the Youth Sports Trust leads on promoting sport for young people. Agencies like the Department of Health and the Department of Transport are asked to promote wider forms of physical activity (such as brisk walking, dancing, recreational cycling and active lifestyles).

This was quite a policy change as for many years Sports Councils like Sport England had been heavily involved in campaigns to encourage wider physical activity as well as sport. Local authorities also often promote sport through sport development departments and healthy lifestyles.

The number of people taking part in regular exercise is still lower in the UK compared to some other European countries. For example Finland has been reported in some surveys to have participation rates as high as 70%. The lack of participation in the UK is a concern because around a quarter of the population are obese, childhood obesity levels continue to grow and diabetes has been increasing since the mid 1990s.

Sport campaigns

'Sportivate' is a joint programme between Sport England and County Sports Partnerships which aims to establish a legacy of participation following the London 2012 Olympics. It will run until 2015 and gives 14–25 year olds access to six–eight weeks of coaching in a range of sports and is aimed at those who are not currently active in their own time.

'Creating a Sporting Habit for Life' is another programme between Sport England and County Sports Parnerships which aims to capitalise on the London 2012 Olympic Games to encourage a legacy of mass participation. The programme will run until 2017 and is projected to cost £1billion. It is intended to instil a sports habit in young people that will last a lifetime by offering all secondary schools in England at least one community sport club on the school site (a satellite club), which is distinct from PE and run by community volunteers. The programme also aims to have at least 150 further education colleges with a full-time sports professional.

School Games

Organised by the Youth Sports Trust, the aim of the School Games is to 'motivate and inspire millions of young people across the country to take part in more competitive school sport' following the London 2012 Olympics. It is sponsored by Sainsbury and organised at four levels:

- Level 1 – Competition in each school
- Level 2 – Competition between schools
- Level 3 – Multi-sport School Games festivals at county/area level
- Level 4 – School Games Finals: a national multi-sport event sponsored by Sainsbury.

For more information visit the School Games website at www.yourschoolgames.com

Promoting physical activity for health

As mentioned earlier, the prime responsibility for promoting wider physical activity (as opposed to promoting more traditional sports) has been delegated to different agencies such as the Department of Health/NHS and the Greater London Authority.

'From Couch to 5K' is a nine-week exercise programme for beginners that is available through the NHS website with a podcast of a personal trainer providing guidance that can be downloaded. It is designed to gradually build up your running ability so that you can run 5K without stopping.

The Greater London Authority Cycling Campaign aims to increase cycling on London's roads by 400 per cent by 2025 compared to 2001 levels. It is hoped that people will become active by cycling instead of using their car or public transport. This is being done through a range of measures:

- installing 12 cycle superhighways into Central London
- improving cycle parking facilities in Central London
- the Barclays Bike hire scheme where bikes can be rented and left at set locations when the journey is completed.

Topic A.2 Role of the media in the promotion of sport

P2

Communication through different forms of media

Studied ☐

- **Television**: One of the most effective ways that the media promotes sport is through the saturation television reporting and broadcasting of major events such as the Football Premier League. This level of publicity creates superstar status for the players and provides high levels of exposure for sponsors so that football becomes very attractive to them. Previously sport was only available on the **free to air channels** such as the BBC and ITV. However, when the number of channels broadcasting sport increased as a result of the new **subscription channels** (such as Sky Sports 1) and **pay-per-view** (for special events like World Championship boxing bouts), media companies were forced to bid higher to obtain the rights to broadcast. This led to a huge influx of money into sports such as the Football Premier League, meaning the upgrading of stadia, high earning international stars being enticed to play in the Premier League and therefore greater promotion of the sport, which in turn made the sport even more attractive to sponsors.

- **Internet websites:** The home page of internet sites such as Yahoo carry sports news and in some cases video footage of action from the latest fixtures, while organisations like the BBC and Sky Sports have sports websites that are continually updated. These all help to promote sports events to a wide audience. At local level sport can also be promoted through websites. For example, a university may have details of their sports teams' progress on their website as well as news and results of their internal competitions.

- **Newspapers:** Both **tabloids** and **broadsheets** report on sport and feature up-and-coming events and so they both promote sport but often with a different style.

- **Radio:** Broadcasters such as BBC 5 Live and Talk Sport feature sports coverage as well as sports debate and sports news and phone-ins. Live coverage of sport is broadcast on national stations as well as on local radio services.

- **Magazines:** Sport is a high profile feature in many magazines. For example, interviews with stars such as Wayne Rooney or Jessica Ennis or endorsements of products by sports stars will be seen by people who might not normally switch on to sports media coverage.

Key terms

Free to air channels – television channels that are funded either by a licence (BBC) or advertising (ITV).

Subscription channels – you need to pay a fee to gain access to these television channels.

Pay-per-view – payment made to watch a specific one-off sports event broadcast by a television subscription channel.

Tabloids – popular newspapers that often feature celebrity or sensational stories.

Broadsheets – papers that contain more serious news items.

Imagery

Promoters of sport will often try to create a certain image in order to help promote the sports event. For example, when Channel 4 promoted its coverage of the London 2012 Paralympics, the television trailer for the event built up this by saying, 'forget all you know about strength, forget all you know about humans ... Meet the super humans'. This is an example of a media organisation creating an image of an event. Portraying paralympians as super humans was aimed at building up the special nature of the paralympians' achievements on the back of the BBC coverage of the 2012 Olympics, where outstanding human feats were seen.

The UEFA Champions League is billed as a supreme football club tournament. UEFA and the television companies in Europe reinforce that brand image by placing the Champions League logo on the centre of the pitch before all matches and playing the specially composed Champions League anthem, which includes lyrics in English, French and German, at all games and on all TV stations. This helps provide a common image that announces the match as part of a bigger European-wide product.

Presentation

When promoting a sports event it is important to choose the right form of media. Where a sports event has sold the broadcasting rights to a major broadcaster, this media organisation will probably promote the event because having bought the rights to broadcast it they will want to ensure that the viewing or listening figures are as high as possible. This makes it more attractive to advertisers. The BBC hypes Wimbledon coverage and ensures that there is coverage of both male and female stars to attract as wide an audience as possible and to ensure women tennis stars are promoted.

Smaller events targeting a more local audience might use local newspapers or newsletters to promote the event. Many councils also publish their own magazines that are distributed free and local organisers will often promote sports events through this medium. An event held within a college or a university, on the other hand, could be promoted through the institution's intranet site or through the college newsletter.

Topic A.3 Effects the promotion of sport has on spectators

Well promoted and high profile events can attract large numbers of people and this can have an effect on spectators in a number of ways.

Constraints

- **Cost:** Top sporting fixtures can be an expensive day out. When events are heavily promoted demand can increase and this will further push up costs. Not only are the tickets themselves expensive but added to this is the cost of travel, refreshments, programmes, etc. For example, the 2012/13 season ticket prices at Premier League grounds ranged from £325 at Aston Villa up to £1955 for a top price season ticket at Arsenal.
- **Availability:** Obtaining tickets for popular events is not always easy. The London Olympics sold out for many events and many people did not get tickets but there was huge controversy when television pictures revealed empty seats that had not been taken up by corporate partners.
- **Accessibility:** Highly attractive events might not be easy to get to. For example, as part of the Football Association plan to pay for the reconstruction of Wembley Stadium, the ground is used for all FA Cup Semi Finals, even when two teams from the north of England are playing. Previously, neutral grounds like Villa Park or Old Trafford were used.
- **Targeted groups:** 'Kids for a Quid' is a scheme that many professional football clubs use to encourage young people to attend matches. The price of a ticket for a junior is priced at £1 but this is usually only done at games where there is likely to be a low attendance.

Psychological effects

Sports spectators are normally focused on enjoying the sports event or on supporting and admiring the achievements of great athletes. This means they are more likely to be susceptible to psychological influences such as advertising, role models, brand sponsorship and merchandising.

- **Advertising:** In today's world of commercialised sport, spectators are exposed to a constant stream of advertising around the perimeter of grounds, in match programmes or, watching on television, through TV adverts.
- **Using role models to promote events to spectators:** Sports stars can quickly become role models because of the huge levels of publicity they obtain through global broadcasting, newspapers, magazines, radio and the internet. This goes way beyond the exposure they would otherwise get through the people that have seen these top athletes performing live. In addition, the commentary that the media provides to go along with the action, as well as an analysis of their

qualities or an account of their life story all add to their attraction. This creation of role models helps to promote the sport itself. In the 2012 London Olympics the 5,000 and 10,000 metres finals would not have received the same hype in the UK without Mo Farah taking part. Similarly, British cyclists like Sir Chris Hoy, Bradley Wiggins and Victoria Pendleton, the gold medal winning female boxer Nicola Adams or great Paralympians like Ellie Simmonds and David Weir, all helped to promote the events in which they compete, thus increasing the number of viewers. This also exposes spectators to the influence of these role models.

- **Brand sponsorship:** Sports fans are exposed to huge amounts of brand exposure through the sponsorship of top athletes, for example, top footballers are sponsored to wear particular brands of football boots – this is known as **brand sponsorship**. This is also known as **product endorsement**. Athletes also endorse other products away from sport. For example, Jessica Ennis has endorsed products like Olay beauty products and British Airways. Victoria Pendleton, who retired from competitive cycling after the Olympics, has had deals to endorse brands such as Pantene beauty products, Halfords bikes and Hovis bread.

- **Merchandising:** Spectators are also open to powerful advertising from **merchandising**. Many of the Football League clubs have mega stores at their grounds and in some cases in shopping malls too, where a wide range of goods featuring the club colours, name and badge are sold.

Key terms

Brand sponsorship – attaching the name of a famous sports personality to a product.

Product endorsement – famous sports personalities are paid to wear the clothing and footwear or use equipment of a particular supplier, or to recommend a particular product, which may or may not be connected with their particular sport.

Merchandising – selling products that contain the name, colours and logos of the event or of the club, such as mugs, replica shirts, car stickers, etc.

Topic A.4 Effects the promotion of sport has on participants

Availability and accessibility

'Inspire a generation' was the slogan of the London 2012 Olympics. It reflects the extent to which the broadcasting of a major event on television can have an inspirational effect in persuading people to take up a sport. However, is there the capacity to cope with this extra demand?

> ## Real world connection
>
> Each year great enthusiasm for tennis can be seen when the Wimbledon Tennis Championships are broadcast on the BBC. A sports centre manager describes the effect of the coverage of Wimbledon on the usage of the centre's tennis courts:
>
> *'During Wimbledon we can't cope with tennis demand. We have six tennis courts but during the rest of the summer we often take the nets on three of these down and use the area for other sports as the demand for tennis can be comfortably met by the other three courts. However, during the Wimbledon Championships, and for about two weeks after, we have to reserve all six courts just for tennis and it is simply not enough at peak time. We see people playing tennis that we do not otherwise see. Many of them seem to have gone out and bought new rackets or the latest tennis clothing. However, by mid to late July the enthusiasm begins to drop off as people start to forget about Wimbledon. When the football season restarts in August demand is back to normal.'*

This account shows us both the strength of televising elite sport in inspiring youngsters and its limitations in that the enthusiasm can soon fade. Unless the coverage is continuous, or there are programmes to tap into this enthusiasm, such as coaching sessions, then there is a real risk that the inspiration will not result in a long-term increase in participation. Indeed, there is very little evidence that participation increased in many countries after they hosted the Olympics.

At a local level, well promoted events can place additional pressures on facilities. Continuing the tennis example from above, a local tennis tournament at the above leisure centre would make it more difficult for casual users to book courts. Well promoted events might also attract higher numbers of entries which may make it difficult for regular participants to get a place. This may also make qualifying for a tournament harder for participants. Similarly, a well promoted school summer holiday football coaching programme might be very popular and therefore places could become very limited. Swimming pools are careful to get the right balance between hosting events that promote competitive sport like swimming galas and keeping the pool time available for recreational and casual swimmers.

Under-represented groups

Studied ☐

The broadcasting of the Paralympics provided huge exposure for disability sport and made household names of people such as Ellie Simmonds and David Weir. A record 11.9 million viewers watched the opening ceremony of the Paralympics in the UK, making it Channel 4's most viewed programme in a decade. Ellie Simmonds' victory was watched on television by 2.9 million people and Jonnie Peacock's gold by 6 million. This exposure will have significant benefits in inspiring new Paralympians to come forward and in raising the profiles of the successful Paralympians.

Women's football has grown hugely in recent years and participation levels have soared. Events like England games and the Women's FA Cup Final are shown on free to air television, but despite this, mainstream media coverage has not kept pace. For example, League games are only shown on subscription channels and while a single tennis or athletics programmes will feature men's and women's sport, women's football does not get coverage on mainstream football programmes. Press reporting of the women's game has also not kept pace with other developments. This shows how difficult it is for growing sports like women's football to break the mould of media coverage. As such, the new Women's Super League had difficulty getting a sponsor when it began in 2010. Higher media exposure would mean women players and women's football itself would be more attractive to advertisers and sponsors. With disability sport too, the mass coverage of the Paralympics is not matched by a commitment by the media to report disability sports events that take place in the intervening time between the Olympic and Paralympic Games.

Perceived status

Studied ☐

Perceived status means how the public view a team or a person. The media can affect the status of athletes by making them favourites or underdogs in order to try to build up interest in their coverage. For example, the media might build up the England football team when they reach the knockout stages of a major tournament or build extra pressure on a tennis player such as Andy Murray when he reaches the later rounds of Wimbledon. In 2011 the media branded the David Haye versus Wladimir Klitschko fight a 'David versus Goliath' contest in order to hype the promotion.

> ### Key term
> **Perceived status** – how a team or sports person is viewed by the public, especially as a result of media coverage.

Check your understanding

1. Are the following statements true or false?

   An active lifestyle can:

   a. reduce the risk of some types of cancer
   b. increase the risk of coronary heart disease
   c. reduce the risk of early death
   d. increase the risk of osteoarthritis
   e. assist with a programme of weight control.

2. Match up the national organisation with their main role.

Sport England	Promoting sport among young people
NHS/Department of Health	Promoting sports participation in the community
Youth Sport Trust	Promoting active lifestyles

3. A sports event has been heavily promoted. Match the effect of this promotion to the correct effect on the spectators.

Cost	The event has been moved to a bigger venue further away
Availability	Souvenirs and t-shirts with the name of the event are widely available
Accessibility	One of the stars of the event is promoting it on television
Targeted groups	The programme for the event features lots of adverts
Advertising	The price of tickets has increased
Role models	Some tickets are discounted to encourage children to attend
Brand sponsorship	Tickets are almost sold out
Merchandising	One of the stars is endorsing the footwear that will be worn in the competition

Summary

In this section we have looked at the benefits of sport to the community in terms of healthy living, prevention of antisocial behaviour and the creation of local and national identity. We have also looked at the role of the media in the promotion of sport and the effects of promotion on participants and performers. The key learning points include:

- participation in regular exercise can reduce the risk of disease and some mental health conditions
- sport contributes to the economy, improves our quality of life, contributes to active citizenship and enhances a country's national identity
- sport events are communicated and promoted through a variety of media and well promoted events can push up demand
- mainstream coverage of major events involving under-represented groups has helped to promote them but it is still difficult for under-represented groups to obtain regular mainstream coverage or reporting outside of major events or fixtures in order to promote their sport
- some promotions focus on targeted groups of spectators and role models are often used to promote sport to spectators
- spectators are often exposed to large amounts of brand sponsorship when watching popular sports events
- well promoted events can place additional pressures on facilities, stimulating demand which in turn takes up facility time
- broadcasting can help promote under-represented sports, such as women's football or disability sports events
- the media can affect the perceived status of participants by hyping pressure on teams or players which may affect their performance or by branding teams or players as underdogs.

Activities

Activity A.1

Tested

A local councillor is about to visit your school or college. You and your class will be trying to persuade her that you want to see more sports facilities installed in your neighbourhood. Write a letter that includes the following four reasons why you are promoting sport:

- A description of the national pride your community felt after London 2012 and then describe how sport could help enhance the identity of your local area.
- A description of how sport could make your community healthier.
- A description of how sport could help the community, for example by reducing crime or promoting active citizenship.
- A description of how healthy living campaigns could help your community.

Activity A.2

Tested

Part 1

Produce some fact sheets that could be handed out at a presentation that explain the role of the media in the promotion of sport in terms of:

- communication: how sport is promoted through televisions, newspapers, radio, etc.
- imagery: how the media portray the image of different sports events.
- presentation: which forms of media are favoured to promote different types of sports events.

Part 2

Select two sports events and assess the role of the media in promoting each of these events.

Activity A.3

Tested

For ONE of the events that you examined in Activity A.2, Part 2, produce a report that describes the effects promotion has had on the following:

Participants in terms of:

- availability, such as opportunities to enter a competition
- accessibility, such as the location of the event (or has promotion led to better facilities?)
- under-represented groups
- perceived status, for example, did the promotion of the event make any participants favourites or underdogs?

Spectators in terms of:

- cost, e.g. travel, entrance fee/tickets, merchandise, food, drink
- availability, such as availability of tickets
- accessibility, such as is the venue convenient to get to?
- whether the event is promoted to underrepresented groups.

Psychological effects in terms of:

- advertising the spectators are exposed to
- role models that promote the event
- brand sponsorship that spectators are exposed to
- merchandising that is promoted to spectators.

Learning aim B: Explore sponsorship in sports promotion

Topic B.1 Sources of sponsorship for individuals, teams, organisations or events

Public sponsorship and funding

Studied ☐

Groups and organisations such as local sports clubs, community organisations and voluntary groups and schools are eligible to apply for a range of grants and awards from different public sources, for example:

- The Sport England Small Grants Programme makes awards of between £300 and £10,000. Application forms and details are available through the Sport England website: www.sportengland.org
- 'Sportsmatch' from Sport England was developed to encourage further sponsorship of sport. It does this by matching the funding of a sponsor from between £1,000 and £100,000. As a result of **matched funding**, sponsorship can go much further, suiting both the sports organisation and the sponsor.
- 'Awards for All' offers grants of between £300 and £10,000 for projects that improve communities and the lives of people within them. Awards for All have their own website where details and application forms can be obtained: www.awardsforall.org.uk

Local authorities sometimes have their own schemes to give out grants to support local organisations too.

> **Key term**
> **Matched funding** – the money a sponsor gives is matched by another organisation that provides the same amount.

Private sponsorship

Studied ☐

At a local level, sports teams might be sponsored by local businesses such as sports shops, retailers or pubs, etc. From the club's point of view, this brings in much needed income to pay for things such as pitch permits, kit and equipment. From the business's point of view the sponsorship will bring them publicity and possibly increased business in the local area.

In the funding of sport the word **partner** is often used instead of sponsor. This is because the partner agrees to work with the sports organisations in a variety of different ways. For example, elite athletes who are sponsored by sports manufacturers will not only publicise the company name through wearing the company logo but will also be seen winning tournaments while wearing the company's clothing and using their equipment.

> **Key term**
> **Partner** – a sponsor who works with a sports organisation in a variety of ways.

UNIT 8 Promotion and Sponsorship in Sport

Football provides us with examples of sponsorship at different levels. At the more local level it is often companies with strong local connections that sponsor the leagues. Some examples are given below.

- The Sheffield and Hallamshire League is sponsored by Windsor Foods Services which is a company based in South Yorkshire.
- The Teesside League is sponsored by sport outfitters in Middlesbrough called Jack Hatfields Sports.
- The Essex and Suffolk Border League is sponsored by a company based in Colchester called KentBlaxhill Building Products.

Regional sponsorship

`Studied ☐`

The Greater London Authority bike hire scheme is sponsored by Barclays Bank. The bicycles are painted in the Barclays colours and the bikes are known as Barclays Bikes. This gives the company huge exposure around the capital and helps to associate the company with a scheme that is environmentally friendly and healthy.

Higher up the football pyramid there are just 14 Leagues covering England, each covering a region or perhaps four or five counties. As can be seen from the following examples, the sponsor's name at this level often becomes the name of the League:

- Thurlow Nunn Eastern Counties Football League
- Midlands Football Alliance sponsored by Baker Joiner
- Ebac Northern League
- Baris Northern Counties East Football League
- Toolstation Western Football League
- Sydenhams Football League (Wessex)

National sponsorship

`Studied ☐`

Sponsorship at national level is more attractive to larger sponsors and multinational companies because of the media coverage that sport at this level receives. Some examples of the highest national level sponsorship in England are given below.

- Barclays Football Premier League
- Cricket: LV County Championship, Clydesdale Bank 40, Friends Life T20
- Rugby Union Aviva Premiership Heineken Cup
- Rugby League: Stobart Super League

At the national level the government-sponsored Talented Athlete Scholarship Scheme (TASS) provides funding of up to £3,500 per year for around 600 young athletes each year competing at national and international level. This may include areas such as coaching, strength and conditioning and sports medicine. Forty-seven different sports are covered by the scheme.

Team GB Olympic athletes receive an Athletes Personal Allowance (APA) and services such as sports science are provided through the World Class Performance Programme.

International and global sponsorship

Unlike the single sponsors for the national leagues mentioned above, the UEFA Champions League has up to eight sponsors. These are all large multi-national companies and include Ford, MasterCard and, in countries that do not restrict alcohol advertising like Spain and Turkey, Heineken. They each receive:

- four over-size advertising boards around the pitch at Champions League matches
- their logos placed on the boards behind pre- and post-match interviews
- priority on television advertisements in Europe during television coverage of matches.

Many Premier League clubs also have multi-national sponsors. This is because the Premier League is shown across the world on television and these companies sell their goods across the world. For example, look at where some of the partners of these Premier League clubs are based:

- Chelsea: Samsung (South Korea) and Adidas (Germany)
- Arsenal: Emirates (Dubai – includes naming rights to stadium), Nike (USA)
- Everton: Chang Beer (Thailand)
- Manchester City: Etihad (United Arab Emirates – includes naming rights to stadium)
- Real Madrid: Bwin (Gibraltar).

Procedures to secure sponsorship

Studied ☐

So why do companies sponsor sport? The procedures to attract sponsors will vary according to level, for example, the up-and-coming athlete in a minority sport will be in a somewhat different position to a famous Olympic superstar that has a sports agent working for them. We will now consider how an up-and-coming athlete might approach a sponsor in their local area.

- **Stage 1:** The athlete should send a letter or an email that outlines their reason for contacting the company as well as a document of their potential or achievements. The athlete could perhaps include an invitation for the company to come to their next competition.
- **Stage 2:** They should follow up the letter or email with a phone call to check the information was received and to arrange a meeting.
- **Stage 3:** Attend the meeting which has been arranged to present the opportunity for sponsorship to the company. After the meeting the athlete should follow up with a letter or an email thanking the company for their time.

Things the athlete could offer a company when asking for sponsorship:

- Making the company name visible at events (although the athlete must be careful to follow the branding rules of their sport).
- Promoting the company's products by using their equipment or clothing while competing (product endorsement).
- Give the company tickets to events. This is even better if the athlete can get tickets to VIP areas. The company might be able to use this to impress or entertain their business associates or to motivate their staff.
- The athlete could offer to make personal appearances at company events.
- The athlete could be used to motivate staff by giving a talk.
- The sponsorship could help the company to show they are supporting their local community.
- The athlete could offer special coaching sessions for staff, the children of families of the sponsor or do demonstration events.

Things the athlete could ask for when asking for sponsorship:

- Funding or supplying products like clothing, footwear and training equipment.
- Funding or supplying services such as free or discounted membership of a local gym or health club.
- Subsidised travel costs.
- Subsidised accommodation expenses.

It is important that athletes do not compromise their performance while meeting or even exceeding the expectations of their sponsor. The athlete needs to keep the sponsor up to date with events and performances and give the sponsor as much recognition and publicity as they can, such as thanking them in press interviews or when making speeches.

If you are Interested in finding out more about sponsorship, go to the UK Sport website and download a pdf document, 'Get Sponsored' – www. uksport.gov.uk/docLib/Information-Zone/Athlete-Zone/GetSponsored.pdf

Topic B.2 Ethical issues arising from sponsorship

Link between sponsorship and alcohol, tobacco and gambling

Alcohol sponsorship

Alcohol companies have for a long time been keen to promote themselves through sport. Old photographs of the first football grounds in the late nineteenth century show breweries that paid to have their products or names painted in huge letters on the roofs of stands at football grounds. This trend continues today with companies such as Carlsberg, Carling and Budweiser heavily involved in sport sponsorship. By sponsoring sport, alcohol companies can associate themselves with something that is associated with sports stars and a lifestyle of health and fitness.

However, beer producing companies are also very keen to associate their products with sports spectating. This is because they hope that those watching something like Premier League matches at home, on TV or in a pub will then choose to buy their brand of drink while they are watching the game or will become familiar with the brand name and so buy this product at a later date. These companies are also keen to show drinking beer as a social activity where groups of friends are drinking their brand while watching the sport. Many adverts during Premier League matches, for example, show fans consuming alcohol as part of the entertainment of watching sport on TV.

So while alcohol sponsorship is good for the alcohol industry as it promotes their product, good for the TV companies who gain advertising revenue and good for the sports club as the alcohol company may be paying them as one of their partners, the ethical question is: *If alcohol misuse, or overuse, is harmful to health, is it right that a healthy activity like sport should be used to promote alcohol consumption in this way?*

Tobacco sponsorship

Tobacco sponsorship of sport is banned in the UK and in the EU. Until the 1990s tobacco sponsorship was a huge source of income in many sports such as cricket and Formula 1. This was because tobacco companies liked to be associated with highly skilled or exciting activities and competitions often took the name of the tobacco company. For example, Rugby League's Challenge Cup was once known as the Silk Cut Challenge Cup.

Gambling sponsorship

One of the main areas to grow in sports sponsorship following the ban on tobacco sponsorship was the gambling industry.

In recent years football has been associated with gambling sponsors such as 188 Bet (Bolton Wanderers) and Genting Casinos (Aston Villa).

In 2012 William Hill announced that they had secured a two-and-a-half-year deal to became the 'Official Supporter' of the England football team, as well as the 'Official Supporter' and 'Official Betting Partner' of The FA Cup. Added to their sponsorship of the William Hill Scottish Cup and several horse races, this gives the company a large degree of exposure on sports where betting is popular.

Furthermore, the rise in internet, telephone and in-play betting has meant that the gambling industry has high exposure through TV and other media. However, there are ethical considerations because betting can be addictive and irresponsible gambling can lead people into severe financial difficulties.

So while gambling sponsorship is good for the gambling company in terms of promotion and good for TV companies who gain advertising revenue the ethical question is: *Is it right that sport events or teams should be used to promote gambling to possibly young and vulnerable people or people who cannot afford it that may be persuaded to gamble?*

Ethics in sports marketing

Sport can carry with it images of excellence, health, excitement, fame, wealth, glamour, winning and many other qualities. It is therefore not surprising that major companies are keen to have their names associated, with this but such associations must be **ethical**, so where should the line be drawn?

Nike like to portray themselves as a company that has a 'street edge'. In order to promote this image they sometimes use sports stars that have been associated with some form of controversy in their advertising campaigns, feeling this will boost their image among younger customers who want that edge.

Read the following British newspaper report which appeared in its online version in September 2012.

> ### Real world connection
>
> ## High fashion...or just promoting drug use? Mayor's fury at Nike after it unveils 'Get High' and 'Dope' T-shirt range
>
> Encouraging people to 'get high' is rather an odd stance for one of the world's best known sports brands.
>
> But it seems that's the message Nike are selling with a new range of men's T-Shirts emblazoned with pill bottles and the phrases 'Get High' and 'Dope.'
>
> Boston Mayor Thomas M Menino is not amused and has called on Niketown in the city to pull its display of the T-shirts from its windows ...
>
> (Daily Mail Online 21st June 2011)

The ethical question to consider is:

Is it right that companies should be using sports stars that have been associated with controversy to sell their products or causing controversy with their sports marketing to gain publicity, as in the case above?

Another ethical issue is the changing of football kits by professional football clubs. For example, in 2000, the Premier League Charter stated that new replica kits would be in use for at least two seasons so that fans would not have to replace expensive shirts too often. This has not been followed and many clubs have been changing home kits more frequently. On top of this, second and third strips are often changed. This places huge pressure as the new products are worn by the players and backed

Key term

Ethical – the extent to which something is morally right or not.

up through advertising campaigns such as on the club's website. This can make the old kit seem quickly out of date.

The ethical question to consider is:

When fans are loyal to just one club, is it fair to keep changing expensive kits regularly so that fans need to keep replacing them?

Contracts and ethical behaviour

Unethical conduct by players can seriously damage the reputation of the player, the sport and the club. For this reason the contracts of sportsmen and women will often contain clauses restricting their off-the-field activities, as well as their behaviour on the field. Players that 'step over the line' may therefore be subject to fines, suspension or contract termination. For example, in November 2012 the BBC reported that four Peterborough United players had been fined and placed on the transfer list following behaviour in which, *'two of the four players were cautioned by police for an incident in Peterborough city centre in the early hours of Sunday morning'*.

Influence of sponsors

Those putting money into sport will gain huge influence over how that sport is played. This is particularly true of media companies who can change the timing of matches to suit themselves and their advertisers. Consider the following examples:

At the Wimbledon Tennis Championships top British players like Andrew Murray or Laura Robson are often placed third on the schedule on Centre Court or Court One so that they are likely to be playing during peak TV viewing time in the evening. While the BBC does not allow advertising, this is good for their viewing figures as more people can see the match, good for the British players who will get greater exposure, good for the sponsors and products that the players endorse and advertise, and good for the sponsors associated with Wimbledon Championships. But is it fair?

Following the intervention of Sky TV, Rugby League changed from being a winter sport to a summer sport.

The schedule of Premier League Football Games has been changed and now matches are rescheduled to suit the needs of TV.

The ethical question to consider is:

Is it right and true to the spirit of fair play that sport schedules should be influenced by media and sponsors?

Influence of sponsors on a sporting organisation

Getting the balance right when it comes to sponsorship is not easy because it is important for large sporting events to attract income from sponsors. However, the main attraction or appeal of the event is that it is a sporting contest, so it is important that the event should not be seen as being too dominated by the sponsors. When this happens the event can be said to be **over commercialised**.

The Olympic Games is very concerned about its relations with sponsors. In 1976 the Montreal Games made a loss which took years to pay off and this could have threatened the Olympic Movement. By the time of the 1984 Olympics in Los Angeles, The Olympic Programme (TOP) had begun where top companies became partners of the Olympic Games. This was an attractive offer because when companies such as Coca Cola or McDonalds become TOP partners, they are associated with an elite sporting event that claims to bring the youth of the world together. This has major benefits for the image they try to portray of themselves around the world. However, when the Games returned to the USA in 1996 the Atlanta Games were thought by some to be over commercialised.

Sports administrators must therefore strike a balance and this varies from event to event. For example, the FA Cup is the oldest and most prestigious competition of its kind and for many years the FA felt it would tarnish the FA Cup competition to let its name be changed to that of a sponsor. While it has kept its name, it is now known as the FA Cup with Budweiser. The Premier League is known as the Barclays Premier League, although there are restrictions on how much sponsorship can be placed on shirts.

The ethical question to consider is:

Where do you draw the line? Would you like to see the rules relaxed so that football kits can be covered in sponsor's logos like a Formula One driver?

> **Key term**
>
> **Over commercialised** – where a sponsor's names are too prominent or the sponsors or other businesses are dictating the sport or the event to an unacceptable level.

Codes of practice for sponsorship

In order to protect themselves and their events, sports governing bodies issue rules concerning sponsorship and advertising, called a **code of conduct**. Every sport has different rules for personal sponsorships, such as motor racing with their branding on clothing, sailing with the branding on sails or cycling with the branding on bikes.

> **Key term**
>
> **Code of conduct** – a set of rules for behaving in a particular way that an organisation must abide by.

Real world connection

The Lawn Tennis Association (LTA) has strict rules for those running LTA Staged Tournaments and LTA Approved Tournaments. Some examples of these LTA rules are provided below.

- The LTA will be the owner of all the commercial rights of the tournament. Commercial rights cover things like broadcasting rights, new media rights, interactive games rights, sponsorship rights, merchandising rights, advertising rights, ticketing rights and hospitality rights.
- The LTA will allow the sponsor's name to be used in the title of the tournament but only if the sponsorship is more than £500 in respect of open events and £250 in junior events.
- All on-court advertising should be discreet and in good taste and should not in any way provide a distraction or hindrance to the players.
- In no circumstances should any banner or advertisement which contains either white or yellow colours be placed at the end(s) of a match court.

Advertising standards

Studied ☐

The organisation responsible for enforcing the rules on advertising is called the Advertising Standards Agency. It states that 'Alcohol ads are banned from appearing in and around programmes commissioned for or principally targeted at audiences below the age of 18, as well as programmes likely to appeal particularly to audiences below the age of 18.'

However, alcohol companies that sponsor football teams or competitions are creating awareness of themselves by sponsoring events and teams and the Advertising Standards Agency has strict rules about how alcohol adverts are portrayed on TV during sports events.

Topic B.3 Impact of sponsorship

It is difficult to distinguish between the impact of the media on sport and the impact of sponsorship because the two feed so closely off each other. Greater media exposure means a sport is more attractive to sponsors, but how has this affected popular sports events like the Wimbledon Tennis Championships and the Football Premier League?

Wimbledon Tennis Championships

Studied

As discussed earlier, it suits broadcasters and sponsors that top British players are scheduled to play during peak viewing time in the evening. Greater sponsorship allows Wimbledon to pay top price money and so retain the quality of the product and its status as an event at the top of tennis. The income that the Championships earn help it to improve the stadia, such as placing a roof on Centre Court. This in turn is attractive to broadcasters and sponsors as it means play is not disrupted by poor weather.

The sponsorship also means that Wimbledon can retain mass coverage on TV for early rounds and does not need to search for other broadcasting deals. This wider audience maintains Wimbledon as a centre piece of summer sport viewing whereas if some matches were moved to subscription channels it would become more marginalised. The income from broadcasting and sponsorship means Wimbledon can survive as a top sporting fixture in a very competitive environment.

The Wimbledon Championships has thirteen partners including:

- Slazenger: supplies the tennis balls (has done so for more than a hundred years)
- Robinsons: supplies drinks such as barley water (has done so for over seventy years)
- Rolex: supplies the familiar clocks and scoreboards on each court (since 1978)
- IBM: provides information such as schedules, player statistics and the speed of serves
- Hertz: supplies the vehicles to transport players to and from the grounds
- Lanson: official supplier of champagne to the Wimbledon Championships
- Polo Ralph Lauren: provides the clothing for the umpires and officials (since 1975)
- HSBC: provides onsite banking services during the Wimbledon Championships and sponsors the 'Road to Wimbledon National 14 & Under Challenge'.

Other partners include Evian mineral water, Jacobs Creek wine and Sony 3D, who obtain 3D footage, along with the BBC, for distribution to global media networks.

Football Premier League

Studied

The Football Premier League on the other hand has been more heavily influenced by sponsors and the media. It is sponsored by Barclays but all the clubs within the League have a wide range of partners too. In the 1990s many football grounds were crumbling and desperately needed money to upgrade to all-seater grounds following the Taylor Report and the 1989 Hillsborough disaster.

The new income from broadcasters and sponsorship has transformed the quality of the product by enabling clubs to build better stadia and entice top international players. Scheduling has been affected with matches now rearranged to suit the demands of TV, many of which are only available on subscription televisions services, but regular highlights programmes help prevent football becoming marginalised from the mass audience.

Table 8.1 compares the impact of sponsorship on Wimbledon Tennis Championships and the Football Premier League.

Table 8.1 Comparison of the impact of sponsorship on two sporting events

Wimbledon Tennis Championships	Football Premier League
Wimbledon are keen to ensure that sponsors do not have too great an impact and so their visibility around the ground and on TV is more subtle	Football has sponsors' names around the ground which are highly visible for TV audiences
Some of Wimbledon's partners like Slazenger are very long standing	Football Clubs tend to change their partners more frequently
Wimbledon has sponsors such as Rolex and Lanson which help to reinforce Wimbledon's image as one of the events of the season for the more affluent, as well as appealing to the masses	Football tends to attract more mass-market sponsors
Wimbledon do not allow sponsorship on clothing apart from a small logo	In the Premier League shirt sponsorship is allowed, although it is controlled
A key similarity is that both competitions are made available to a global audience and therefore are very attractive to large multinational corporations	Another similarity is that while both competitions have their own sponsors, players within each sport have their own deals to endorse products by using them when playing

Check your understanding

1. Match up the type of sponsorship to the correct example.

Public sponsorship	AC Milan sponsored by Emirates Airlines
Private local sponsorship	Grant for Sport England
Regional sponsorship	Rugby Union Aviva Premiership
National sponsorship	A high street sport shop sponsoring a football league
International/global sponsorship	Lees Brewery Lancashire County League

2. Are the following statements true or false?
   a. Alcohol sponsorship of sport is banned in the UK.
   b. Tobacco sponsorship of sport is banned in the European Union.
   c. There are no restrictions as to how alcohol can be advertised on TV during football matches.
   d. Sponsorship in sport by gambling companies has decreased in recent years.

Summary

In this section we have looked at sources of sponsorship for individuals, teams, organisations or events and the ethical issues arising from sponsorship. The key learning points include:

- non-profit making groups and organisations may get funding from organisations such as Sport England, Awards for All and local councils
- private sponsorship can be available at the local level from local businesses such as sports shops
- at the elite level athletes will get sponsorship from major companies and will be supplied with equipment
- multinational companies like to be associated with elite sports events and teams because their name is portrayed around the world.
- athletes must be careful about what they can offer a potential sponsor because they must not compromise their training or performance
- alcohol sponsorship is huge in sport, but we should consider the ethics of a healthy activity like sport being used to promote alcohol consumption
- tobacco sponsorship of sport is banned in the UK and in the EU, but the ethics of encouraging people to gamble when watching sport must be considered too
- sports marketing companies sometimes sponsor sport personalities associated with negative or bad behaviour to give the company an edge
- sponsors are able to influence match schedules and playing times but this is not always fair to players and fans
- event organisers must get the balance right between obtaining income from sponsors and not letting the event appear to be too dominated by the sponsors
- the Advertising Standards Agency publishes strict rules on advertising.

Activities

Activity B.1

Tested

Part 1

Prepare and deliver a presentation that describes in general terms the following sources of sponsorship in sport:

- public
- private
- regional
- national
- international and global.

Part 2

Describe how an athlete or an event organiser might secure sponsorship.

Activity B.2

Tested

Part 1

Select *two* sports individuals, teams or events. Provide fact sheets to hand out that summarise information on the sponsorship of your chosen sports individuals, teams or events.

Part 2

For *one* of these individuals, teams or events, describe and explain the range of different ethical issues which can arise from sponsorship.

Part 3

Compare and contrast the impact of sponsorship on your *two* selected sports individuals, teams or events by explaining their similarities and differences.

Learning aim C: Plan the promotion of a sports event or scenario

Topic C.1 Create a plan to promote a sporting event or scenario

For the assessment you are required to provide a plan of how you promoted a planned sports event. The best way to approach the creation of this plan is to link it to Unit 11 Running a Sports Event. Your plan must include the elements outlined below.

Aims and objectives

Studied ☐

This could be fund raising for a good cause or a promotional event to encourage healthy lifestyles. See Unit 11 for more details on selecting event objectives.

Choice of media

Studied ☐

In your plan you will need to provide reasons for the media you have selected. Each form of media has its advantages and disadvantages.

Table 8.2 The advantages and disadvantages of each form of media

Media	Advantages	Disadvantages
Posters	Do not get scattered or lost	Cannot be distributed like leaflets
Leaflets	Can be distributed	Can get scattered and lost; can be expensive to print
Internet/intranet	Saves on printing costs	Might not be seen by people outside the organisation
Press advert	Can be very effective	Expensive
Video promotion	Can be persuasive	Time consuming to make well; you need to think where it will be shown and who will see it
Personal selling (i.e. going around selling tickets)	Can be effective	Time consuming
Mailshot	Reaches the target audience; internal mailshots can be done through pigeon holes, e.g. to different school or college departments	Might be expensive

When deciding on your choice of media consider:

1. Will the right people see the advert?
2. Will the advert persuade people to come?
3. Can we produce the material to a reasonable standard?
4. Can we afford to produce the materials?

> **Key terms**
>
> **Personal selling** – selling tickets or handing out cards face to face.
>
> **Mailshot** – sending promotional materials to people or organisations by mail.

Press release

A copy of the **press release** should be included in the plan. The press release might be sent to a newspaper, a newsletter, a council magazine or all three. Newspapers are more likely to promote charity and community events than profit-making events. The press release is written in the style of an article and must contain all necessary information, such as time, date, place and entry fees, etc. The name of the sponsor will also help.

> **Key term**
>
> **Press release** – written as a press article but drafted by the event organisers and sent to newspapers and newsletters so they can write up an article about the event.

Contacting sponsors

A contact list of local sponsors should be included in your plan. An example contact list is shown below.

Table 8.3 An example of a contact list

	Contact details	Sponsorship required	Offer to sponsor
Dennis's Trophies	2 High Street Newtown Tel: 427009	Trophies	Announce name of sponsor at presentation. Place name of shop on all leaflets
Ryan's Supermarket	4 High Street Newtown Tel 789143	Drinks	Name sponsor in press release

When contacting sponsors it is important to be clear what you are offering. This might include announcing their name at the presentation, placing their name on posters and leaflets or promoting them in a mailshot or email distribution, mentioning that they are sponsoring the event in the press release or promoting them during the event by including adverts around the venue or handing out their business cards.

Advertising timeline

An **advertising timeline** shows the times when different parts of the promotional plan will happen. Your plan will need to include an advertising timeline and you can amend it as things happen. An example timeline is shown below.

> **Key term**
>
> **Advertising timeline** – a timeline showing when different stages of the plan will be carried out.

Table 8.4 Example of an advertising timeline

Week 1	Week 2	Week 3	Week 4
Select choice of media for promotion Draw up list of sponsors Agree what sponsors can be offered and what we are asking for	Contact sponsors Produce rough drafts of posters and leaflets Draw up distribution list for materials	Replies from sponsors. Ann's Bakery agreed to sponsor food. Dennis Trophies will supply medals Finish draft of leaflets and posters – send for printing	Write and issue press release
Week 5	**Week 6**	**Week 7**	**Week 8**
Leaflets and posters ready Leaflets arrived three days late Start distributing leaflets and posters	Ask for press release in newspaper and council magazine one week before event Press release appeared	**Event day** Place sponsor's adverts around venue Distribute sponsor's business cards Thank sponsors at presentation	Issue an after-event press release as a news story. Thank sponsors in press release Send thank you letters to sponsors

Evaluation questionnaire

After the event it is important to evaluate how well your promotional strategy worked. One way to do this is to include in the evaluation questionnaire some questions that will help the event team to plan future events, for example, asking how the person found out about the event and were they aware of who the sponsors were.

Topic C.2 Review the plan

Strengths and areas for improvement

Studied ☐

When reviewing your plan you need to consider its strengths and areas for improvement. In order to do this, ask yourself the following questions.

- Did the timeline work as planned or was it all a bit of a rush?
- Did the choice of promotional material attract the target audience? Was the event well attended?
- Were the right forms of media used?
- Were the promotional materials distributed in the right places?
- Were the materials produced in the right way? For example, were the materials too expensive and were any not effective?
- Were the promotional materials attractive?
- Which promotional materials attracted people to the event? (You will need to look at the questionnaire responses to find out the answer to this question.)
- Did you contact the right sponsors? Were there other sponsors that could have been approached?
- How many sponsors said yes? Why do you think this was?
- How many sponsors said no? Why do you think this was?
- Could you have offered the sponsors other benefits?
- Could you have asked sponsors for other things?
- Were the sponsors happy?
- Was the press release well written?
- Did the press release go in the paper at the right time?
- Could other newspapers or newsletters have been contacted?

Answers to these questions will provide you with either a strength or an area of improvement to comment on.

Recommendations for future promotions

Studied ☐

When reviewing your plan you need to think about what could be done differently if the event was to be organised again. You can act on areas for improvement by recommending alternative promotions for the same event, by using different approaches or by recommending new ideas for the future. In order to do so, ask yourself if any of the following would help you to change your promotional plan:

- Changing the timeline or the order things were done. State why you would change them.
- Changing the types of media used. Recommend other types of media that weren't used. State why this might help.
- Suggest other places the promotional material could have been distributed. State why this would be more effective.
- Suggest changing the content of the promotional material, for example the colour, the text, how they were produced. State why this may help.

- Suggest other sponsors that could have been approached. State why they might have been interested.
- Suggest other benefits that could have been offered to sponsors.
- Suggest other things that could have been asked of sponsors.
- Suggest how the press release could have been better written.
- Suggest that the press release should have been sent out at a different time so it appeared in the press at a more suitable time. Explain why this would have helped.
- Suggest other newspapers or newsletters that the press release could have been sent to. Why is this? Is it because these other newspapers or magazines would have been likely to give more space to your piece or because they would be more likely to be seen by your target audience.
- Could personal selling have been done better or differently? Maybe personal selling was not used at all or was used at the wrong time or in the wrong place. Explain how and why this would have helped with the promotion.

The suggestions that you put forward to any of the above will contribute towards your work for D2. For each of these suggestions you should explain how following your idea would have led to a better promotion plan.

Check your understanding

1. State one advantage and one disadvantage of each of the following forms of media.

	Advantage	Disadvantage
Posters		
Leaflets		
Internet/intranet		
Video promotion		
Press advert		
Personal selling with cards		
Mailshot		

Summary

In this section we have looked at planning the promotion of a sports event or scenario. The key learning points include:

- a promotional plan must contain details of the event's aims and objectives, the types of media chosen and why, a copy of the press release, examples of advertisements, a contact list for sponsors, an advertising timeline, feedback to sponsor and an evaluation questionnaire
- after the event it is important to review the plan
- reviewing strengths and areas of improvement can help to inform the planning of future events.

Unit 8 Model assignment

This assignment will assess the following learning aims:

A investigate issues involved in promoting sport

B explore sponsorship in sports promotion

C plan the promotion of a sports event or scenario

Note

It is recommended that consideration be given to assessing this unit alongside Unit 11 Running an Event, as there are opportunities for linkage between Task 5 and the event that is run in Unit 11.

Scenario

You have obtained a work experience placement as an assistant in the office of a sports marketing company. The company has agreed to provide information to a visiting High School group from the USA who are researching sport in the UK. You have been asked to help by performing a series of tasks.

Task 1

Prepare a PowerPoint presentation to welcome the group which explains why sport is promoted in the UK. Your presentation should include the following:

- why participation in sport can make people healthier
- how sport can help the community, for example by reducing crime or promoting active citizenship
- details of organisations running healthy living campaigns that can help the community
- how sport has helped promote national and local identity.

Task 2

Produce a fact sheet that explains the role of the media in the promotion of sport, in terms of:

- communication: how sport is promoted through television, newspapers, radio, etc.
- imagery: what image do the media portray of different sports events
- presentation: which forms of media are favoured to promote different types of sports events.

Select two sports events and assess the role of the media in promoting each of these events

Task 3

For one of the events you chose in Task 2b, produce a report that explains the effects the promotion has on:

1. Participants in terms of:

- availability, such as opportunities to enter a competition
- accessibility, such as locations, or has the promotion led to better facilities?
- Under-represented groups,
- Perceived status, e.g. did the promotion of the event make any participants favourites or underdogs?

2. Spectators in terms of:

- Cost, e.g. travel, entrance fee/tickets, merchandise, food, drink
- The availability - such as availability of tickets
- The accessibility, such as is the venue convenient to get to
- Whether it is promoted to underrepresented groups
- The advertising the spectators are exposed to
- The role models that are promoting the event
- The brand sponsorship spectators will be exposed to
- The merchandising that will be promoted to spectators

Task 4

Prepare and deliver a presentation to the group that describes:

1. In general terms the following sources of sponsorship in sport

   - private
   - regional
   - national
   - international and global sources

2. How an athlete or an event organiser might secure sponsorship

Select TWO sports individuals, teams or events.
Provide fact sheets to hand out that summarise information on the sponsorship of these TWO sports individuals, teams or events.
For ONE of these individuals, teams or events describe (P5) the range of different ethical issues which can arise from sponsorship. If you can explain this you will obtain M3. Explore the similarities and differences of the impact of sponsorship on TWO selected sports individuals, teams or events.

Task 5

Create a plan to promote an event that you can show the visitors that includes the following:

- The aims and objectives of the event
- The choice of media you intend to use
- A copy of the press release
- A copy of the advertisements
- A contact list for local businesses to supply prizes or trophies
- A timeline showing specific times of advertising activity
- What you are asking from the sponsor and what you will provide in return.

Write a report describing the strengths and areas for improvement of your promotional plan.

- You will need to explain the strengths of the plan and areas for improvement, providing recommendations for future promotion.
- You will need to justify your recommendations for future promotion of events.

Unit 9

Lifestyle and Well-being

This unit gives an overview of what is required to lead a healthy lifestyle. You will explore what is meant by positive lifestyle choices, including following a healthy lifestyle, maintaining a healthy body weight and undertaking physical activities. Negative lifestyle choices will also be covered, such as smoking, excessive alcohol consumption and recreational and performance enhancing drugs. Finally, you will look at how negative lifestyle choices can be reduced.

Learning aims

By the end of this chapter you will:

✓ be able to apply recommended guidelines for physical activity

✓ explore what makes a healthy diet and carry out dietary planning

✓ know the health risks associated with smoking and excessive alcohol consumption

✓ know the impact of drugs on health and sports performance.

Assessment criteria

Assessment and grading criteria		
To achieve a **PASS** grade the evidence must show that the learner is able to:	To achieve a **MERIT** grade the evidence must show that, in addition to the pass criteria, the learner is able to:	To achieve a **DISTINCTION** grade the evidence must show that, in addition to the pass and merit criteria, the learner is able to:
P1 Assess whether three selected individuals are undertaking sufficient physical activity to benefit their health	**M1** Explain recommendations for how three selected individuals could increase their physical activity levels	**D1** Justify recommendations for how three selected individuals could increase their physical activity levels
P2 Make recommendations for how three selected individuals could increase their physical activity levels		
P3 Explain the functions of the essential nutrients and why a healthy diet is important for a healthy lifestyle		
P4 Collect dietary information for a selected individual for one week, documenting via a food diary		
P5 Independently design a healthy meal plan for a selected individual, for one week	**M2** Design a healthy meal plan for a selected individual, for one week, making reference to the eatwell plate, and describing suggested recommendations for change	**D2** Justify the design of a healthy meal plan for a selected individual, for one week, justifying suggested recommendations for change
P6 Describe four health risks associated with smoking and effects of smoking on sports performance		
P7 Describe four health risks associated with excessive alcohol consumption and effects of alcohol consumption on sports performance		
P8 Explain two techniques an individual can use to stop smoking, and two techniques to cut down on excessive alcohol consumption	**M3** Compare and contrast different techniques used to stop smoking and for cutting down on excessive alcohol consumption	
P9 Describe four different types of drugs and their impact on sports performance	**M4** Evaluate the impact of four different performance-enhancing drugs on performance in four different types of sport	**D3** Discuss, using relevant examples, why some individuals may resort to using performance enhancing drugs in sport

Topic A.1 Recommended guidelines for physical activity

Taking part in regular **moderate exercise** is essential for good health. In 2011 the Department of Health set physical activity guidelines for:

- adults (those aged 19–64 and those aged 65+)
- children and young people (those aged under 5 years and those aged 5–18 years).

Recommendations for adults and older people

Studied ☐

Adults aged 19–64 should aim to:

- be active every day
- do at least 2½ hours of moderate intensity activity each week in sessions that last at least 10 minutes or more, for example, 30 minutes of exercise at least five days a week
- take part in physical activity to improve muscle strength on at least two days a week
- spend as little time as possible sitting down for long periods of time.

Older adults aged 65+ should aim to:

- be active every day
- do at least 2½ hours of moderate intensity activity each week in sessions that last at least 10 minutes or more, for example, 30 minutes of exercise at least five days a week
- take part in physical activity to improve muscle strength on at least two days a week
- take part in physical activity to improve balance and coordination on at least two days a week
- spend as little time as possible sitting down for long periods of time.

Recommendations for children and young people

Studied ☐

Children aged under 5 should be encouraged to:

- take part in play on the floor that involves physical activity
- spend as little time as possible sitting down or restrained such as in a car seat or buggy.

> **Key term**
>
> **Moderate exercise** – exercise at an intensity that raises heart rate but the person is not so out of breath that they are unable to carry on a conversation.

Children aged 5–18 years should aim to:

- take part in at least 60 minutes of moderate to vigorous intensity physical activity every day
- take part in activities that strengthen muscle and bone at least three days a week
- spend as little time as possible sitting down for long periods of time.

Topic A.2 Ways to increase physical activity levels in daily life

Simply making some lifestyle adjustments can lead to an increase in physical activity levels.

Lifestyle adjustments

Studied ☐

These are things that can be carried out regularly without having to make any specific time for sport and exercise activities, such as walking or cycling to school/work rather than travelling by car or bus and walking up stairs rather than taking lifts or an escalator.

Increasing sports and exercise participation

Studied ☐

School and work commitments can make it difficult for us to spare time to take part in sports activities but there are ways that sports activities can be fitted into our busy lives:

- Take part in lunchtime sports and exercise activities such as an aerobics class, going for a walk or a swim.
- Early morning swim, jog or bike ride before school or work.
- Take part in regular family physical activities such as a family bike ride or swim at the weekend.

Check your understanding

1. How much physical activity should the following take part in?
   a. Child aged 10
   b. Adult aged 40
   c. Adult aged 70
2. Suggest some physical activities that the above could include in their weekly activity programme.
3. Suggest suitable ways in which a 16-year-old student who travels one mile to school by bus each day could increase his activity levels.

Summary

In this section we looked at the recommended guidelines for physical activity. The key learning points include:

- the Department of Health has set physical activity guidelines for adults (19–64 years and 65+) and children and young people (aged 5–18 years and under 5 years).
- physical activity levels in daily life can be increased by walking or cycling to school/work, gardening, playing active games and taking the stairs rather than a lift
- increased physical activity levels can be fitted into daily life by taking part in lunchtime exercise classes, family activities at the weekend and early morning exercises.

Activity

Part 1

Carry out an assessment on three different individuals to find out if they are taking part in enough physical activity to provide benefits to their health.

Part 2

From your assessment in Part 1, write a report which recommends how each of the three individuals can increase their physical activity levels and explain and justify your recommendations.

Learning aim B: Explore what makes a healthy diet and carry out dietary planning

Topic B.1 Nutrients

A balanced diet is important in order for a person to maintain and promote good health.

Essential nutrients and their functions

Studied ☐

Food can be broken down into three main groups:

- fats
- carbohydrates
- proteins.

These food groups are also called **macronutrients** because they form the major part of our diet. Within each of these food groups, you will also find the following:

- vitamins
- minerals.

These are referred to as **micronutrients** because we only need to consume them in small quantities.

Fat

Studied ☐

Sources of fat

Figure 9.1 Fatty food

Fat is found in dairy products such as cheese and cream and in and around meat as well as in plant products such as olive oil, fish oils and nuts. Around 30 per cent of your daily calorie intake should come from fats. There are two types of fat: saturated fat and unsaturated fat.

> **Key terms**
>
> **Macronutrients** – nutrients required in large quantities such as carbohydrates, fats and proteins.
>
> **Micronutrients** – a nutrient required in small quantities such as minerals and vitamins.

- Saturated fats: these are usually called the 'bad fats' because if you eat too many they will raise your cholesterol level and thereby increase your blood pressure. Saturated fats are mainly found in products such as meat, cheese, cream, butter, lard and chocolate.
- Unsaturated fats: these are the 'good fats' and some types can actually help to reduce cholesterol levels, which will usually have the effect of decreasing blood pressure. They usually come from plant sources and examples include olive oil, rapeseed, nuts and oily fish.

Function of fat

The main function of fat is to provide energy, insulate the body and protect the internal organs. Some vitamins are also stored in our body fat and fat is used in the production hormones. Fat is also used as an energy source but it produces energy at a much slower rate than carbohydrates; therefore fats supply the energy when we are taking part in low-intensity exercise.

Carbohydrates

Studied ☐

Sources of carbohydrates

Figure 9.2 Carbohydrate food

Around 45–50 per cent of our daily calorie intake should come from carbohydrates. Foods that are high in carbohydrates include sweet tasting foods such as biscuits and cakes and also foods that do not taste sweet such as bread, pasta and potatoes.

Types of carbohydrates

There are two types of carbohydrates: simple or complex.

- Simple carbohydrates: these carbohydrates taste sweet and can be found in a wide variety of foods such as fruits, sweets, jam, biscuits and fizzy drinks and they are broken down in the body quickly and easily. As a result, when we eat sugary foods they give the body a quick burst of energy which is sometimes referred to as a 'sugar high'. Milk also contains sugar but does not taste as sweet as the foods described above.
- Complex carbohydrates: these take longer to break down in the body so give a slow and prolonged supply of energy. They do not taste sweet and can be found in a wide variety of foods such as bread, pasta, potatoes, rice and cereals.

Function of carbohydrates

The main purpose of carbohydrate is to give us energy to enable our bodies to move and take part in sports. Carbohydrate is broken down into glucose which is carried around the body in the bloodstream and transported to the working muscles, where it is used to make the muscles produce movement. Any carbohydrates that are eaten and not used are stored in the muscle and liver as glycogen or turned into fat and stored in the fat cells in the body.

Proteins

Studied ☐

Around 10–15 per cent of our daily calorie intake should come from proteins.

Figure 9.3 Protein-rich food

Sources of protein

The majority of protein-rich foods come from animal sources and include meat, chicken, fish, eggs and milk. Soya and tofu are examples of vegetable-based foods that contain high levels of protein.

Function of protein

Protein is required in our diet mainly for growth and repair of body tissues. Taking part in sport and exercise, particularly resistance exercises, actually causes our muscle tissue to tear – these tears are microscopic but act as the stimulus to make our muscles grow. The protein we eat in our diet is used for muscle repair and growth.

Vitamins and minerals

Studied ☐

Vitamins and minerals are present in very small quantities in many of the foods that we eat. Our body cannot make vitamins or minerals (with the exception of Vitamin D, which the body can make from sunlight) so it is essential that we eat a diet that contains all the vitamins and minerals that we need. There are many different types of vitamins and minerals and each helps us to maintain a healthy body which can work effectively. Table 9.1 gives details of the sources and function of vitamins and Table 9.2 gives details of the sources and function of minerals.

Table 9.1 Vitamins

Vitamin	Sources	Function
A	Carrots, apricots, liver, dark green vegetables, mackerel	Helps to maintain good eye health and vision and helps maintain the function and production of skin
B	Whole grains, milk, nuts, meat, Marmite, cereals, liver, yeast, eggs, beans	Helps to break down food to produce energy and helps with the function of the nervous system, helps with the formation of red blood cells
C	Citrus fruits – oranges, lemons, grapefruit, most fresh fruits and vegetables	Helps our immune system to fight infection, maintains healthy skin and gums and helps wounds to heal
D	Oily fish, eggs, sunlight	Helps to build strong bones and teeth

Table 9.2 Minerals

Mineral	Sources	Function
Iron	Liver, lean meats, eggs, dried fruits, nuts, chicken	Helps with the formation of red blood cells
Calcium	Milk, cheese, yogurts, fish bones, green leafy vegetables	Helps to build strong bones and teeth and helps blood clots to clot
Sodium	Salt, sea food, processed foods, celery	Helps to maintain fluid and electrolyte balance in cells, helps in muscle contraction
Potassium	Bananas, meat, shellfish	Works with sodium to maintain fluid balance, aids muscle contraction, maintains blood pressure
Zinc	Milk, cheese, eggs, shellfish, meats	Tissue growth and repair and helps the immune system to fight infection

Water

Studied ☐

We are able to live without food for several days, but we could only survive for around three days without water. Although water has no nutritional value in terms of energy, it is essential to life and plays many roles within the body. Water helps to maintain the body at a constant temperature through sweating, it transports nutrients around the body and is used to get rid of waste products from the body in the form of urine and faeces. We take water into our body via drinks and the food we eat. For our body to work at its best we need to consume around 2.5 litres of water per day; however, this amount must be increased if we live in hot conditions or are exercising.

Topic B.2 Food groups

The eatwell plate

Studied

The eatwell plate (see Figure 9.4) splits food into the five main food groups and can be used to ensure a person's diet is balanced according to the different types of food and their proportions.

Figure 9.4 The eatwell plate

The five main food groups on the eatwell plate are:

- fruit and vegetables
- bread, other cereals and potatoes
- milk and dairy products
- meat, fish and alternatives
- foods containing fat and foods containing sugar.

The eatwell plate is suitable for most people, whatever their ethnic origin, but does not apply to children under the age of 2 years old.

Topic B.3 Collecting dietary information and meal planning

Maintaining a food diary

A good way to assess your own diet is to keep a food diary (see below). This is a record of everything that you eat over a period of time, usually two weeks, because that gives a truer picture of what you normally do. If you do keep a food diary it is vital that it covers both weekdays and weekends because we tend to eat differently at these times. The food diary should contain the following details:

- type of food: for example, toast, biscuit, sausage
- food group: as described on the eatwell plate
- amount: this refers to portion size, such as one apple, small bowl of cereal, two pieces of toast, one egg
- timing of food intake: note down the time that you ate the food
- personal feelings: it is important to note down how you were feeling when you decided to eat a particular food, as this can indicate whether you are a 'comfort eater' in that you choose to eat 'treat foods' that are not healthy when you feeling unhappy.

Table 9.3 Example of a food diary

Day	Time	Type of Food	Food Group	Amount (portion size)	Feelings
Monday	08.30	scrambled eggs on brown toast, no butter	Bread, rice and pasta Eggs	2 eggs 2 pieces of toast	Hungry
	11.00	Mars bar	Fat and sugar	1 normal sized bar	Tired
	13.00	Ham toasty	Bread, rice and pasta Meat	2 slices of bread 1 slice of ham	Hungry
	15.00	Apple	Fruit and vegetables	1 large apple	Fine
	17.30	Spaghetti Bolognaise	Bread, rice and pasta Meat	Medium portion of spaghetti and medium of meat	Hungry
	20.00	Chocolate bar	Foods containing fat and sugar	small 100g bar	Worried about my homework

Healthy meal plans for one week

When choosing foods to include in a healthy meal plan, use the following guidelines to help you make good choices:

- eat foods which are naturally occurring rather than processed
- eat foods that look as they occur in nature
- limit processed or take-away foods
- the best foods will not have a label containing ingredients

- avoid additives or E numbers
- eat organic foods where possible as they will usually contain more vitamins and minerals.

What you eat will become part of your body or affect the way your body functions, so be very particular about what you choose to eat.

Type of food and food groups

- Bread, cereals and potatoes: the majority of the food you eat should be from this group of foods and every meal should include at least one food from this group. You should aim to eat 6 to 11 portions of food per day from this food group. The best types of foods to eat from this food group are the whole grains such as wholemeal bread, brown rice and oatmeal as these contain more vitamins, minerals and fibre compared to processed foods such as white bread and white rice.
- Fruits and vegetables: you should aim to eat at least five portions of fruit and vegetables per day. You can eat fresh, frozen, canned or juiced fruit and vegetables. When buying canned vegetables avoid vegetables canned in brine as they contain high levels of salt too much of which is bad for health.
- Milk and dairy foods: you should eat servings from this food group around two to three times per day. Foods in this group include milk and any products made from milk such as cheese, yogurt and cream.
- Meat and fish and pulses: this food group includes all kinds of meat and meat products such as sausages, poultry, eggs and fish. For vegetarians, this group should incorporate foods such as soya products, lentils, pulses and tofu products. Around two portions of food from this food group should be eaten each day.
- Fats and sweets: this food group includes all foods containing high quantities of fats and sugars. Examples of fatty foods are butter, margarine, olive oil, cakes, biscuits, pastries, ice-cream, cream and fried foods such as chips. Examples of sugary foods include sweets, jam, cakes, biscuits and fizzy drinks. You should only eat small quantities of foods from this group.

Making improvements to meal plans
that don't meet the guidelines

Studied ▢

It is possible to change meal plans so that foods that are not good for you and which should only be eaten in small quantities are replaced by foods that are good for you. For example, a chocolate bar can be replaced with fruit, chips should be limited to once a week and at least one type of vegetable should be included in every evening meal.

Importance of a healthy diet in leading a healthy lifestyle

Studied ☐

A healthy diet contributes significantly to a healthy lifestyle as it can help with maintaining a healthy body weight and prevents some types of disease such as type 2 diabetes and heart disease. There is also a strong link between good nutrition and sports performance and most elite sports performers will have a nutritionist who advises them on what to eat and devises appropriate meal plans for training and competition. Consuming the right type and amount of fluids is very important for sports performance as dehydration has a negative effect on performance. Different types of sports require different quantities of carbohydrates and proteins, depending upon the requirements of the sport. For example, long distance runners and cyclists need lots of carbohydrate foods for energy production and need to consume many more calories than the average person as they are using up thousands of calories while exercising. Sports which require large muscle bulk will usually require higher protein consumption in order to help with muscle growth and repair.

Recommendations for change

Studied ☐

Food preparation

The way food is prepared has a huge impact on its nutritional value, for example, we should eat a reasonable amount of potatoes, but if these are fried to make chips then they will become high in fat and therefore unhealthy. Changing the way we prepare foods can help to make them much healthier, for example:

- Pasta dishes can be prepared using wholemeal pasta and a small portion of sauce.
- Sandwiches can be prepared using wholemeal bread.
- Dried fruit, fresh fruit or vegetable sticks (e.g. carrot sticks) make healthy snacks.
- A selection of vegetables or salads can accompany each main meal.
- Puddings can be fruit-based, such as poached pears or apple and blackberry crumble.
- Using lean meat with the skin and fat removed where possible.
- Grilling meats wherever possible helps to reduce their fat content.
- Eating two portions of oily fish per week is recommended.
- Semi-skimmed or skimmed milk and low-fat or reduced-fat cheeses are healthier than full fat products.
- Cream can be replaced with lower fat fromage frais or yoghurt in cooking.

Timing of food intake

Eating before taking part in sports can be beneficial to performance. You should aim to eat one to four hours before taking part in sports. Choose a starchy carbohydrate food that is easily digested, such as a banana or a bowl of cereal. The more you eat, the more time you need to give the body to digest the food before taking part in sports.

While taking part in sports, most people will sweat in order to cool down, so it is important to drink plenty of water. If the sport you are taking part in lasts for 90 minutes or more (an **endurance sport**), or if you feel that you have low energy levels, drinking a sports drink or eating sugary foods during the course of the event will help to maintain your energy levels.

After you have taken part in strenuous sport, the body's carbohydrate store will be low and will need to be replenished. Eating foods and drinks high in carbohydrates within the first two hours of stopping exercising will help to maximise the replenishment of these carbohydrate stores.

Key term
Endurance sport – any sport that lasts 90 minutes or more, such as football, marathon running and distance swimming.

Check your understanding

1. Complete the eatwell plate with the different food groups.

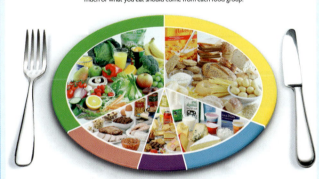

The eatwell plate

Use the eatwell plate to help you get the balance right. It shows how much of what you eat should come from each food group.

2. Which food groups do the following foods belong to?

Food	Food group
Brussels sprouts	
Eggs	
Olive oil	
Bananas	
Milk	
Fish	
Beans	
Bread	
Potatoes	
Nuts	
Butter	

Summary

In this section we looked at what makes a healthy diet and what is involved in dietary planning. The key learning points include:

- the essential nutrients are fats, carbohydrates, proteins, vitamins, minerals and water
- macronutrients refers to fats, carbohydrates and proteins and micronutrients refers to vitamins and minerals
- the eatwell plate is made up of five food groups – fruit and vegetables, bread, other cereals and potatoes, milk and dairy products, meat, fish and alternatives, foods containing fat and foods containing sugar
- we can collect dietary information by maintaining a food diary for a period of two weeks, which describes each type of food eaten, as well as the food group it belongs to, the amount eaten and the timing of the food intake
- it is easy to make improvements to meal plans that don't meet guidelines, by replacing certain types of food or changing the way we cook food
- a healthy diet is important for weight management and the prevention of disease
- consuming the right fluids and foods in the right quantity is essential to perform well at sports
- different sports have different nutritional requirements.

Activity

Part 1

Design a leaflet that can be handed out to clients which explains the functions of each of the essential nutrients including fats, carbohydrates, proteins, vitamins, minerals and water and which also explains why a healthy diet is important for a healthy lifestyle.

Part 2

To help you to learn about assessing food intake, a nutritionist has asked you to keep a food diary which contains information on what you eat for one week.

Part 3

Using the information provided by your food diary, design a healthy meal plan for yourself for one week.

Part 4

Write a report to accompany your meal plan which refers to the eatwell plate and describes and justifies the design of your plan and the recommendations for changes to the foods, fluids, timings of food intake or methods of food preparation that you have suggested.

Topic C.1 Health risks associated with smoking and drinking alcohol

There are many health risks directly linked with smoking and as such smoking is the currently the biggest cause of preventable death and disease in England. Drinking excessive amounts of alcohol is also linked to a number of diseases.

Health risks associated with smoking

Studied ☐

The products in a cigarette that appear to do the most damage include tar, nicotine and carbon monoxide.

Figure 9.5 The lungs of someone who smoked (right) compared with someone who has never smoked (left)

Cancer

Smokers are much more likely to suffer from a range of cancers including lung, mouth, bladder, oesophagus, kidneys, pancreas and cervical cancer.

Coronary heart disease

Coronary heart disease is the main cause of death in smokers due to the excess cholesterol produced from smoking narrowing the blood vessels. When the blood vessels become narrower, blood clots are more likely to form which can then block the coronary blood vessels. A blockage in these vessels can lead to a heart attack. Alternatively, a blood clot may travel to the brain leading to a stroke, or it could travel to the kidneys, resulting in kidney failure. A blood clot that blocks the arteries in the legs can lead to gangrene, for which the main treatment is amputation.

Emphysema

This disease causes breathlessness because the alveoli in the lungs have become damaged.

Bronchitis

This makes the person cough excessively because of increased mucus production in the lungs.

Health risks associated with excessive alcohol consumption

Alcohol is a poison and if too much is consumed it can lead to coma and even death. Alcohol consumption in excess of the recommended daily guidelines will often cause physical damage to the body and increase the likelihood of disease, health risks include cancer, mental health issues, stroke, weight gain, stomach ulcers, gastrointestinal complications and liver complications.

Liver complications

The liver is the largest organ in the body and excessive alcohol consumption can result in liver complications. The liver is responsible for getting rid of poisons from the blood, helps our immune system in fighting infection, makes proteins that help our blood to clot and produces bile, which helps with the breakdown of fats. Damage to the liver will produce scar tissue and this scar tissue replaces the normal tissue and prevents the liver from working as it should.

Cancer

Cancers associated with excessive alcohol consumption include cancer of the mouth, larynx, oesophagus, liver, breast and bowel.

Mental health issues

Excessive alcohol consumption has been linked with anxiety and depression. One in three young people who have committed suicide drank alcohol before they died, and more than two out of three people who attempt suicide have drunk excessively.

Weight gain

Alcohol contains a lot of calories so if a person drinks excessive amounts of alcoholic drinks they may well be consuming more calories than are required and will therefore gain weight.

Topic C.2 Effect of smoking and alcohol consumption on sports performance

Effect of smoking on sports performance

Research clearly indicates that smoking over a period of time will adversely affect health and, in most cases, will decrease sporting performance, especially in sports that use the aerobic energy system. The aerobic energy system requires oxygen, so if the alveoli in the lungs are blocked and damaged by tar from cigarettes, they will not function and this will decrease the amount of oxygen that can be taken into the body and used for aerobic energy production. Red blood cells contain haemoglobin whose function is to transport oxygen around the body to where it is required, such as the muscles. Cigarette smoke contains carbon monoxide and this attaches to the haemoglobin, preventing it from working and thereby reducing the amount of oxygen that can be transported around the body.

Effect of alcohol consumption on sports performance

Once sports participation has finished for the day, alcohol consumption in moderation is thought not to have too much of a detrimental effect on a player's health or sports performance. However, if alcohol is consumed in excess, the 'hangover' effects and damage to the liver will reduce sporting performance. Excessive alcohol also has a dehydrating effect on the body and dehydration has clear links with a reduction in performance. There is also a greater risk of a person suffering from muscle cramps after excessive alcohol consumption which can have a significant effect on sports performance.

Alcohol consumed prior to or during sports performance will negatively affect performance by slowing down reaction times and affecting balance and coordination, which could lead to accidents or injuries.

P6

P7

Topic C.3 Techniques to stop smoking

Techniques and aids used in primary health care

People become addicted to smoking through a physical addiction to the nicotine in cigarettes and the psychological addiction to the act of smoking, both of which makes stopping the habit very difficult. To try to overcome nicotine addiction, a person can either slowly decrease the number of cigarettes they smoke over a set period or they can use a nicotine replacement therapy, such as nicotine gum and/or a nicotine patch (see Figure 9.6). This process helps the person break the cigarette habit and also slowly reduces the amount of nicotine being taken into the body.

There are also a number of campaigns set up by the Department of Health to help people to stop smoking, such as 'Stoptober', national 'No Smoking Day' as well as support groups.

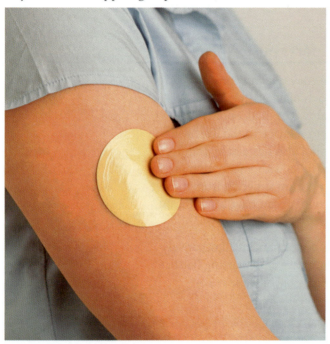

Figure 9.6 Nicotine replacement therapy can help to break the addiction to nicotine

Alternative techniques

Hypnotherapy can be used to help a person to stop smoking and involves the person being put into a state of deep relaxation so that the therapist can help the person to overcome their addiction to smoking.

Acupuncture is another technique used to help a person stop smoking and involves placing tiny needles in various parts of the body which, when stimulated, remove or reduce a person's craving for nicotine.

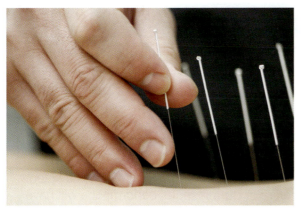

Figure 9.7 Acupuncture treatment

Cutting down on alcohol consumption

Studied

Keeping a 'drinking diary' of the time and number of units of alcohol consumed in a week can help a person to cut down on their alcohol consumption. It is then possible to see whether excessive weekly amounts are being consumed. The amount of alcohol consumed can be reduced by modifying drink choices, for example:

- choose low alcoholic drinks
- drink regular lager rather than export strong lager
- dilute drinks with non-alcoholic beverages to create drinks such as shandy or wine spritzer
- drink a non-alcoholic drink such as water or lemonade between each alcoholic drink.

It is recommended that a person has several alcohol-free days a week. Another way to reduce alcohol consumption for a person that regularly meets with friends in a pub, is to find alternative venues to meet, such as a juice bar or coffee shop where alcoholic drinks are not on offer.

Counselling and support groups can help a person to reduce or stop their alcohol consumption. Most people who are addicted to alcohol will have to stop all alcohol consumption. Attending support groups such as Alcoholics Anonymous will help them to deal with their addiction and stay sober.

Check your understanding

1. Identify three health risks associated with smoking.
2. Identify three health risks associated with excessive alcohol consumption.
3. Explain why smoking has a negative effect on sporting performance.
4. Describe four different methods that an individual could use to reduce their alcohol consumption.
5. Describe four different methods that an individual could try to stop smoking.

Summary

In this section we have covered the health risks associated with smoking and excessive alcohol consumption. The key learning points include:

- smoking poses a risk to health because it is associated with such diseases as lung cancer, bronchitis, coronary heart disease and emphysema
- excessive alcohol consumption can lead to cancer, mental health issues, stroke, weight gain and liver complications
- smoking has a negative effect on sports performance
- reasonable consumption of alcohol following sports performance will not have too much effect, although consumption before or during sports performance will have negative effects
- techniques and aids to stop smoking include counselling, nicotine patches/gum as well as hypnotherapy and acupuncture
- alcohol consumption can be reduced by having alcohol-free days, by consuming low alcohol/non-alcoholic drinks and by planning alternative activities, such as meeting in cafes rather than pubs.

Activity

Part 1

Design a poster which describes four health risks associated with smoking. You should include illustrations and text which describe the effects of smoking on sports performance.

Part 2

Design a poster which describes four health risks associated with excessive alcohol consumption. You should include illustrations and text which describe the effects of alcohol consumption on sports performance.

Part 3

Prepare a leaflet which explains and compares and contrasts two different techniques that a person could use to a) stop smoking and b) reduce their alcohol consumption.

Topics D.1 and D.2 Performance-enhancing drugs and their impact on sports performance

There are many types of **performance-enhancing drugs** and the requirements of the sport will depend on the type of drug an athlete may choose to use.

The main effects of the different groups of performance-enhancing drugs are:

- build up muscle mass
- increase the delivery of oxygen to exercising tissues
- provide stimulation
- provide relaxation
- reduce weight.

Table 9.4 gives details of the various performance-enhancing drugs and their impact on sports performance together with the harmful effects they have on the body.

> **Key term**
>
> **Performance-enhancing drugs** – used to improve an athlete's performance, they include anabolic steroids, EPO, stimulants, beta blockers and diuretics.

Table 9.4 Performance-enhancing drugs

Drug	Impact on Sports Performance	Harmful effects on the body
Anabolic steroids	Build muscle mass. Muscles recover more quickly from training, allowing the athlete to train at a higher level and for longer than if they were not taking these drugs	Liver and kidney tumours, jaundice, high blood pressure, severe acne, trembling, increased aggression
Erythropoietin (EPO)	EPO increases a person's red blood cell count, resulting in increased blood haemoglobin concentrations. After taking EPO, a person's blood will have an increased oxygen-carrying capacity	Increased thickness of the blood so can increase the risk of the athlete suffering a heart attack
Stimulants	These ensure more blood is directed to the working muscles and increase the amount of air that a person can inhale while exercising. They also increase a person's mental alertness and stop a person feeling exhausted	It is possible for athletes to over-exert themselves so that they can suffer heat stroke and cardiac failure. Increased blood pressure and body temperature, increased and irregular heartbeat, aggression, anxiety, loss of appetite
Beta blockers	Used to lower heart rate and blood pressure and reduce anxiety which can help with sports such as shooting and archery where accuracy and precision is important	Side effects include lowered blood pressure, slow heart rate and tiredness. In extreme cases, the heart may actually stop because it has been slowed down too much

Diuretics	Diuretics help to get rid of excess water from the body. They can be used to reduce the weight of competitors in sports where weight categories are involved as this can allow competitors to remain in their weight category. An athlete whose body weight is only slightly above the category lower limit will be competing against athletes who are larger than them and who presumably have a greater muscle mass, which could be a disadvantage for the athlete	Side effects include dehydration, leading to dizziness and fainting, vomiting and muscle cramps. If the athlete becomes severely dehydrated through taking diuretics, the effect on the kidneys and heart can lead to death
Growth Hormone	In males, growth hormone acts to increase testosterone levels and results in increased muscle development, as with anabolic steroids. Excessive growth hormone levels increase muscle mass by stimulating protein synthesis, strengthen bones by stimulating bone growth and reduce body fat by stimulating the breakdown of fat cells.	The side-effects of growth hormone in males are the same as those of anabolic steroids together with enlarged internal organs. The athlete taking the drug may also develop acromegaly, which results in the person's hands, feet and lower jaw growing much larger than normal.

Topic D.3 How performance-enhancing drugs can affect different types of sport

The physical requirements of different sports will usually determine which drugs can have a performance-enhancing effect (see Table 9.5).

Table 9.5 Performance-enhancing drugs and the sports they affect

Type of sport	Example of sport	Drugs that could be used for performance enhancement
Endurance	Distance running and cycling	EPO to improve aerobic energy system
Strength/ power sports	Javelin, high jump	Anabolic steroids and/or growth hormone to increase muscle mass which will increase the force that the muscle can exert
Sports with weight limits	Wrestling, judo	Diuretics to help a competitor remain in their weight category
Target sports	Shooting, archery	Beta blockers to reduce heart rate and anxiety and help the performer to remain focused and accurate
Team sports	Football, hockey	Stimulants to help the performer to be alert and stay focused for the duration of the game

Why some performers may resort to using performance-enhancing drugs in sport

Studied ☐

The practice of using banned substances to enhance athletic performance is called **doping**. The first drug tests on athletes were conducted at the 1968 Olympic Games in Mexico. Since then, drug testing has become a major part of sporting competition and new methods of detecting drugs are always being sought. As sport has become increasingly pressured, with a 'win at all costs' approach taking over from the old ideals of athleticism (playing fairly as an amateur), so we have seen a rise in the use of performance-enhancing drugs, as the rewards for winning are so great. Pressure on athletes to succeed comes from fans, managers and, in world competitions, the nation, all of whom are desperate for a

Key term

Doping – using illegal substances such as performance-enhancing drugs to improve sports performance.

win. Many athletes do not understand the health risks associated with such drugs and are concerned only with the benefits they bring to their improved performance.

Real world connection

Lynne works as a sports development officer. Part of her role is to encourage people in the local community to increase their participation in sport so that they meet the government guidelines to improve health. Her work is with people of all ages, from children to older adults aged 60+, so she has to make sure she introduces the correct types of physical activity to each group of people so that it is suitable and engaging for them. She also gives talks to different groups of people, including parents, teenagers, adults and older adults, to give them tips and ideas on how they can improve their physical activity levels by changing their lifestyle choices, such as walking to school instead of driving.

Check your understanding

1. For each of the questions below, select the correct answer from the boxes.
   a. This type of drug could be taken by an athlete who wants to increase the size of their muscles.
   b. A boxer may take this type of drug to try to get into a lower weight category.
   c. An archer may take this type of drug.
   d. An athlete taking part in the Tour de France may take this drug to try to reduce feelings of exhaustion.
   e. An athlete who runs for long distances may take this type of drug to improve their performance.
   f. The name given to the practice of using banned substances to enhance athletic performance.
   g. One of the main issues with drugs is that they all have side effects which can do what to an athlete?
   h. A group that determines which drugs are legal and which ones should be banned.

Stimulant	EPO	Anabolic steroid	Doping
Beta blocker	Damage health	Diuretic	International Olympic Committee

Summary

In this section we have looked at the impact of drugs on health and sports performance. The key learning points include:

- performance-enhancing drugs include anabolic steroids, erythropoietin (EPO), diuretics, beta blockers and stimulants
- taking drugs to improve sports performance can have a harmful effect on the body
- different types of performance-enhancing drugs have different effects and so the type of drug taken will depend on the type of sport
- sport performers may resort to using performance-enhancing drugs because there is a lot of pressure on them to succeed.

Activity

Part 1

Write an article describing four different types of performance-enhancing drugs and evaluate how they impact upon sport performance in four different types of sport.

Part 2

In your article, discuss, using examples, why some individuals may resort to using performance-enhancing drugs.

Unit 9 Model assignment

This assignment will assess the following learning aims:

A be able to apply recommended guidelines for physical activity

B explore what makes a healthy diet and carry out dietary planning

C know the health risks associated with smoking and excessive alcohol consumption

D know the impact of drugs on health and sports performance.

Scenario 1

You are working as a personal trainer and have clients of differing ages and abilities. You have recently been asked to give personal training advice and guidance to three new clients who wish to improve their physical activity levels and diet. You will need to carry out some research to find out the recommended guidelines for physical activity for people of different ages and devise an interview or questionnaire to find out the amount of physical activity each of the three clients is taking each week and compare this with the recommended guidelines.

Task 1

For three different clients, assess their physical activity levels and write a report that indicates if they are carrying out enough activity to benefit their health.

For each client, explain and justify recommendations for how they could increase their physical activity levels by making everyday life changes as well as specific exercise sessions, if appropriate.

Task 2

Prepare a leaflet that explains the functions of the essential nutrients, such as fats, carbohydrates, proteins, vitamins, minerals and water and why a healthy diet is important.

Keep a food diary to collect dietary information for one person for one week, documenting this via a food diary. Include in your diary the type of food, food group, portion sizes, timing of food intake and personal feelings.

From the information provided in the food diary, design and write up a healthy meal plan for this person for seven days, using the eatwell plate to help your design. Include in your write up suggested recommendations for change, justifying these suggested improvements to the person's food intake in the healthy meal plan that you have designed.

Scenario 2

You are working as an assistant sports coach at an athletics club. The athletes that you work with are aged between 16 and 30 years and some compete at a very high level. Some of the teenagers in the athletics squad have friends outside of athletics who smoke and drink excessively and the coach is concerned that these teenage athletes may be tempted to try smoking and drinking alcoholic drinks when they are out with these friends, which will not only affect their sports performance but also their health.

Task 1

You have been asked by the head coach to prepare a leaflet that can be handed out to athletes in the club which covers the health risks associated with smoking and drinking alcohol.

a. In your leaflet you should include four health risks associated with smoking and four health risks associated with excessive alcohol consumption and the effects of both on sports performance.

b. The leaflet should also include information on at least two techniques to help people to stop smoking and two techniques to help reduce their alcoholic intake. The leaflet should compare and contrast the different techniques available for stopping smoking and reducing excessive alcohol consumption.

Task 2

In your role as assistant coach it is important that you are aware of different performance-enhancing drugs so that you know why some athletes may be tempted to take these drugs and the impact that they have on performance.

a. Write a report that describes four different performance-enhancing drugs such as anabolic steroids, erythropoietin (EPO), growth hormone, diuretics or beta blockers.

b. In your report evaluate the impact of these four performance-enhancing drugs on sports performance in four different types of sport.

c. Using information from media stories where possible, discuss why some individuals may resort to using performance-enhancing drugs in sport.

Unit 10

Injury and the Sports Performer

Any person who undertakes a sporting activity will find that they are at risk of many different types of injuries. It is therefore very important that people who take part in sports or who wish to pursue a career in sports industries have a good grasp of health and safety, know how to avoid sports injuries occurring and are able to deal with basic sports injuries when they do occur.

Learning aims

By the end of this unit you will:

✓ understand risks and hazards associated with sports participation

✓ know about different injuries and illnesses associated with sports participation

✓ know about the response to injury and injury management

✓ know about rules, regulations and legislation associated with health and safety in sport.

Assessment criteria

Assessment and grading criteria		
To achieve a **PASS** grade the evidence must show that the learner is able to:	To achieve a **MERIT** grade the evidence must show that, in addition to the pass criteria, the learner is able to:	To achieve a **DISTINCTION** grade the evidence must show that, in addition to the pass and merit criteria, the learner is able to:
P1 Explain three different risks or hazards that relate to each topic of people, equipment and the environment, respectively		
P2 Explain three different physiological, and three psychological, causes of injury in relation to sport		
P3 Describe two different types of basic injury and two different types of complex injury associated with sports participation	**M1** Using sports-specific examples, discuss the relationship between causes of injury and basic and complex types of injury	**D1** For a selected injury or illness give a detailed account of how it might occur, analysing the associated types and signs of injury or illness
P4 Explain four types and signs of illness associated with sports participation		
P5 Describe the physiological and immediate and long-term psychological responses to injury in sport		
P6 Describe how to manage physiological and immediate and long-term psychological responses to injury in sport	**M2** For a selected sports injury, explain the responses and process of physiological and psychological management	**D2** Justify selected methods used to manage physiological and psychological responses to a selected injury in a sporting context
P7 Discuss reasons for having health and safety rules, regulations and legislation in sport	**M3** Explain how two selected rules, regulations or pieces of legislation help maintain the health and safety of participants in a selected sport	**D3** Analyse the impact of two selected rules, regulations or pieces of legislation on participants in a selected sport

Learning aim A: Understand risks and hazards associated with sports participation

There are many potential **hazards** and **risks** associated with participating in sporting and outdoor activities, many of which can result in a sports injury.

Risks and hazards can be categorised into three groups: people factors, equipment factors and environment factors.

Topic A.1 People-related risks and hazards

These are hazards that are caused by people, for example:

- not warming up or cooling down correctly which can lead to muscle strains
- mismatch of physique between opponents or an inappropriate physique for a sport or playing position.
- an opponent playing recklessly: a high tackle in rugby could cause a serious neck injury
- playing under the influence of alcohol or drugs
- playing sport wearing jewellery: this could catch on another player and injure them or yourself
- playing sport while chewing gum: this could result in choking
- overtraining and not allowing time for recovery leading to an overuse injury
- poor technique giving rise to inappropriate movements, such as overstretching, over-striding or injury through incorrect technique lifting weights
- differences in skill level: injuries can occur if opponents have very different skill levels (e.g. children playing against adults; elite athletes against recreational athletes).

Topic A.2 Equipment-related risks and hazards

Many sports require special equipment, which can lead to injury if not used or used incorrectly, for example:

- not wearing the correct protective equipment
- using gym equipment without knowing how to use it correctly
- equipment not being set up correctly, such as climbing ropes and harnesses
- not having the correct clothing for the conditions.

It is important that all equipment is checked prior to being used to ensure that it is complete, in working order and not faulty or damaged.

> ### Key terms
>
> **Hazard** – something that is dangerous and has the potential to affect someone's safety or cause an injury.
>
> **Risk** – the possibility of the hazard causing an injury.

Topic A.3 Environment-related risks and hazards:

Environmental hazards are often beyond our control, but it is important to assess any potential hazards before starting an activity. Where the environment could have a big impact on your sporting activity, such as in mountain climbing or sailing, you should make sure you receive local weather forecasts for that day in order to determine whether you should continue with the planned activity. Some examples of environmental hazards are as follows:

- The weather can cause sports fields to become a dangerous environment to play sport on. An icy or waterlogged field has the potential to cause many types of injury.
- Undertaking exercise in hot conditions can cause participants to become tired more quickly and can cause problems such as dehydration and heat exhaustion.
- Extreme wet and cold weather can lead to hypothermia.
- High winds can cause a potential hazard to people undertaking water-based activities such as sailing.
- Cold weather conditions increase the risk of muscle strains.
- A playing surface can be hazardous, for example astroturf can produce skin abrasions if a player slips and falls onto it.

Figure 10.1

Check your understanding

1. Decide whether the examples below are a people, equipment or environment risk or hazard by placing a tick in the appropriate column.

Example	People risk/ hazard	Equipment risk/ hazard	Environment risk/ hazard
Hot weather conditions			
Adults playing against children			
Icy hockey pitch			
Not doing a warm-up before a basketball game			
Picking up gym weights incorrectly			
Not wearing shin pads for football			
Wet patch on the gym floor			
Chewing gum while playing sport			
Skiing on a dry ski slope			

Summary

In this section we looked at the risks and hazards associated with sports participation. The key learning points include:

- people-related risk factors include failing to do a warm-up and/or cool down, overtraining taking drugs, mismatched physiques of opponents, mismatched skill level and poor technique
- equipment-related risk factors include a lack of protective clothing or equipment, using the wrong equipment, using damaged equipment and using equipment incorrectly
- environment-related risk factors relate to extremes of temperature, the weather and the playing surface used for a sports activity.

Activity

Select one of these sports:

- Squash
- Rugby
- Football
- Basketball
- Hockey.

For your selected sport write a report that explains three different risks or hazards that are associated with

a. people-related risk factors
b. equipment-related risk factors
c. environment-related risk factors.

Topic B.1 Causes of injury

Injuries can be divided into two types: those that have a physical effect on the body's systems – physiological injury – and those that affect the mind – described as psychological.

Physiological causes

Studied ☐

Gravity

The effect of gravity means that if you lose your balance when playing sports then you will probably fall over. You may then suffer injuries as a result of this fall, such as cuts, bruises or even fractured bones.

Overuse

An overuse injury is caused when a sportsperson does not take time to recover after exercise. Not allowing the body to repair itself means it becomes weaker and injuries occur. Overuse of a specific body part over time can make repair more difficult. A runner, for example, puts a lot of pressure and strain on their body and particularly their knees. Injuries to the knee joint can be a problem if a runner has trained or competed for a long period of time, even allowing for rest periods within training.

Intensity

If a sports performer exercises or plays at too high an intensity they are at a greater risk of injury as they are pushing their body to such an extent that it can result in acute injuries such as a strain or a sprain. Intensive activity over a prolonged period of time can result in overuse injuries.

Intrinsic injuries

Intrinsic factors result from stress inside an individual's body.

Body alignment

Having good movement patterns and maintaining body alignment and good posture by keeping your back straight, shoulders back, stomach in and head looking forwards minimises the risk of injury.

UNIT 10 Injury and the Sports Performer

Effect of levers

The effect of levers is a principal that primarily concerns the way in which we lift equipment. A lever consists of a rigid bar that rotates around a pivot point. Force is applied to the lever in order to lift a load. In a human, the rigid bar is the bones, the pivot point is the joint and the muscles apply force in order to produce movement.

Think of your back as a lever: the fulcrum is at your waist and the muscles in your arms apply the force. If you are lifting a piece of equipment that weighs 4 kg and you stoop to lift the equipment, the fulcrum will be in the centre and the stress on your back will be equal to the weight of the equipment plus your body weight.

However, if you stretch out further with your arms to pick up the piece of equipment, it will take more force to lift the piece of equipment which will place even more stress on the back which may result in injury.

In order to reduce the length of the lever and therefore place less stress on your back, you should keep your back straight and vertical and bend your knees to lift the equipment. Reducing the strain on your back means you are less likely to sustain a back injury.

Extrinsic injuries

These are caused by an outside force such as equipment or other participant. Examples of injuries caused by extrinsic factors include a head injury due to a collision with another player, a black eye from being hit in the face by a squash ball or a cut knee from falling over on a dry ski slope.

Psychological causes

Studied ☐

If an athlete feels stressed this can alter their focus and narrow their attention so that they do not notice other players, making them more likely to mistime a tackle for example, which can result in injury. Stress can also increase muscle tension which affects a person's coordination and therefore the risk of injury.

Personality factors can also have an impact on injury. An athlete who has high trait anxiety will often view situations as threatening, is more likely to feel stressed while taking part in sport and is therefore more likely to get injured when playing sport.

Topic B.2 Types of injury

Basic injuries

- **Bruises** are normally a result of an extrinsic force that squashes the muscle between the impact and the bone. This impact causes damage to the blood vessels, which leak blood into the tissue under the skin. It is the blood leakage that causes the swelling and discoloration.
- **Strains** are muscle injuries caused by muscle fibres becoming torn. The more muscle fibres that are torn the greater the severity of the injury and the longer the recovery time.
- **Sprains** are injuries to the ligaments. Ligaments link bones together and give stability to your joints. Ligament injuries often occur in sports that involve quick changes in direction, such as football. The most common ligament sprain is the ankle.
- **Cuts** are normally the result of falling or impact with another player or a piece of equipment. Most cuts are minor and can easily be treated at home. They will need to be cleaned and covered with a plaster or dressing. If the bleeding is excessive, stiches may be required to close the cut.
- **Blisters** are small pockets of fluid in the upper layers of the skin. They usually occur on the feet from continued rubbing of shoes or boots where the skin has been damaged. Most blisters are filled with a clear fluid which acts to cushion the tissue underneath which protects the tissue from further damage and allows it to heal.
- **Grazes** are where the top layer of skin is scraped off, leaving a raw, tender area. This type of injury often occurs as a result of a sliding fall.

Complex injuries

- **Tendonitis** – tendons join muscles to bones. Overuse from repetitive muscle contractions can lead the tendon to become inflamed and sore, making it difficult to perform the contraction without it hurting. Tendonitis is common in the Achilles (the tendon connecting the heel to the calf muscle) and in the elbow joint (tennis elbow).

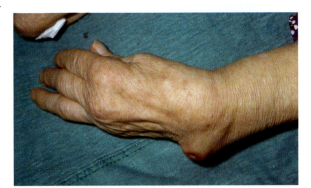

Figure 10.2 Fractured forearm

- **Fractures** – a fracture is a break in a bone. A bone that is broken in more than two places may have to be operated on and pinned together. A cast is used to immobilise the bone and help reset it, allowing the broken ends to join together. After wearing a cast you will often lose strength in the area around the broken bone. Doctors will usually prescribe strength and flexibility exercises to help regain the strength in the injured area.
- **Concussion** – an injury to the brain caused by a blow to the head that damages blood vessels in the brain. Often the person will have a headache, feel dizzy, groggy and disorientated and possibly feel

or be sick. In some cases they may become unconscious (pass out). Following concussion it is important to rest. Any person who gets a head injury should be referred to hospital or a doctor. This is why it is important to wear a helmet when undertaking activities such as cycling, climbing and canoeing.

- **Spinal injury** – an injury to the spinal column. Spinal injuries are often associated with head injuries and can occur in such sports as rugby and horse riding. It is important not to move a person with a back injury, unless it is really necessary to do so, because of the possibility of further damage to their spinal cord.

Topic B.3 Types and signs of illness

When taking part in any sports activity, whether as a coach, player or leader, it is important to recognise the symptoms of different illnesses because a quick diagnosis can help ensure the health and safety of the group.

Asthma

This is an illness that affects a person's airways and their ability to breathe easily. A person who has asthma normally has sensitive bronchial breathing tubes. Irritation or allergic reactions cause the tubes to become inflamed and narrow, making it difficult to breathe. The muscles around the airway tighten, which causes the tubes to produce excess phlegm.

Symptoms include a tight chest, being short of breath and wheezing. Tablets and sprays can be taken that help to stop the tubes from being sensitive and becoming inflamed. Sprays and pumps can also be used during an asthma attack. These help relax the muscles around the airways, helping the person to breathe more easily.

Asthmatics should carry their medication with them at all times. It is important that a coach or sports leader is aware of any asthmatics in their group.

Figure 10.3 Asthma affects a person's ability to breathe

Hypoglycaemia

Hypoglycaemia occurs when the level of glucose (sugar) in the blood drops below an individual's ideal level. This is common with people who suffer from Type 1 diabetes.

Hypoglycaemia occurs for a number of reasons, including not eating enough food, too much exercise, drinking too much alcohol and having too much insulin in the blood. This leads to insufficient energy (glucose) going to the brain and the body. Symptoms of hypoglycaemia include confusion, shaking, paleness, hunger, irritability and temporary unconsciousness.

It is important for a person experiencing the above symptoms to eat some simple carbohydrates straightaway as this will help to reverse the condition. A person with hypoglycaemia will normally recover within ten minutes of eating.

Viral infection

The most common types of viral infections are colds and sore throats. These occur as a result of viruses (microscopic germs) that invade our cells and multiply. We can pass on these germs through sneezing, touching somebody and touching food.

Symptoms of viral infections include a high temperature, muscular aches and pains, a blocked nose, fever, sickness and diarrhoea. There is no medication available for viral infections, so the best advice is to stay at home, drink plenty of water to help flush the virus from your system, and take some paracetamol or ibuprofen to reduce the aches and pains and bring down your body temperature.

Heart attack

A heart attack occurs when the blood vessels that provide the heart with oxygen and nutrients become blocked, stopping the blood from getting through. If you suspect someone is having a heart attack you must get medical help immediately as a heart attack is often fatal if not treated quickly.

Symptoms of heart attack include:

- chest pain in the centre of the chest
- pain in the left arm which also affects the jaw, neck, back and abdomen
- shortness of breath
- feeling sick
- coughing and wheezing.

Check your understanding

1. For each of the questions below, select the correct answer from the boxes.
   a. This is an injury to a ligament.
   b. Shin splints is an example of this type of risk factor.
   c. Swelling and discoloration of the skin as a result of damage to the blood vessels.
   d. This is the name of an injury to a muscle.
   e. This type of injury occurs from a blow to the head.
   f. An example of this would be if a person said they were *feeling* sick.
   g. An example of this would be if a person was *actually* sick.
   h. A bad tackle in football is an example of this type of risk factor.
   i. A person suffering from this condition would have the following symptoms: a tight chest, shortness of breath and wheezing.
   j. Symptoms of this type of illness include a high temperature, muscular aches and pains, a blocked nose, fever, sickness and diarrhoea.

Extrinsic risk factor	Bruise	Strain	Sign	Asthma
Intrinsic	Symptom	Sprain	Viral infection	Concussion

Summary

In this section we looked at different injuries and illnesses associated with participation in sports. The key learning points include:

- physiological causes of injury include overuse, intensity, gravity, intrinsic factors such as body alignment and the effect of levers and extrinsic factors such as other participants and the equipment used
- the psychological causes of injury include stress, reduced concentration and personality factors such as trait anxiety
- basic injuries include muscular injuries such as strains, sprains, bruising and skin injuries which include grazes, cuts and blisters
- complex injuries include over-use injuries such as tendonitis and shin splints, concussion, dislocations and fractures, back and spinal cord injuries
- recognising signs of illnesses is important whether you a coach, player or sports leader.

Activities

Activity B.1

Part 1

Prepare a PowerPoint presentation which explains three different causes of physiological injury and three different psychological causes of injury that you have witnessed while taking part in sport or supervising other people taking part in sport.

Part 2

Describe two different types of basic injury and two different types of complex injury associated with taking part in sport.

Part 3

Explain four types and signs of illness that you would look out for to check if a person was suffering from a specific illness while they were taking part in sport.

Activity B.2

Tested

Part 1

Write a report which discusses the relationship between the sports shown below and the possible causes of basic and complex injuries that could result from taking part in the sports.

- Rugby
- Cricket
- Hockey on astroturf pitch
- Rock climbing on a climbing wall

Part 2

Select one injury or illness that could occur while a person is taking part in sport. Write a detailed account of how the injury or illness might occur and provide an analysis of the types and signs of your chosen injury or illness.

UNIT 10 Injury and the Sports Performer

Topic C.1 Physiological responses to injury

One of the responses to injury is pain which is caused by the release of a chemical from the damaged cells, leading to swelling of the injured area (see Figure 10.4). The swelling creates pressure on the nerves surrounding the damaged tissue which causes the pain. The swelling occurs because the surrounding blood vessels are ruptured, allowing blood to bleed into the area and tissue fluid to gather around the injury site. The injured area will usually look red because the blood vessels surrounding the site dilate (vasodilation), which also has the effect of making the injured area feel hot. The injured area will show a reduced function or a total inability to function because of the pain and swelling.

The degree of swelling and pain is directly related to the degree of the injury – the greater the degree of damage, the greater the effects of the swelling and pain felt.

Figure 10.4 Swelling causes the pain associated with an injury

Topic C.2 Psychological responses to injury

Short-term responses to being injured

Studied ☐

The immediate response to injury varies from individual to individual. The initial reaction is usually negative as they will be unable to participate in short-term physical activity. The first reaction is usually shock, followed by disbelief and denial as many athletes tend to play down the significance of any injury and deny that it will cause a problem. These initial responses are then followed by possible further responses including anger directed towards themselves or other people and blaming themselves or other people for doing something wrong which resulted in their injury.

Long-terms responses to being injured

Studied

In the long term, when athletes realise that they are not able to participate in their sport for a length of time, their responses to being injured can include:

- loss of self-confidence as they may think they will be unable to achieve the level of fitness and skill they had before the injury
- lowered self-esteem as they may worry they are not good enough to play in the team any more
- frustration as they want to recover more quickly than is actually possible as well as tension and helplessness as they become frustrated at not being able to continue as normal with training or playing
- depression as they may feel that they will never play again because recovery takes longer than anticipated. An injured individual who belongs to a team may start to feel isolated from the 'group' and this in turn can lead to depression

Eventually the athlete begins to move towards an acceptance of the injury and adaptations to their lifestyle while injured. The focus then turns to rehabilitation and a return to sports activity. This stage tends to mark the transition from an emotional stage to a problem-coping stage as the individual realises what needs to be done to aid recovery. The timescale through these stages can vary considerably depending on the individual and the severity of the injury.

Figure 10.5 It can take time to recover from an injury

Topic C.3 Management of physiological injuries

Appropriate professional help

When an **emergency** occurs it is important that you remain calm in order to minimise the risk of injury to yourself and others. Your initial assessment could save somebody's life. Upon finding a **casualty** or when a person is injured, it is important to summon medical assistance as soon as possible.

Calling the emergency services

If a person is injured and you believe the injury requires professional attention, you must ensure that someone calls for an ambulance. If you are dealing with a casualty by yourself, minimise the risk to them by taking any vital action first (check their airway, breathing and circulation), then make a short and accurate call to the emergency services.

- Dial 999 and ask for an ambulance.
- Give your exact location.
- Give clear details of the accident and the severity of the injuries sustained by the casualty.
- Give the telephone number you are calling from and the gender and approximate age of the casualty.
- If you get someone else to make the call, always ask them to report back to you to confirm that the call has been made.
- When the paramedics arrive, tell them as much as possible about how the casualty has behaved, such as if they temporarily lost consciousness, whether they needed artificial resuscitation, and so on.

Often people who have been involved in an accident will suffer from shock. Shock usually makes it difficult for a person to focus on anything and both their heart rate and blood pressure may drop, which will make them feel faint. It is important that anyone who has been in an accident is looked after. By keeping the person warm and getting them to sit or lie down you will help reduce the risk of shock. It is also important to talk to the casualty and reassure them that help is on its way.

First aiders

Most sports providers have their own qualified first aiders who will deal with any injuries or illnesses that occur. Most minor injuries can often be dealt with on the spot, but major injuries will require further treatment. If the injured person is not admitted to hospital they should still be referred to a doctor.

Key terms

Emergency – a serious incident that happens suddenly or unexpectedly which requires urgent assistance from the emergency services.

Casualty – a person injured as a result of an incident.

Basic treatment for soft tissue injuries

SALTAPS

The sooner an injury is treated, the greater the chances of a complete recovery and the faster rehabilitation can begin. The immediate treatment of an injury is summarised by the acronym **SALTAPS**:

- **S**top play
- **A**sk the player what is wrong and where they have pain
- **L**ook (evaluate the appearance of the injury and look for signs of bleeding, deformity of limbs, inflammation, swelling and redness)
- **T**ouch the injury or close to the injury to establish signs of heat, tenderness, loss or change of sensation and pain
- **A**ctive movement – ask the player if they can move the injured area
- **P**assive movement – try to move the injured limb; if they are able to, ask the player to move it through its full range of movements
- **S**tand up – if the player has been taken through the steps above with no pain, use resisted movements to assess loss of function; for example, with an injured ankle you would assist the casualty to their feet, then ask them to stand unaided, then progress the test to walking and running. This process will determine the extent and severity of the injury, although it may be obvious.

Further treatment at this stage should consist of PRICE, which is described below.

In minor injuries all stages of SALTAPS can usually be completed, but if a person sustains a serious sports injury, such as a fracture or dislocation, the assessment should not be completed because further injury may occur.

PRICE

If a person has suffered from a soft tissue injury such as a strain or a sprain, ensuring that they follow the **PRICE** regime will help to limit the severity of their injury:

- **P**rotect the injured body part from further injury.
- **R**est: as soon as a person has injured themselves they should be told to discontinue their activity because further activity could cause more injury, delay healing, increase pain and stimulate bleeding.
- **I**ce: an ice pack or cold compress should be applied to the injured area to help reduce the swelling and pain of the injury.
- **C**ompression: gentle pressure should be applied to the injury site by surrounding the area with padding, a compressive bandage or a cloth. Compressing the injured area will reduce blood flow to the injury site and help to control swelling by decreasing fluid seeping into the injured area from adjacent tissue. After applying a compression bandage, the casualty's circulation should be checked by squeezing the nail beds of the injured limb. If blood is seen to return to the nail bed on release, the compression bandage is not too tight. The

> **Key terms**
>
> **SALTAPS** – Stop, Ask, Look, Touch, Active movement, Passive movement, Stand up.
>
> **PRICE** – Protection, Rest, Ice, Compression, Elevation

compression bandage should be reapplied after 24 hours in order to maintain compression over the injury site.

- Elevation: the injured area should be supported in a raised position above the level of the heart in order to reduce the blood flow to the injury. This will further help to minimise swelling and bruising at the injury site.

Topic C.4 Basic treatments to help support rehabilitation through to recovery

Cold therapy

Studied ☐

Cooling an injured body part to minimise the swelling and bruising and to reduce pain is essential. By cooling the injury site, the local blood vessels are constricted, thereby reducing blood flow to the area. This has the effect of decreasing the flow of this fluid into the tissues and also helps to slow the release of chemicals that cause pain and inflammation. Cold also decreases the feeling of pain by reducing the ability of the nerve endings to conduct impulses.

Cold therapy should be used immediately after injury has occurred for 48–72 hours. Ice bags (plastic bags with ice cubes in or a bag of frozen vegetables) or chemical cold packs can be used. Never apply ice directly onto the skin; cover the injured area with a cloth towel to prevent a blister or 'ice burn'. The cooling procedure should be repeated every two hours during the day.

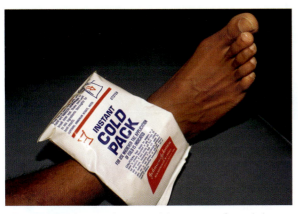

Figure 10.6 Ice packs can aid recovery from injury

Heat therapy

Studied ☐

The application of heat to an injury site will dilate the local blood vessels, increasing blood flow to the area. This type of treatment should only be given once the swelling has gone down, usually around 72 hours after injury. The increased blood supply will have the effect of absorbing the swelling and removing dead cells from the injury site. It will also help to increase the growth of new blood vessels in the area and help scar tissue to form. The application of heat to muscles allows them to relax and aids pain relief. Heat treatment is not suitable for an open wound or where tissues are very sensitive, such as in the genital region.

Contrast bathing – heat and cold therapy

Contrast bathing is the process by which alternating treatments of both hot and cold therapy are applied to the injury site. They should be used when the swelling has gone down – around 72 hours after the injury occurred. The application of a hot treatment increases the blood flow to the area and, when this is followed by a cold treatment, the blood flow to the area is decreased, taking with it the debris from the injury site. The injured site should be immersed in alternating hot and cold water for periods ranging from one to four minutes, with increased time initially in the cold water.

Basic strapping for support

The injured area can be strapped with a bandage or a tubigrip which gives the injured area support and protection. Joints are usually strapped as this stablises the joint and keeps it in the correct position, helping to prevent further damage to the soft tissue surrounding the joint.

Figure 10.7 Strapping provides support to an injured joint

Sports creams

Sports creams contain medication to treat and soothe injuries. They are usually applied to bruises, painful areas and aching muscles to ease pain and reduce swelling. These creams should not be used on broken skin such as cuts and grazes.

Topic C.5 Management of psychological injuries

Goal setting within a rehabilitation period

Goal-setting strategies and relaxation techniques have been shown to help many injured athletes with their psychological response to injuries. With the right knowledge, support and patience, an injury can be overcome without it being a totally negative experience.

Most sports people set themselves targets and goals to achieve. Injury does not mean that this goal setting should stop and it can be a very positive focus. Rather than viewing the injury as a crisis, it can be made another training challenge. The goal is now focused on recovery rather than performance. This will help keep the individual motivated. By monitoring these goals it becomes easier to notice small improvements in the rehabilitation of the injury, encouraging confidence in the recovery process. It is important that realistic goals and targets are set so this should always be done in conjunction with the person in charge of the physical rehabilitation process. Most athletes have a tendency to try to speed up their recovery by doing too much too soon. It is important that the injury is accepted and that the individual takes professional advice and knows their own limits.

Relaxation techniques

Relaxation techniques can be used by the recovering sports person to alleviate frustration and depression. Methods of relaxation include mental imagery and visualisation and both of these techniques involve creating pictures in your mind which work to influence how you feel. Imagining yourself in a relaxing place, such as on the beach during a holiday, should help you to feel the symptoms of relaxation.

Check your understanding

1. Are the following statements true or false?
   a. A first aid provider should always ensure they are safe before administering first aid.
   b. If a person appears to be having a heart attack you should contact their GP.
   c. PRICE treatment should be used if a person has stomach cramps.
   d. A fractured bone can be treated and dealt with on site.
   e. When calling the emergency services, you must tell the operator where you are and what sort of injury the casualty is suffering from.

Summary

In this section we looked at the response to injury and injury management. The key learning points include:

- the physiological response to injury is pain, swelling, redness, heat, loss or partial loss of function/range of movement
- long-term responses to being injured include loss of self-confidence, lowered self-esteem, frustration and depression
- basic treatments for soft tissue injury are PRICE, hot and cold therapy, strapping and sports creams
- SALTAPS should be used to assess an injury
- the management of psychological response to injuries includes goal setting within a rehabilitation period and using relaxation techniques.

Activity

a) In preparation for work experience with a local football club's physiotherapist you have been asked to carry out some research and write a report describing the possible responses of one of the club players to getting injured during a game. Include in your report a description of the immediate physiological responses to a specific injury of your choice and the immediate and long-term psychological responses that the player may have to this injury and how these can be managed.

b) Explain the responses and process of physiological and psychological management used to manage your chosen sporting injury. Justify the methods used to manage the physiological and psychological responses of your chosen sporting injury.

Topic D.1 Purpose

Maintain a safe environment

The leader of an activity is responsible for the planning and preparation and smooth running of the event in order to maintain a safe environment. Before the activity the leader should:

- determine who will be taking part in the activity
- undertake a risk assessment of the proposed activity
- determine the staffing requirements of the activity; this should include an appropriate number of qualified first aiders
- plan contingency and emergency arrangements
- if the activity is for children then inform parents and obtain parental and medical consent.

The site chosen must be suitable for the activity. Indoor facilities must be an appropriate size and have suitable lighting, changing facilities and first-aid provision. All the necessary equipment needed for the activity and the participants should be available and adhere to health and safety guidelines. Equipment must be checked before use to ensure that it is not faulty or damaged.

For outdoor activities environmental factors should be taken into account as these may adversely affect the activity. For example, a lot of rain could cause a sports field to become waterlogged, making it dangerous to play on. Always have a contingency plan that allows you to still run your activity without putting participants' health at risk. For example, a football game that was due to be played outside could be changed to a indoor five-a-side match.

Rules

Rules exist to protect the health and safety of sports participants and sports leaders. It is therefore important that all participants know the rules and stick to them. Rules will vary according to the sport, organisation, location and facility.

Specialist equipment and protective clothing

Specialised equipment or protective clothing can be worn to maintain or increase the health and safety of participants, such as a gum shield in rugby or pads in cricket and safety equipment such as ropes in rock climbing.

Figure 10.8 Protective clothing

Different equipment may be required for different age groups. For example when playing cricket with primary-school-aged children you would use soft balls – children are likely to be less experienced in throwing and catching than adults and hard balls are more likely to cause injuries. More staff would be needed to supervise the children and ensure their health and safety. By contrast, a group of 18-year-olds you would use the usual cricket equipment and follow standard rules. The only staffing required would be to umpire the event and to ensure appropriate first-aid provision.

Risk assessment

A risk assessment is carried out before an activity to consider what could go wrong during an event and to establish the steps to be taken to try to prevent such an incident occurring. A risk assessment looks at the possible hazards and associated risks and reduces or eliminates them where possible.

A hazard is something with the potential to cause harm such as water in a swimming pool. A risk is the chance of somebody being harmed by that hazard such as drowning in the swimming pool.

The level of risk is categorised by how severe the injury could be. The categories are:

- Low – minor injury
- Medium – injury requiring medical assistance
- High – major injury or fatality.

Control measures can be put in place to reduce the impact of the hazards or the level of risk. This could include using protective equipment and safety equipment or planning to keep away from or preventing access to identified hazards. For example, warning signs can be put up to make people aware of wet and slippery floors. This brings attention to the hazard and reduces the risk of injuries such as slips, trips and falls.

Table 10.1 An example of a risk assessment template

Risk Assessment Form					
Location of risk assessment:			Risk assessor's name:		
Date					
Activity	Participants	Hazard	Associated risk	Level of risk	Control measures

After an event has taken place, it is always good practice to review health and safety planning and implementation to see whether they were effective or if they could be improved. Examine if there were any injuries or near misses, how they occurred and if you could have done anything to reduce the likelihood of that incident happening.

Real world connection

Kate works as a part time first aider for a local semi-professional rugby league team. Her full time job involves teaching sports therapy at a university. She has always enjoyed watching rugby so when she was asked to work in this role she jumped at the chance! Kate has to be available to administer first aid during matches so she has to go to each match at the weekend and must be prepared to travel for away matches so that she can deal with any sports injuries that the team may suffer from. She also has to help to rehabilitate rugby players who have been injured and get them back to being match fit which means she often has to work one or two evenings a week too. Kate is able to deal with basic sports injuries herself, but she also has to be able to make a judgement and decide if the injury sustained is a complex injury that requires hospital treatment.

Topic D.2 Legislation and regulations

There is much government legislation relating to people's health, safety and well-being. The following legislation is relevant to the sports industry.

The Health and Safety at Work Act (1974)

Studied ☐

This Act ensures that employers take reasonable steps to ensure the health, safety and well-being of employees at work, including the provision of a safe working environment free from anything that could cause harm or risk. For example, a leisure centre must ensure that its employees:

- have the correct number of breaks of a sufficient length depending upon the hours that are going to be worked in a set shift
- are provided with an appropriate uniform
- are provided with the relevant training.

The act also includes responsibilities for the employee, who must stick to the rules set and not to put themselves or others at risk of injury or harm. Employees of a leisure centre such as lifeguards and gym instructors must ensure they:

- wear the uniform that is provided
- attend all training that is required to perform their job role properly
- follow and enforce the health and safety rules in respect of all people using the leisure centre.

The Management of Health and Safety at Work (Amendment) Regulations (1994)

Studied ☐

This act makes the Health and Safety at Work Act (1974) more explicit in stating what employers are required to do to manage health and safety in this act. The main requirement is that employers with five or more employees should carry out a risk assessment and record any significant findings of the risk assessment. Employers also need to appoint competent people to implement the health and safety measures identified in the risk assessment. They need to set up emergency procedures, provide clear information and training to employees and work together with other employers that are sharing the same workplace.

Health and Safety (First Aid) Act (1981)

Studied ☐

This Act requires companies and organisations to have sufficient first aid facilities and equipment in case of injury or illness affecting their employees. The number of qualified first aiders will be related to the number of employees working in the organisation.

Control of Substances Hazardous to Health Regulations COSHH (2002)

Studied ☐

Hazardous substances are anything that can cause ill health such as asthma, skin irritation and poisoning. COSHH covers substances that can be used directly in work (for example, cleaning materials), arise from the work (for example, dust or fumes) or occur naturally. Swimming pool chemicals, for example fall under these regulations.

The regulations also tell employees how to control hazardous substances, including labelling hazardous products clearly and storing them in a locked cabinet.

Safety at Sports Grounds Act (1975)

Studied ☐

The Safety of Sports Grounds Act 1975 was introduced following a number of disasters at football grounds. It introduced licensing of sports grounds and ensures they adhere to certain guidelines. Sports grounds holding more than 10,000 must have set capacities and may be used for only a set purpose. If they satisfy this they are granted a safety certificate, which states the number of people each section of the stadium can hold, the location of all exits including emergency exits and the number of crush barriers required.

The Act also highlights problem areas that need to be dealt with efficiently. These include:

- potential hazards to individuals that could cause them to trip or fall at a sports ground
- being able to evacuate the ground quickly in the event of an emergency.

This Act has been revisited since the Bradford and Hillsborough tragedies, which saw the introduction of the recommendations contained in the Taylor Report.

Children Act 2004

Studied ☐

This Act ensures there are consistent standards of care given to children. It requires organisations to provide training and ensure standards of care are maintained. For example a Summer Sports Coaching Camp for children requires qualified, competent and CRB-checked staff.

Many outdoor activities such as climbing and water sports have regulations and policies set by their governing bodies. These have become more vigorous since the Lyme Bay Disaster in 1993, where four teenagers drowned while kayaking on a school trip. Changes in the law have meant that schools need to ensure that they have undertaken a thorough risk assessment because teachers will be liable for any accidents that may occur.

Fire Safety and Safety of Places of Sport Act (1987)

Studied ☐

This Act requires that all sports arenas and stadia have sufficient means of escape in the event of a fire. The venue must also provide adequate equipment for fighting fire.

P7

M3

D3

1. For each of the questions below, select the correct answer from the boxes.

   a. This ensures that employers take reasonable steps to ensure the health, safety and welfare of their employees while they are at work.

   b. This law requires companies and organisations to have sufficient first aid facilities and equipment.

   c. This law aims to ensure that consistent standards of care are given to children.

   d. This regulation ensures hazardous substances are stored in a locked cabinet.

   e. This is something that is dangerous, and therefore has the potential to affect someone's safety or cause an injury.

   f. Something that is this type of risk means that it is likely to happen.

Children Act 2004	Health and Safety at Work Act 1974	Hazard	COSHH (2002)	Health and Safety (First Aid) Regulations 1981	High risk

Summary

In this section we looked at rules, regulations and legislation associated with health and safety in sport. The key learning points include:

- rules, regulations and legislation help to maintain a safe environment, protect participants and those leading the activity and minimise the risk of injury occurring
- risk assessment depends on the type of sport, the skill and age of the participants and the environment
- you need to be aware of the legislation which is relevant to the sports industry.

Activity

Part 1
Design and present a poster with text and illustrations which discusses the reasons for having health and safety regulations and legislation in sport.

Part 2
Write a report about the sport played at your local sports ground that explains and analyses the impact of two rules, regulations or pieces of legislation that help to maintain the health and safety of the participants in this sport.

Unit 10 Model assignment

This assignment will assess the following learning aims:

A understand risks and hazards associated with sports participation

B know about different injuries and illnesses associated with sports participation

C know about the response to injury and injury management

D know about rules, regulations and legislation associated with health and safety in sport.

Scenario 1

You are working as an assistant first aider for your college basketball team. In your role you are expected to have a basic knowledge of first aid and the different types of injuries that a sports performer may suffer from. You also need to know how to keep the team safe by adhering to health and safety guidelines and regulations.

Task 1

You have been asked by the basketball team manager to carry out research into sports injury and produce a leaflet to help to educate the team on sports injuries and illnesses

a. Many injuries occur because of risks or hazards associated with people, equipment and the environment. In your leaflet explain three different risks or hazards for each of these topics.

b. Explain three different physiological and three psychological causes of sports injury.

c. Describe two different types of basic injury and two different types of complex injury associated with participation in basketball. You should include sports-specific examples in your descriptions and discuss the relationship between causes of injury and basic and complex types of injury.

d. Explain four types and signs of illness associated with sports participation. You need to provide a detailed account of how this injury or illness could occur, analysing the associated types and signs of injury or illness.

Task 2

Prepare a presentation to the basketball team to help them know what to do if they get injured so that they can deal as effectively as possible with the situation. In your presentation you should describe the physiological and immediate and long-term psychological responses to injury and how to manage these responses.

For one sports injury explain how to manage the responses and process of physiological and psychological management. You need to justify the selected methods used to manage the physiological and psychological responses for your chosen injury.

Scenario 2

You are working as a leisure centre assistant and are hoping to be promoted to a senior assistant. This role requires a good knowledge of health and safety so that you can check that junior leisure centre assistants are following health and safety guidelines to keep the customers safe while taking part in sport.

Task 1

Write a report that includes a discussion on the reasons for having health and safety rules, regulations and legislation in sport.

Explain how two selected rules, regulations or pieces of legislation help to maintain the health and safety of participants in a selected sport. You should select two from the list below. You should analyse the impact of these two rules, regulations or pieces of legislation on participants in a selected sport.

Choose two from the following:

- Health and Safety at Work Act 1974
- Management of Health and Safety at Work (Amendment) Regulations 1994
- Health and Safety (First Aid) Regulations 1981
- Control of Substances Hazardous to Health (COSHH) 2002
- Safety at Sports Ground Act 1975
- Children Act 2004.

Unit 11

Running a Sports Event

Running an event as part of a team can be a very rewarding and a challenging thing to do. It opens up many exciting possibilities of what you can do for your school, college or community. Running the event is also about teamwork and overcoming the obstacles that are bound to occur in the planning process. Even the most experienced event organisers encounter obstacles at the planning and organising stages, the skill is that these problems are overcome without any damage to the event. If the event is well run on the day it will look quite easy and straightforward to those that see it or take part. The event can take many forms from a large tournament to some coaching sessions in a community centre. Whichever event is chosen you will need to plan the resources, get everything together, and contribute to running and leading it on the day.

It is your event so plan it carefully and properly, and it may cause quite a stir!

Learning aims

In this unit you will:

✓ plan a sports event

✓ contribute to the organisation of a sports event

✓ assist with running and leading a sports event

✓ review your own contribution to running a sports event.

Assessment criteria

Assessment and grading criteria

To achieve a **PASS** grade the evidence must show that the learner is able to:	To achieve a **MERIT** grade the evidence must show that the learner is able to:	To achieve a **DISTINCTION** grade the evidence must show that the learner is able to:
P1 Produce a plan for a selected sports event, outlining the planning process to meet event aims and objectives	**M1** Produce a plan for a selected sports event, describing the planning process to meet event aims and objectives	**D1** Justify the plan for a selected sports event, explaining the planning process
P2 Contribute to the organisation of a selected sports event		
P3 Contribute to the running and leading of a selected sports event, demonstrating the application of leadership attributes	**M2** Contribute to the running and leading of a successful sports event, demonstrating the application of leadership attributes	
P4 Collect qualitative and quantitative feedback from participants using four different methods		
P5 Review feedback obtained, describing strengths of the event and areas for improvement	**M3** Assess feedback, evaluating strengths of the event and areas for improvement, providing recommendations for future events	**D2** Analyse strengths of the event and areas for improvement, justifying recommendations for future events

Learning aim A: Plan a sports event

Topic A.1 Sports event

Selecting which event to organise is probably the most important decision that your group will make. It can be very difficult, or even impossible to change your decision afterwards, so as an event organiser it is essential that you consider the options and the issues involved very carefully.

Why are you running the event?

Studied ☐

One of the key issues to think about is the reason for running the event. This is sometimes called the aims and objectives. Reasons for running an event include:

- to encourage people to take up a new sport or an active lifestyle
- to raise funds for a charity or a good cause
- to raise awareness of the benefits of an active lifestyle
- to promote an organisation such as a youth club
- to improve skills through coaching sessions
- to organise a competition, event or tournament.

You must also think about the timing of your event. You will need to allow plenty of time to plan, organise and promote it properly (you could link this promotion to Unit 8 Promotion and Sponsorship in Sport, learning aim C: Plan the promotion of a sports event or scenario). However, the planning of an event should not be too drawn out as it is far more exciting and motivating if the event date is not too far away. Therefore, depending on the plans of your tutor, it might work best if the planning of the event lasts for one term or semester, with the event scheduled to take place at the end of that term or semester.

Which events are possible?

Studied ☐

You may come up with lots of suggestions for events that meet the aims you have chosen. But which of these suggestions are possible or 'feasible' and which are not? Finding out information and deciding which ideas for events are possible or feasible in advance is sometimes called a **feasibility** study.

Event organisers need to ask some detailed questions at the outset to do this properly and some of the answers may require people in the group to undertake some investigations before reporting back to the group their findings. For example, somebody may need to check which days the local community centre is free to stage the event.

> **Key term**
> **Feasibility** – whether something is possible.

Another important thing to find out is what **resources** you have available to run the event:

- **physical resources**: such as a sports hall or a football pitch and equipment such as balls, bibs, whistles, cones, etc.
- **human resources**: you need enough people with the right skills such as coaches, referees, fitness trainers, etc.
- **financial resources**: this simply means the money required. This might include payment for people who will work as referees or money to hire the facility. It is important before deciding on the event to add up the likely costs and see if the money will be available to run it. Sources of money include a grant, help from the school or college, sponsorship from a local company or through the money raised by entrance fees and other fundraising activities.

You also need to ask yourselves who the event will be aimed at. Your target group could therefore be, for example women or primary school children.

You also need to consider whether the event will attract sufficient interest. The event needs to be exciting enough that people will want to come and take part. This is not always easy to find out in advance.

Key terms

Resources – things you need to run an event which can be split into financial, physical and human.

Financial resources – sources of money available to pay for an event.

Physical resources – facilities and equipment needed for the event.

Human resources – the people and skills needed for the event.

Check your understanding

1. Fill in the blank spaces to complete the sentences about planning to run an event. The objects and facilities that you need to run an event are known as _____ resources. The people that are needed and the skills that you must have available are called the _____ resources. The money that you will need to run the event is called the _____ resources. Finding out information in advance to see what events are possible and what are not can be called a _____ study

2. For each of the objectives shown below, choose the event which would best meet that objective.

Objective	Event
A fundraising activity	A 5-a-side football competition
Supporting local community organisation	A community badminton coaching programme
A skill improvement activity	A 'come and try' sports day in the sports hall
A competitive activity	Raising money to go towards the setting up of a new playgroup
Encouraging sports participation	Holding an open day at the local youth club to attract new members

Topic A.2 Planning process

Now that the event has been chosen you will need to produce a plan of how it will be organised. The plan will consider a range of factors.

Nature of event and aims and objectives

Studied ☐

The plan should start by stating the nature of the event (i.e. the type of event, the event size and its location) and the event's aims and objectives.

- An Aim is the overall mission of the event.
- The Objectives break this down into smaller things that lead to the aim.

For example, the aim might be 'To encourage young people at Key Stage 3 to take up new racket-based sports.' This could be broken down into a series of objectives.

Your group could decide that the objectives leading toward this aim would be:

1. To encourage young people at Key Stage 3 to take up tennis.
2. To encourage young people at Key Stage 3 to take up badminton.
3. To encourage young people at Key Stage 3 to take up squash.

Each objective takes you towards your original aim. After agreeing the objectives we now have a clearer idea of how we will reach that aim and everybody should focus on working towards these objectives. This also helps prevent people from selecting different ideas half way through the planning process that might get confusing or distracting.

Target audience

Studied ☐

The next thing to agree and to put on the event plan is the **target audience**. These could include; toddlers, primary schools, secondary schools, colleges, local sports teams, adults or older adults.

Agreeing this is important because it will affect how you promote and run the event.

It is also important to think not just about who will take part but who the customers are. For example, for an event called 'A Sports Fun Day' for Key Stage 2 Primary School children that is organised on a Saturday morning and to which parents need to bring their children, you need to convince both children and their parents. However if the same event were organised in school, than you will more likely be trying to sell the event to the teachers in the primary school.

> **Key term**
>
> **Target audience** – the group of people you are aiming the event at.

Resources

Studied ☐

You will need to make a list that includes where you are going to get all the resources you will need. You will also have to state whether each resource needs to be paid for. For example, will you need to hire or buy equipment or is it freely available?

Budgeting your event

You will need to include in your plan a breakdown of the costs of the event. A **costing** is a calculation of the likely cost of something. The **budget** is the amount of money you have to spend. Perhaps the simplest way to work out how much your event is going to cost is to itemise the cost of everything and the income or budget that you will receive in the form of an **income and expenditure chart**. Table11.1 shows a simple chart for a 5-a-side football tournament.

> ## Key terms
>
> **Costing** – a calculation of the likely cost of something.
>
> **Budget** – the money available to spend.
>
> **Income and expenditure chart** – a breakdown showing all the income and expenditure involved in organising an event.

Table 11.1 Example of a budget

Income		Expenditure	
Grant from College	£50	Hire of sports hall 3 hours x £12 an hour	£36
Entry fees £2 per team x 8 teams	£16	Equipment: balls, bibs, goals, first aid kit supplied by leisure centre	£0
		Drinks (sponsored by Neal's Foodstore)	£0
		Printing Leaflets	£0
		Referees (from local football club)	£10
		Trophies	£14
Total	£66	Total	£60
		Balance for contingency	£6

Check your understanding

1. A group has decided that the aim of their event is 'to raise money for local junior sports clubs'. The group has chosen three objectives to meet this aim. Which of the following do you think they chose to meet their aim?
   - To raise money for the British Heart Foundation
   - To raise money for the NotOut Junior Cricket Club
   - To raise money for the Bees Junior Rugby Union Club
   - To improve the skill level in local sports clubs
   - To raise money for the Old Town Girls Football Team

Staffing roles, meetings and gathering evidence

Studied

Roles and responsibilities

The event plan should include an outline of the roles of each of the group members and who is responsible for different tasks. These may include coordinator, chairperson, secretary, finance officer, publicity officer and marketing officer. Sometimes people may be placed in a team responsible for a specific aspect of the event, for example, the publicity team that is responsible for distributing the promotion materials, the catering team that is responsible for organising the refreshments or perhaps the resources team that is responsible for organising and collecting the equipment. More details on the roles and responsibilities of the group is given in learning aim B, Topic B.1 later in this unit.

Records of meetings

Planning meetings may take some time – it is unlikely that all the arrangements will be made in one meeting. It is a good idea to keep records of these meetings so that people know who is responsible for different things and that people are reminded of decisions that have been taken. The records of meetings are normally called the **minutes**. As part of the evidence your tutor might suggest that records of meetings are kept by members of the group taking minutes. The minute taker could be rotated each meeting.

It is not possible to record what everybody said at a meeting. The important thing is to record what was decided and who is responsible for carrying out tasks so everyone knows what is happening and who is responsible. An example of part of the minutes of a meeting could look something like this.

> **Key term**
>
> **Minutes** – a written record of what was agreed at a meeting.

Table 11.2 Example of meeting minutes

	Action by Whom	Action by When
Item 4 Publicity		
It was decided that we would not print posters but would have 100 leaflets printed. It was agreed that these would be in black and white as colour printing is too expensive.		
A draft copy of the artwork will be drawn up for us to see	Sandra & Kyle	9th Nov
Agreed that we find out from the Media Resources Officer if the printing can be done cheaply	Will & Mohammed	6th Nov
Agreed that we would write up an advert to be put into the school website	Tracey & Darren	9th Nov

At the next meeting it is also a good idea to go back over the records of the previous meeting to ask if people have successfully carried out their tasks.

Maintaining a personal diary

Apart from the general minutes that apply to the whole group, you should keep a **personal diary** in which you record notes of what role you performed, what jobs you have done or been asked to do, and a record of your attendance and contribution at each team meeting. This will help provide evidence of your own contribution to the event and so is important to your achievement of the unit. An example of a personal diary is shown in Table 11.3.

> ### Key term
>
> **Personal diary** – a record that you must complete to provide evidence of your contribution to the organisation of an event.

Table 11.3

Date	My Contribution
Nov 11th	I attended our 4th team meeting. The meeting decided to distribute leaflets to local community centres and libraries and the Humberston Leisure Centre. I was given this role along with David, Sandra, Rahana, and Kyle as we are the publicity team.
Nov 12th	As part of the marketing team I went with Sandra and delivered leaflets to Giraud Street Library.
Nov 15th pm	I attended the 5th team meeting. When it came to the group discussing publicity I told the group which places I had delivered to so far and where I was going to deliver to in the following week.

Check your understanding

1. Why is it a good idea to place the names of the people responsible for a task on the records of meetings (minutes)?

2. Why is it a good idea to place the date by which something must be done on the records of meetings (minutes)?

3. Why do you think is it helpful to look at the records of the last meeting before starting a meeting?

Risk assessments

You will need to enter your risk assessments in your event plan. A **risk assessment** is a method of trying to ensure that possible accidents are anticipated in advance so that something can be done to avoid them. They force event organisers to sit down and think ahead and entail thinking about the possible **hazards** and **risks**. A hazard is something that could cause harm and a risk is the likelihood of the hazard causing harm.

Begin by making a list of all the possible hazards that could exist at your event. Write them all down, no matter how remote you think the chances might be. It should be quite a long and thorough list!

You then need to work out the risk of each of the hazards, including:

- the probability of the accident happening: this could be on a scale of Very unlikely, Unlikely, Medium likelihood, Likely, Very likely
- how harmful the hazard might be: this could be on a scale of Very harmful, Harmful, Some danger, Slightly harmful.

The first part of a simple risk assessment for a summer sports day on a playing field is shown below.

Table 11.4 Example of a simple risk assessment

Hazard	Risk	
	Likelihood	**How harmful**
Broken glass on playing fields	Very likely	Very harmful
Sunburn	Medium likelihood	Some danger
Falling goalposts	Unlikely	Harmful

There is not much point doing all this if it does not result in any action. You should weigh up the risks and agree on what measures to take – these are often called **control measures**. For example a control measure for the hazard of broken glass on playing fields might be for all group members to check the pitch and remove dangerous objects before the event starts and to only allow plastic bottles into the area. You should include these control measures and who is responsible for them in your risk assessment.

When all this is done the event should be a great deal safer.

> ## Key terms
>
> **Risk assessment** – a list of all the possible dangers connected with an event.
>
> **Hazard** – something that could cause harm.
>
> **Risk** – the likelihood that a hazard will cause harm.
>
> **Control measures** – what you can do to control or eliminate a risk

Informed consent

Sometimes the event that you run might carry with it a risk. As such, it is best if you tell people about the risk beforehand and ask that they agree to take the risk. This is known as **informed consent**. For example, if you run fitness sessions for older adults it is a good idea to devise a form that tells them of the risk and suggests they get clearance from their doctor before participating. Normally a person is asked to sign a form to show that they have read and understood the risk. The point of the signature is that you can prove that you obtained informed consent should you need to.

First aid procedures

In your plan you need to include details of what the first aid procedures are for injuries. The level of first aid cover required depends on the size of the event and the numbers present. If you are holding the event in a college or leisure centre you need to find out who the first aiders are and where they can be contacted. If you are holding an event in an unsupervised area you may need to state who the first aiders are. The largest events will normally have crews present from the St John's Ambulance Service (you will need to arrange this); smaller events might just require a first aider with a first aid kit.

You should also find out the procedure for major injuries at your venue and where these must be reported to so that the emergency services can be called.

Check your understanding

Match up the following risk assessment statements with their correct definition.

Statement	Definition
Tripping over a trailing cable to the PA system at a sports day	The risk of damage
Harmful	The control measure
Likely	The hazard
Moving the PA system beside the power point so the cable does not trail	The risk of likelihood

Timings

Studied ☐

The plan should include the timings of different parts of the event. If you are a coach or a sports leader that has written a session plan you will know the importance of breaking this down into separate parts for warm-ups, main activities and cool downs, etc. The same applies whether your event is a tournament, a sports day or a healthy lifestyle awareness day. You must break the overall time down into different parts and include this schedule in your plan. Remember to begin the timings before the event begins with the setting up, and to end the plan after the end of the event with the taking down and clearing up. An example could be as follows:

Table 11.5 Example of a schedule

10 am	Team briefing to ensure everybody knows their duties
10.15 am	Setting up sports hall, safety checks, check changing rooms and sports hall are clean and tidy, getting equipment and welcome desk ready. Organising the refreshments
11 am	Doors open. Ready to welcome teams
11.30.	Start group stage matches. Refreshment stand open for players
1 pm	Start Knock out Games
2.30 pm	Final
3.00 pm	Presentation of trophies. End of Event
3.15 – 3.45 pm	Clearing Up
3.45 pm	Return equipment we borrowed
4 pm	Debrief meeting

Constraints

Studied ☐

Constraints refer to things that limit what you can do at your event. You could be constrained by things like lack of facilities, such as insufficient space in the sports hall, a lack of certain skills, such as there being no qualified play leaders available, or a lack of money. For example, if only three badminton courts are available this might limit the number of entries you can allow into a badminton tournament.

> **Key term**
>
> **Constraints** – things that set limits on what you can do.

Contingency planning

Studied ☐

A **contingency plan** simply means having a back-up plan in place if things go wrong. This might include booking the sports hall so you can take the event inside if the weather is too bad to complete the event outside. Having arrangements in reserve is important. For example, you may be running a tennis tournament and are expecting a delivery of new balls that have been ordered. A few days before the event the balls have not arrived. One possible contingency is to contact a local school to see if you can borrow some baskets of older balls from them if the new balls do not arrive. They will certainly not be perfect for your event but they may save the day if the new balls do not arrive.

> **Key term**
>
> **Contingency plan** – back up plans in case things go wrong.

One of the key points to remember when planning an event is that circumstances can change as the event approaches. For example, a 5-a-side football competition is organised and the draw is made a week in advance. However, the draw is then messed up as some teams pull out the day before the event. On the day, some teams turn up with only three players and ask you to wait because some of their players are late. The problem for the event organiser is that these teams were meant to be playing first and time is short. Clearly in this case it might have been better if the organisers had done the draw on the day for those teams that had turned up on time. Thinking ahead of possible problems can save a great deal of trouble on the day itself.

Promotional activities

Studied ▢

The group will need to decide what promotional materials to use for the event. You will need to think about constraints like the cost of materials and how you will attract your target audience to come. For more information about **promotional activities** for an event see Unit 8 Promotion and Sponsorship in Sport, learning aim C: Plan the promotion of a sports event or scenario.

> **Key term**
>
> **Promotional activities** – how you publicise your event to your target audience.

Methods for obtaining feedback

Studied ▢

As part of your review you will need to look at the information and feedback that customers have provided about the event. This could be done through questionnaires, or comment cards that you have made or by interviewing participants during or after the event. You should discuss and agree on the best way to gather this information at a meeting and decide who is given the job of designing these cards or questionnaires, or obtaining feedback. One effective way of gaining feedback is to use a questionnaire with scales, for example:

Very Good [ ]   Good [ ]   Satisfactory [ ]   Poor [ ]   Very Poor [ ]

Check your understanding

1. Fill in the blank spaces to complete the sentences about planning to run an event.

   One of the main _____ we have in running our sports day is that there is limited space available on the playing fields so that has limited the number of entries we can accept. However, we have been able to book the sports hall which we can use as a _____ in case it rains heavily and we are unable to use the playing fields. We carried out _____ assessments to ensure the event will be safe and the promotional materials have been distributed to our _____ audience so we expect to have a good turnout.

Summary

In this section we have looked at the planning process involved in organising a sports event. The key learning points include:

- selecting the right event is important because it can be difficult to change your plans at a later date
- when planning an event you need to consider your reasons for running the event, who the target audience is, what resources are available and what budget is available
- you need to prepare a plan for the event which includes details of the nature of event, its aims and objectives and how these will be achieved, a list of resources needed and costings of the event together with a budget
- you must remember to keep records of all meetings and record details of the roles and responsibilities of different group members
- a risk assessment is an important part of the event plan
- timings for the event must be carefully considered and included in the plan
- contingency plans should be put in place to provide an alternative if things go wrong
- details of your promotional activities should be included in your plan together with the methods you will use to obtain feedback (you should make sure you have at least four methods of obtaining feedback to assist your review later).

Activity

You are working as a sports leader in a local youth club and suggest to the management of the club that you should run a 'come and try' sports day to boost sports participation at the youth club among local youths aged 14–16. Produce a plan to organise the event which covers the following:

- aims and objectives of the event
- target audience
- resources needed
- costings of the event and a budget
- records of meetings
- roles and responsibilities of different group members
- risk assessment
- first aid procedures you will have in place
- timings of what will happen and when
- details of constraints
- contingency plans
- promotional activities
- methods you will use to obtain feedback (make sure you have at least four methods to assist your review later).

Learning aim B: Contribute to the organisation of a sports event

Topic B.1 Event organisation

Learning aim B is a practical activity so your tutor will be keeping an assessor record of your contributions. To add to this you will have your personal diary of your contributions and you should also include some photos or digital evidence showing your part in the event preparation.

Participation

Studied ☐

It is a good idea to allocate roles at one of the first meetings when planning an event. Roles can be divided into two types: those involved with the planning and organising of the event and those involved with the running of the event. Everybody should have a role in both of these areas in order to best meet the requirements of the unit.

Table 11.6 below shows some of the roles involved with organising and planning an event.

Table 11.6 Roles involved in planning an event

Title	Role
Chairperson	Chairs the meetings and may have a leadership role
Secretary	Writes letters to external organisations and keeps records of the meetings
Finance officer or Treasurer	Looks after the money
Publicity officer	Distributes the promotional materials
Marketing officer	May design and get the promotional materials ready for the publicity officer

Depending on the nature of the event and your group other roles could include:

Table 11.7 Further roles involved in planning an event

Title	Role
Facilities officer	Responsible for booking venues, sending letters to confirm bookings, etc.
Minutes secretary	To lighten the workload on the secretary, a separate role is sometimes created to keep the records of the meetings
Resources officer	Responsible for obtaining and organising the equipment
Sponsorship organiser	Responsible for trying to get sponsorship for the event (see also Unit 8, learning aim C)

Each of these roles could be shared with one or more others. For example, somebody sharing the role of finance officer would be called the co-finance officer. To keep everybody active teams can also be set up such as:

- a sponsorship team that is responsible for trying to get sponsorship for the event
- a publicity team that delivers all the publicity materials
- a safety team that is responsible for ensuring that the measures on the risk assessments are put into place
- an organising team responsible for the event itself, such as drawing up the session plans and rules for a tournament or drawing up the plans for the displays on an awareness day.

Whatever your role, make sure you record all that you do in your personal diary.

Organising the resources

Studied ☐

On the event plan you will have outlined what resources you will need for the event. Now it is important to put this into action. For example, the sports hall will need to be booked or the shuttlecocks purchased or the t-shirts that the organising team will wear will need to be ordered.

Health and safety

Studied ☐

As part of the planning process your group will have conducted risk assessments. As the event draws nearer and arrangements are being made it is now important to make sure that the risk assessments are up to date. One of the key things to check is that your risk assessments cover the safety of participants, staff and spectators. You should also check that the control measures will be in place, for example, is the first aid kit available?

Contingency plans

Studied ☐

Now is also the time to check and review your contingency plans in case things go wrong.

P2

M2

Topic B.2 Participant requirements

Particular needs

Access

It is important to ensure that all participants can access your event. Access is not just about mobility issues, you need to think about other forms of disability too, and the measures that can be taken to help such people to take part. For example, access to an event should also cover:

- people who are partially sighted
- people who have hearing difficulties
- people who have learning needs.

If people attending your event have a problem with access and the group has not taken reasonable measures to assist them, this will have to be recorded in the review as an area for improvement. As part of the planning process therefore it is advisable to think ahead and decide what reasonable adjustments can be made to your event so that everybody can be included.

Language

Depending on where you live, there may be a higher proportion of people for whom English is not a first language. You need to think about whether this is likely to be an issue that needs to be addressed. For example, do you have a list of other languages that members of your group can speak so you know who to contact for assistance if the need arises?

Ability

You may find that you get a huge range of ability levels at your event and this can spoil the enjoyment for some, so it is important to plan how you can overcome this. Here are some suggestions.

- If you were running a tournament such as 5-a-side football or a table tennis competition, you could plan to organise a plate competition. This is a special competition among those who go out in the first round and it means they do not leave after just one match but instead get to stay around and try again against opposition that is more likely to be closer to their ability level.
- If you are running a fitness session you might have alternative exercises ready for those who are finding it difficult.
- If you are running a squash coaching event you could think about special arrangements for different abilities, for example, by providing different speed balls to cater for different ability levels.

Another way of considering your participants' requirements is to list them in a chart which assesses them by category and the likely needs of that category (see Table 11.8).

Table 11.8 Participants' requirements

Needs	Category	Arrangements
Gender	Both genders	Male and female toilets and changing facilities needed
Languages	There is a large Bangladeshi population in the area so there may be some people for whom English is a second language	Four of our group speak Bengali and will be on hand to assist if needed
Age	Children aged 7–8	High levels of qualified supervision Need to be kept busy with exciting activities
Access issues –mobility	We know of two wheelchair users	Need to ensure that the ramps are in place
Other disabilities	None that we know of at present, but the centre has leaflets in large print for the partially sighted	
Ability levels	It is an open tournament so we cannot tell	Run a plate competition for those that are knocked out in the first round

Using a chart to assess your participants' requirements may also help you to think about how you promote the event in terms of the type of language and imagery that you use. For example, different types of language are appropriate for different age groups.

Satisfaction

Studied ☐

After the event you will need to find out if you have succeeded in meeting the particular needs you have identified. As you are still at the organising stage, check you have included questions on meeting participants' needs on the feedback materials, such as the questionnaire and comment card.

Summary

In this section we looked at how you can contribute to the organisation of the event and the importance of meeting the requirements of the participants. The key learning points include:

- dividing up the roles and responsibilities required to organise the event is important and should be carried out at an early stage in the planning process
- as the event approaches, it is important to revisit the plans you have made, especially with regard to contingencies, health and safety and making sure all resources are in place, particularly those relating to venue, finance, transport, staffing, equipment, information, catering and entertainment
- remember to review the safety arrangements that you have made – these should cover the safety of participants, staff and spectators
- you should check you are still on course to meet your aims and objectives. For the review you will need to measure the results against your targets. All targets set should be SMARTER
- as a group you must make sure your event will meet the particular needs of the participants, particularly with regard to such things as access for those in a wheelchair, those speaking a different language and those of a different ability level
- you should by now have got methods in place to record customer satisfaction, for example, make sure you have the questionnaires and comment cards printed in good time and be sure to include a question on whether the participants who took part were satisfied with the event.

Activity

Following on from the plan you produced in the activity for learning aim A (page 299), you are now required to put your plan into action and organise the 'come and try' sports day as part of a team. To do this you will need to attend meetings and perform practical tasks that have been allocated to you by the group.

To produce evidence for this activity you need to produce:
- the event plan and related materials
- an assessor observation record of your participation in the organisation of the event
- a personal log or diary where you record your participation in organising the event
- photo or video evidence that clearly shows how you contributed to the organisation
- other information such as copies of records of meetings where you were present.

UNIT ⊩ Running a Sports Event

Learning aim C: Assist with running and leading a sports event

Topic C.1 Running a sports event

Learning aim C is a practical activity so you will be given an assessor observation sheet on the day of the event that is signed by you and your tutor. This sheet will outline your contribution to running and leading the event and how you met the requirements of the unit. You should also make arrangements to gather other information. For example, you could bring along a digital camera so that photos can be taken of you setting up the event, during the event and setting down the event.

Before the event begins it is a good idea to have a briefing meeting so that everybody is clear about their role(s). We have already discussed the possible roles that you might have in organising the event. Your role on the day of the event may well be different though. Depending on the nature of the event, your role might be:

- Sports leader
- Coach
- Referee or umpire
- Assistant referee
- Tournament organiser
- Steward
- Supervisor
- Looking after refreshments
- Fitness instructor
- Front of house – greeting people as they arrive, checking tickets, etc.

Setting up

Studied ☐

It is important to allow plenty of time to set up beforehand. Depending on the event, seating areas should be in place, changing rooms checked, sports pitches ready, everything clean and tidy, equipment should be ready, banners tied up in place, sponsors, names in place, promotional materials neatly laid out on the desk, refreshment area set up and so on.

During event

Studied ☐

Depending on your role and the nature of the event you should be very busy going about your duties. These may include serving food and drink, meeting customer requests, instructing, officiating, monitoring or supervising activities.

The one thing that you can expect, no matter how well you have planned and organised the event, is that the unexpected will happen. Do not worry, this is normal, however the important thing is how you respond to unexpected occurrences in the right way.

Setting down

Studied ☐

When the event is finished it is very important that the venue is left as it was found.

You must therefore ensure you have sufficient members of the team available to make sure:

● all sports equipment is returned to the proper place
● the venue is left tidy, such as replacing all the benches in the sports hall in the appropriate places
● all signs, posters and banners are taken down. Remember not to leave Sellotape™, pins or Blu-tac™ on the walls
● you have wiped down surfaces such as tables where drinks may have been placed
● waste is disposed of properly
● you let the host of the venue know when you are leaving and remember to thank them.

Real world connection

An event organiser at a community centre describes the switch between set up mode and action mode when the doors open and customers come in:

'We work as hard as you could imagine during the day getting everything just right, putting out the tables and chairs, setting up the presentation, arranging the food and drink, making sure everything is clean and tidy. We want the hall to look at its best before any customer arrives. An hour before opening all the staff go and clean themselves up and change into clean uniform so that we all look as presentable and professional as can be. No customer arriving on a Friday night must see any last minute setting up. When they arrive everything is done and we are standing there smiling and smart and ready to meet and greet. If only they knew what we looked like an hour before!'

Topic C.2 Leading a sports event

You need to contribute to the leading of the sports event and demonstrate leadership attributes. Your tutor will observe you and will record on your assessor observation record how you did this.

Leading

Studied ☐

How you show your leadership skills will very much depend on the nature of the event. Let us consider some examples of leadership in different events.

- If the event consists of leading a sports session you may take over for part of the session, perhaps by leading the participants for the cool down.
- If it is a coaching event or a 'come and try' sports day you might show leadership by taking some time to instruct a skill or show some people how to play a sport they have never played before.
- If you are running a fitness testing clinic you might give a short talk telling people about things like their body mass index and their body fat composition.
- If it is a sports activity you might be in charge of one of the activities.
- If it is an athletics day you might be in charge of running one of the events like the long jump.

Responsibilities

Studied ☐

You will be responsible for helping to lead the event throughout the programme. This means that you should be professional at all times. You must be aware of health and safety issues and make sure that both the event and venue rules and regulations are followed. For example, you might see that somebody has blocked a fire exit with sports equipment and so you should arrange for it to be cleared.

Measures of success

Studied ☐

The word '**proactive**' means doing something on your own initiative to prevent something going wrong. It is the opposite to reactive where you wait to react by being told to do something or react to something going wrong. You can show leadership by being proactive. You should be constantly aware of how well the event is going and try to do something if the event is not going as well as it might. Showing leadership means looking out for the following:

- Participant enjoyment: have you noticed some participants who are not enjoying the event as much as others? Is there something you can do about this?

> ### Key term
> **Proactive** – doing something on your own initiative rather than waiting to be told to respond to something.

- Meeting aims and objectives: are team members so busy that they have forgotten the objectives of the event? This is not uncommon but is there something you can do about it. For instance, if it is a promotional event you could ask some of your colleagues to begin giving out materials, even if you are too busy yourself.
- Coverage of planned components: is the event covering all it is supposed to? Are the group keeping to the timings in the plan? If not, can you show leadership and get the event back on track?
- Organisation: is the event well organised or do you need to tighten things up? For example, are participants that are not currently active wandering into areas they should not? Could you have a polite word with them about this, using all your customer service skills to make sure they stay where they are supposed to and that they stay good humoured about it?
- Safety: are you keeping an eye on safety? For example, you might notice that participants are wandering with their drinks too near to the electrical PA system.

It is not easy keeping an eye on all these things but it is what successful event organisers must do. Showing an awareness of these areas will mean that you have not just contributed to running the event, but contributed to leading it as well.

Topic C.3 Demonstration of leadership attributes

It is important to be as professional as you can be at all times before, during and after the event. In demonstrating the attributes of leadership there are certain skills and qualities that are expected of you.

P3

Skills

Studied ☐

- **Communication:** You must have good verbal communication skills, if you are to demonstrate leadership attributes, so this means speaking clearly at all times during the event. Your non-verbal communication must also be professional and relate to your expression, body language, posture and appearance. Standing with your hands in your pockets or slouching on a desk while you chat to your friends is not professional behaviour. It is also important that you make the effort to talk to and engage with spectators, participants and customers when appropriate.
- **Use of language:** Appropriate language should be used at all times. Remember that in a public place you may be overheard by others, including young children.
- **Organisation of equipment:** You should ensure all equipment is organised, tidy and in the correct place. All this should be sorted out beforehand so that you can relax and focus on the customers during the event.
- **Knowledge:** Make sure that you are familiar with all the arrangements, even those that are not your direct responsibility. You never know what customers are going to ask you or what information they may need, and it will not look professional if you do not know the answer.
- **Activity structure:** You should be clear about the activity structure, so that you can step in to do something if needed, hurry things along if they are running late or inform people of what time something starts.
- **Target Setting:** You will already have the SMARTER targets that were agreed by the group. But you could still show leadership by setting your own targets during the event. For example, if you are leading a fitness session you might call out that you want an extra five repetitions of an exercise in the next set, or put a time target on the completion of an exercise. Using targets like this is motivational for the participants and can demonstrate good leadership skills.
- **Evaluation:** In topic C.2 we looked at Measuring Success as part of the role of leading the event. If you are to demonstrate good leadership skills you might want to step forward from time to time to ensure that the team is evaluating how well it is performing (look back at this part of C2 for an outline of some of the things that you could evaluate). You might also ensure that team members are collecting the completed evaluation forms that you will need for your review.

M2

Qualities

- **Appearance:** You should be well groomed, tidy and in appropriate clothing. If the team has agreed to have a dress code, such as all wearing red t-shirts, than make sure you follow this.
- **Leadership style:** Different people have different types of leadership style. Some people are louder, while others demonstrate leadership through being softly spoken. Some people like to tell people what to do without consultation, while others collaborate and consult with colleagues. You should use the style that best suits you.
- **Personality:** People have different leadership attributes when it comes to their personality. Some people may be more extrovert, others might be quieter and more introvert. Use your own personality type to demonstrate leadership attributes.
- **Motivation and enthusiasm:** You are an event organiser and should be enthusiastic about what you have helped to create. You should be highly motivated and not need to be told to do something as you are one of those in charge of the event.
- **Humour:** Good humour is a must! This does not mean you need to be funny although a joke at the right time is of course fine. It does mean that you must appear to be approachable and in a good mood, no matter what the circumstances.
- **Confidence:** Even if you are feeling slightly nervous, you must try to show confidence on the outside. Try to look relaxed but engaged with the activity.

Check your understanding

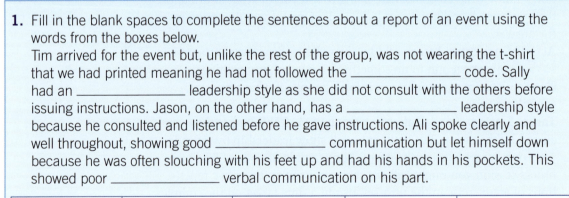

1. Fill in the blank spaces to complete the sentences about a report of an event using the words from the boxes below.

   Tim arrived for the event but, unlike the rest of the group, was not wearing the t-shirt that we had printed meaning he had not followed the _____ code. Sally had an _____ leadership style as she did not consult with the others before issuing instructions. Jason, on the other hand, has a _____ leadership style because he consulted and listened before he gave instructions. Ali spoke clearly and well throughout, showing good _____ communication but let himself down because he was often slouching with his feet up and had his hands in his pockets. This showed poor _____ verbal communication on his part.

non-verbal	democratic	verbal	autocratic	dress

Summary

In this section we have looked at what is involved in assisting with running and leading a sports event. The key learning points include:

- you will need to contribute to the running of the event by setting up, helping during the event and setting down after the event
- when leading the event you need to think about demonstrating your leadership skills through things such as coaching, leading a session or taking responsibility for a particular aspect of the event
- on the day of the event make sure you meet all your responsibilities and help others to do the same
- leadership attributes include being professional, demonstrating good verbal and non-verbal communication, making sure equipment is organised, being aware of the event and the activity structure, taking care with your appearance and demonstrating motivation, enthusiasm and humour.

Activity

Following on from your work in the previous activities, the Youth Club Management are delighted with your plan for the 'come and try' sports day and the report justifying the proposals and want you to run the event. You are to contribute to running and delivering the event. You must also demonstrate leadership attributes in running the event.

To produce evidence for this activity you need to produce:

- an assessor observation record showing exactly how you contributed to running and leading the event
- other evidence such as digital recordings showing how you contributed to running and leading the event
- a collation of four types of information for you to conduct your review that includes qualitative and quantitative feedback (such as completed questionnaires, completed comment cards, etc.).

Learning aim D: Review your own contribution to running a sports event

Topic D.1 Review of the event

It is now time to look back and review the planning and the running of the event. In order to do this you will need to gather feedback from a variety of sources, such as:

- questionnaires
- survey
- observation sheets or witness statements
- participant comment cards
- interviews with event participants (during or after the event)

The views of participants, observers, yourself, your assessor and any other witnesses to the event are all important when reviewing the event.

Qualitative and quantitative feedback

Studied ☐

To review the event you should use both **quantitative** and **qualitative** information. The example of the informal interview above is an example of qualitative feedback. It is not precise and does not have a quantity but it does tell us what participants say, think and feel about the event.

Quantitative information has a quantity. This means that is it is precise and has a numerical value. For example, using scales on questionnaires allows you to easily add up how many people selecting a certain option for each question. For example:

Q4. Did you think the organisation of the event was

Very Good | 8 | Good | 9 | Satisfactory | 5 | Poor | 2 | Very Poor | 0 |

Key terms

Quantitative information – information that is precise and can be measured numerically.

Qualitative information – does not have a quantity and tends to involve feelings and opinions.

Review against aims, objectives and SMARTER targets

After all that work you now have to ask the most important questions: did you achieve what you set out to do and meet your aims, objectives and targets? The extent to which you met your aims and objectives may be the cause of some discussion and there may be differences of opinion as to how well you did.

You should also look back at the event and review it by asking the following questions:

- Did you keep within the budget?
- Were the costings accurate?
- Did you correctly identify constraints when planning or did others crop up that you had not thought of?
- Were your contingency plans sufficient and did you need them?
- Were meetings held frequently enough or too frequently?
- Did you keep proper records of the meetings?

Strengths of the event and areas for improvement

This will depend to a large extent on whether you found that you met your aims and objectives. Looking at all the above things you have reviewed you need to pose some of the following questions: If you did meet most or all of the objectives why was this? What were the strengths that led to this success? Or was it the case that the targets were set at too easy a level? Were there nevertheless some areas of improvement?

If you did not meet any or most of the objectives why was this? Is it the case that the objectives were not well thought out or were not realistic? Even if you did not meet your objectives were there some strengths to look back on?

SMARTER targets

When reviewing the event you should state whether or not it met its SMARTER targets. You will only be able to accomplish this and review targets if you have set some targets in advance of the event.

SMARTER targets are:

- **S**pecific. This means that you should nail down the target more exactly. For example "To increase the numbers of young people at Key Stage 3 playing badminton" becomes "Increase the numbers of Key Stage 3 pupils playing badminton at Old Town Youth Club". The place is specific.
- **M**easurable. The target should be easy to measure. In other words you need to know if you have met the target. This can be done by adding numbers to the target. For example: "Increase by 2000 players every week, the number of Key Stage 3 pupils playing badminton at Old Town Youth Club".

- **A**chievable and **R**ealistic. The target given above is almost impossible to reach in most youth clubs. Targets are pointless unless they are achievable, in that they pose us a challenge, yet realistic in that we can reach them. If they are not set at an achievable and realistic level they are not a fair test of whether your event did well or not. Set the numbers at a realistic and achievable level. For example: "Increase by 12 every week the number of Key Stage 3 pupils playing badminton at Old Town Youth Club". This is challenging for one sport in one youth club but is possible if you work hard.
- **T**ime-related. How long will your goal take to achieve? A cut-off point is needed so we know how long it will take before the benefits of the event have happened or not. A time limit should be placed on when the target will be reached. For example: "Increase by 12 every week the number of Key Stage 3 pupils playing badminton at Old Town Youth Club within two weeks of our event".
- **E**xciting. The target should be exciting so that people are motivated to try to meet it.
- **R**ecorded. The target should be recorded so that at the review stage you can go back and see which smart targets were met.

Recommendations for future events

One way to view this task is to imagine that you are giving advice to a group that are about to run the same event that you did. Imagine what you would say and what advice you would give. Your recommendations do not have to be related just to the areas of improvement. Looking at your strengths and saying that you would repeat something you did well, or do it to a greater degree, is just as much a recommendation as focusing only on the negatives.

Check your understanding

1. Match the target with the reason why it is not SMARTER.

Increase the numbers of youths playing football in the borough within two weeks	not measurable
Increase by 25 the numbers of youths playing football in the borough	not realistic
Increase the numbers of youths playing football so that everybody in the borough plays football at least six times a week within two days	not time bound

Summary

In this section we looked at reviewing your own contribution to running a sports event. The key learning points include:

- collecting participant feedback on your event is essential to find out what went well and what could be improved
- methods to collect feedback include questionnaires, surveys, observation sheets, witness statements, participant comment cards, interviews with participants (during and after the event) and informal conversations with participants during the event
- the information you receive will include qualitative and quantitative feedback
- you will need to review the event against your aims and objectives and your SMARTER targets
- other areas to review include the budget and whether it was accurate, whether the constraints of the event were what you expected, whether you needed to implement your contingency plans, the frequency of group meetings and the records of the group meetings
- reviewing the event will enable you to consider the strengths of the event and areas of improvement and make recommendations for future events.

Activity

Part 1

Following on from your work in the previous activities on completion of the event the Youth Club Management want you to write a report that provides a full review of the event, describing the strengths and areas of improvement. Your report should include the following:

- Aims and objectives
- SMARTER targets
- Did you keep within the budget?
- Were the costings accurate?
- Constraints
- Contingency plans
- Were meetings held frequently enough or too frequently?
- Were records of meetings kept?

Part 2

Assess the feedback you have received, evaluating the strengths of the event and areas for improvement and use this information to provide recommendations for future events.

Part 3

Analyse the strengths of the event and areas for improvement and justify your recommendations for future events.

Unit 11 Model assignment

This assignment will assess the following learning aims

A plan a sports event

B contribute to the organisation of a sports event

C assist with running and leading a sports event

D review your own contribution to running a sports event.

Scenario

You are working as a sports leader in a local youth club and suggest to the management of the club that you should run a 'come and try' sports day to boost the sports participation at the youth club among local youths aged 14–16.

Task 1

Your ideas have been accepted by the management committee of the youth club and they have asked you to produce a plan to organise the event which covers the following:

- aims and objectives of the event
- target audience
- resources needed
- costings of the event and a budget
- records of meetings
- roles and responsibilities of different group members
- risk assessment
- informed consent disclaimers
- first aid procedures you will have in place
- timings of what will happen and when
- details of constraints
- contingency plans
- promotional activities
- methods you will use to obtain feedback (make sure you have at least four methods to assist your review later)
- preparing to cater for the particular needs of customers.

You should produce as evidence of this:

- the event plan and related materials
- an assessor observation record of your participation in the organisation of the event
- a personal log or diary where you record your participation in organising the event
- photo or video evidence that clearly shows how you contributed to the organisation of the event
- other information such as copies of records of meetings where you were present.

Task 2

Write a report to the management of the Youth Club justifying the reasons behind all the decisions you took in drafting your plan for Task 1.

Task 3

The management of the Youth Club are delighted with your plan and the report justifying the proposals and want you to contribute to running and delivering the event. You must also demonstrate leadership attributes in running the event. As evidence you will need to provide.

- an assessor observation record showing exactly how you contributed to running and leading the event

- other evidence such as digital recordings showing how you contributed to running and leading the event

- a collation of four types of information for you to conduct your review that includes qualitative and quantitative feedback (such as completed questionnaires, completed comment cards, etc.).

Task 4

On completion of the event the management of the youth club want you to write a report that provides a full review outlining the strengths and areas of improvement of the event and justification for each recommendation for improvement. This report should include the following:

- Aims and objectives
- SMARTER targets
- Did you keep within the budget?
- Were the costings accurate?
- Constraints
- Contingency plans
- Were meetings held frequently enough or too frequently?
- Were records of meetings kept?

Assess the feedback, evaluating strengths of the event and areas for improvement, providing recommendations for future events.

Analyse strengths of the event and areas for improvement, justifying recommendations for future events.

Unit 12

The Sport and Active Leisure Industry

The sports sector continues to grow and employs over 600,000 people who work across the public, private and voluntary sports sectors. A wide variety of jobs are available in the industry and this unit investigates employment in the sport and active leisure industry.

Learning aims

By the end of this unit you will:

✓ investigate organisations and occupations in sport and active leisure

✓ recognise current trends in sport and sports participation

✓ know about the impact of key issues on sport and active leisure

Assessment criteria

Assessment and grading criteria

To achieve a **PASS** grade the evidence must show that the learner is able to:	To achieve a **MERIT** grade the evidence must show that, in addition to the pass criteria, the learner is able to:	To achieve a **DISTINCTION** grade the evidence must show that, in addition to the pass and merit criteria, the learner is able to:
P1 Describe the different types of organisations in sport and active leisure, and the benefits of each	**M1** Explain, using relevant examples, the benefits of each of the different types of organisations in sport and active leisure	**D1** Compare and contrast the benefits of each different type of organisation in sport and active leisure
P2 Using information from selected sources, describe the requirements for, responsibilities of, and skills required by two occupations in sport and active leisure	**M2** Summarise selected information about occupations in sport and active leisure, describing the advantages and disadvantages of each	**D2** Explain the advantages and disadvantages of occupations in sport and active leisure
P3 Using relevant information, describe reasons for, and growth in, participation in sport and active leisure		
P4 Describe six factors that can affect participation in sport and active leisure	**M3** Explain, using relevant examples, how different factors can affect participation in sport and active leisure	
P5 Describe six different trends that can affect participation in sport and active leisure	**M4** Explain trends in participation in sport and active leisure	**D3** Compare and contrast trends in participation in sport and active leisure
P6 Describe six different key issues and their impact on sport and active leisure	**M5** Explain, using relevant examples, the impact of key issues on sport and active leisure	**D4** Analyse the impact of key issues on a selected sport and active leisure activity or business

Learning aim A: Investigate organisations and occupations in sport and active leisure

Topic A.1 Organisations in sport and active leisure

The three main sectors within the sport and active **leisure** industry are the public sector, private sector and voluntary sector. Each sector differs in its provision of **sport** and active leisure facilities; some of them work together to support the provision of sport and active leisure activities for different groups of people.

Key terms

Leisure – activities carried out for the purposes of enjoyment, relaxation and socialisation during time off from work or school/college. These activities may be active or passive and include activities such as reading, watching television, playing sports, going to the cinema or going out for a meal with friends.

Sport – a physical activity which involves physical skill or physical exertion, which must be played according to rules set down by a governing body. Sport is usually played for reward in terms of winning competitions.

Private sector

Studied ☐

The aim of the private sector is to make money. Private sector sport is provided by individuals or companies who invest their own money in facilities. As a result, these facilities are usually named after people, such as the David Lloyd clubs, although some have a brand name, such as Virgin Active or Cannons and have the latest equipment. Other types of private clubs include private golf clubs and tennis clubs. Many private sector facilities offer membership schemes.

The private sector provides for sports increasing in demand. It provides for active sports (for example tennis, golf, health and fitness suites, snooker and pool or water sports), spectator sports (for example, stadiums for football, rugby, cricket, tennis or golf) and sponsorship for well-known sports personalities so that they wear and advertise branded products and sports goods.

Figure 12.1 shows you how to identify a private sector provision.

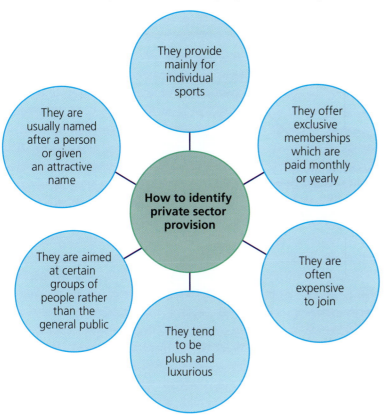

They provide mainly for individual sports

They are usually named after a person or given an attractive name

They offer exclusive memberships which are paid monthly or yearly

How to identify private sector provision

They are aimed at certain groups of people rather than the general public

They are often expensive to join

They tend to be plush and luxurious

Figure 12.1 How to identify private sector provision

Public sector

Studied

This sector is funded by money collected from the public in the form of direct taxes and indirect taxes as well as the National Lottery.

The public sector is made up of national government and local government (or local authorities). Public sector facilities are provided by local authorities with the aim of offering people a positive activity to do in their leisure time. These facilities often do not make a profit as they charge minimal prices to encourage participation in sport and active leisure activities. Figure 12.2 shows you how to identify a public sector provision.

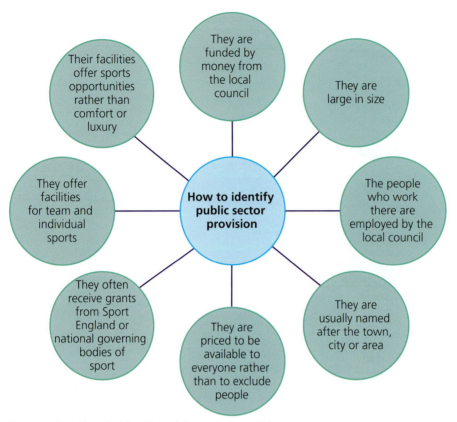

Figure 12.2 How to identify public sector provision

Voluntary sector

The voluntary sector is made up of clubs that operate as non-profit-making organisations and which are essentially managed by and for amateur sportsmen and women. Most people involved in this sector carry out the work as volunteers and do not receive payment for their help and support.

Some voluntary clubs own facilities, but the majority hire facilities which are usually provided by the public sector. Most clubs that people join to enable them to participate in competitive sport are in the voluntary sector. Voluntary sector clubs often work in partnership with the private or public sector; for example, they may use public sector facilities or gain sponsorship from the private sector (e.g. in the evening you may find the swimming pool at your leisure centre being used for swimming club or kayaking club training sessions).

The voluntary sector is funded primarily by its members in the form of subscriptions. Every club will have an annual subscription fee and match fees. These are to cover the costs of playing, travel and equipment. Money can be raised from sponsorship, applying for national lottery grants, applying for a grant from the government or local authority or running fundraising events.

Figure 12.3 shows you how to identify a voluntary sector provision.

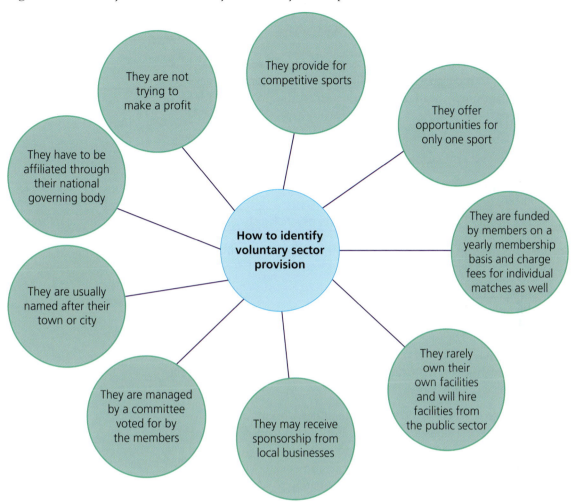

Figure 12.3 How to identify voluntary sector provision

Joint and dual use

Studied

Partnerships occur when two or more of the sectors come together to provide opportunities for sport and **dual use** is where two organisations use the facility. An example of this would be where a school has use of a leisure centre's sports facilities in the day time and then local clubs and fitness classes use it when the school is closed in the evenings, weekends and school holidays.

Joint use is where a school has a purpose-built sports provision which is used by both the school and the local community.

> ### Key terms
>
> **Dual use** – a facility used by two different organisations, such as a school during the day and local clubs and fitness instructors during evenings, weekends and school holidays.
>
> **Joint use** – a purpose-built sports provision at a school, which is used by the school and the local community.

Topic A.2 Occupations in sport and active leisure

A huge range of jobs are available in the sports industry (see Table 12.1 for examples). In order to gain the skills and qualifications you need for a particular job you may need to continue your studies to a higher level or complete a part-time course.

Table 12.1 Jobs available in the sports industry

Fitness instructor	Leisure attendant	Sports centre manager	Kayak instructor	Sports coach
Sports development officer	Sports/PE teacher	Mountain leader	Professional sports performer	Sports massage therapist
Sports scientist	Sports nutritionist	Sports psychologist	Sports groundsman	Sports retailer

Occupations in sport and active leisure will usually have similar responsibilities in terms of:

- Customer care
- Health and safety
- Child protection

The emphasis on how much responsibility is required in each of these will be dependent upon the occupation and the types of people that the professional is working with.

Customer care – Where an occupation includes working with people customer care skills are required. Both verbal and non-verbal communication techniques can be used to communicate with customers. Active listening is also a skill required for customer care which involves making eye contact with the customer and reacting to what the customer has said. This is followed up with questions to show that you have understood what the customer has said or need clarification. A positive attitude is also necessary to provide a high level of service.

Health and safety – Most occupations will require a person to take some responsibility for the health and safety of the people they work with and their customers. They must provide a safe environment and minimise any risks. They must also ensure that they and all participants follow any relevant health and safety legislation.

Child protection – any person who works with children needs to be aware of child protection policies and ensure that the children they are working with are kept safe. The Children Act (2004) details the levels of care required for people working with children.

The skills required by people working in sport and active leisure usually include the following:

- time management skills – examples include, getting to work on time, completing and making sure activities are completed in the time frames provided/expected.
- communication skills – examples include, giving presentations, working with other people and using verbal and non verbal communication to convey messages effectively.

- Leadership skills – examples include, being a sports captain, leading sports or children's activities, leading a team of people to organise an event.
- Team work skills – examples include, collaborating with others in the planning of an event, being a member of a team to set up and take down equipment, supporting other members in the team to achieve a goal.

We will now examine in more detail some of the responsibilities, skills, requirements, advantages and disadvantages of a number of these job roles.

Figure 12.4 PE teacher

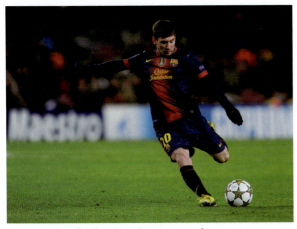

Figure 12.5 Professional sports performer

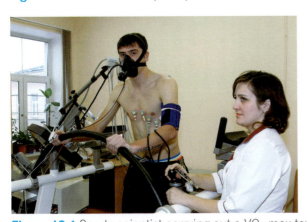

Figure 12.6 Sports scientist carrying out a VO$_2$ max text

Table 12.2 Responsibilities, skills, requirements and advantages and disadvantages of different occupations

Occupation	Responsibilities	Skills	Requirements	Advantages	Disadvantages
Fitness instructor	Assessing people's fitness levels; designing and instructing exercise programmes; teaching classes (e.g. aerobics or circuits); supervising people in the gym.	Good communication skills; friendly; able to remain calm under pressure.	Sound anatomy and physiology knowledge (from a sport science course); a recognised fitness instructor's award (e.g. from Premier Training International, YMCA or Focus); extra qualifications to teach specific skills (e.g. aerobics, circuits or stability ball work), first aid and CPR qualification.	Can be carried out in hours to suit; keep fit while doing your job; free use of equipment/facilities.	Pay can vary (usually less in public organisations than private); if you get injured you may be unable to work; may involve working unsociable hours and weekends.

P2

M2

D2

327

Occupation	Responsibilities	Skills	Requirements	Advantages	Disadvantages
Leisure attendant	Preparing and supervising sports halls, swimming pools and changing rooms; coaching or supervising sports sessions.	Outgoing and people-oriented; good communication skills; ability to deal with a range of people.	Sports qualification (desirable but not essential); National Pool Lifeguard Qualification (compulsory if you want to work poolside); specific national governing body coaching awards for coaching.	Free use of equipment/facilities; good experience for progression onto leisure centre management work; can be carried out from age 16 so is a good source of part-time income while still at school/college.	Shift work and can involve unsociable hours and weekends; pay is usually quite low.
Sports centre manager	Managing and motivating staff; organising the programme of facilities and activities; establishing systems and procedures; preparing and managing budgets, monitoring sales and usage; marketing and promoting the centre; dealing with members and any complaints or incidents.	Personal qualities including confidence, enthusiasm, assertiveness, communication skills, self-motivation, presence and professionalism.	BTEC First or National Diploma or GNVQ. Most managers will hold higher-level qualifications such as a degree or HND in Leisure Management or Business Studies.	Free use of the equipment/facilities; pay levels are quite good; good experience for progression onto other types of management work.	Usually done as shift work and can involve unsociable hours and weekends.
Sports coach	Developing the physical fitness and skills of their athletes; evaluating athletes' performances and offering feedback to improve performance.	Able to motivate athletes and gain their trust; good communication skills; good listener; able to show patience and empathy towards their athletes.	Knowledge of many aspects of sport science, such as anatomy and physiology, bio-mechanics, nutrition, psychology and sports injury. Every sport will have its own system for awarding coaching qualifications and coaches must hold the relevant award. Many coaches also hold qualifications in sport or sport science.	Your work involves a sport you really enjoy; get to see people progress and become better at their sport because of your help and support; work hours vary and can be fitted in around other commitments.	Usually carried out during unsociable hours and weekends; can involve working outside (great in good weather but not so good in cold and wet); pay can vary from nothing for volunteer coaching to very high amounts for coaching professional sports players.

Occupation	Responsibilities	Skills	Requirements	Advantages	Disadvantages
Sports development officer	Works to increase participation rates in sport and provide opportunities for people to play sport in a local area; responsibility for specific groups of people, such as ethnic minorities, women or disabled people.	An interest in and knowledge of a range of sports and the needs of a community; ability to communicate with people from different backgrounds and be sensitive to their needs; good leadership, motivational skills and an organised approach to work.	Most sports development officers have at least a BTEC National in sport or sports science and usually also hold a degree or HND in sport, sport science or leisure management, along with a range of coaching qualifications.	Work is varied; you get to meet lots of different people and take part in sports regularly; helping to improve community sports participation can be very rewarding.	May involve working unsociable hours; travel may be required; pay varies.
PE teacher	Teaching PE in schools to children aged 5–18 years. If you choose to teach younger children you will also usually have to teach a range of other subjects from the National Curriculum. If you teach PE in a secondary school, this will usually be the only subject you will be required to teach. A lecturer teaches in a college or university and usually specialises in a few subject areas such as physiology or psychology.	Patience; ability to deal with young people and their various needs; organised; able to maintain discipline; able to adapt communication skills to the group you are teaching; good level of personal fitness; enjoy working with young people.	Educated to degree level – Bachelor of Education (BEd) or a Bachelor of Arts with Qualified Teaching Status (BA (QTS)); or take a three-year degree in sport science or sport studies and then complete a one-year Postgraduate Certificate in Education (PGCE). You must have passed English, maths and a science at GCSE grade C or above and have passed at least two A levels.	Longer holidays than most other professions; get to play sports every day; helping children to get better at sports can be very rewarding.	Teachers can only take holiday time during scheduled school holidays; most PE teachers run after-school clubs and take children to interschool sports events which can mean they do not finish work until late; time is spent after school marking children's work.

Occupation	Responsibilities	Skills	Requirements	Advantages	Disadvantages
Professional sports performer	Play sport full-time at a professional level. There are a limited number of sports where you can play professionally and most professional players have to have a second job to ensure their income.	Technical efficiency at the chosen sport; physical fitness; self-motivation; commitment; determination.	No formal qualifications are needed, although you need to investigate the best route into your sport, as every sport will be slightly different in terms of the way it recruits young players.	Salaries for professional sport performers can be very high indeed and the person is paid to play a sport they love!	The career of a sports performer is short-lived (many retire soon after or even before the age of 30); if a player is injured it can stop them playing their sport completely which means they will have to find another job to earn money; high profile sports performers lose their privacy and anonymity.
Sports massage therapist	Using massage skills to prepare athletes for competition; helping them to warm down after competition; dealing with any injuries or soreness they may suffer; treating members of the public who have injured themselves as a result of non-sporting activities such as gardening.	A professional approach, as the job involves physical contact with people; should be patient, caring and sensitive to an individual's needs; a high standard of personal hygiene; good communication skills.	A sports therapy diploma. These courses are accredited by the Vocational Training and Charitable Trust (VTCT) and can be studied at most colleges of further education. Private training organisations, such as Premier Training International, also offer these courses in an intensive 12-week format. It is possible to do a degree in sports therapy or sports rehabilitation at a limited number of universities.	Can arrange work hours to fit in around other commitments; pay varies depending upon the area and organisation; you may be able to work with elite sports players.	Can involve working unsociable hours and weekends.

Occupation	Responsibilities	Skills	Requirements	Advantages	Disadvantages
Sport and exercise scientist	To maximise the performance of an individual in their care; applying their knowledge and skills in physiology, biomechanics and psychology to give the performers all possible advantage. Physiology will involve fitness testing and monitoring physical condition; biomechanics will involve examining the performer's technique and equipment to analyse where improvements can be made; psychology will be applied to ensure the performer is mentally prepared.	Must work well with people and have good communication skills; be patient, caring and sensitive to an individual's needs.	A degree in sport science and possibly a Master's degree or a PhD in their chosen field of expertise.	Working with elite athletes to improve their performance and knowledge of a subject area that interests them.	Pay can be quite low depending upon which sports the scientist works with, although high profile sports such as football can offer high salaries.
Sports retailer	Working in a sports shop selling sports goods; using knowledge of sport and matching a client's needs to specific products.	An ability to deal with members of the public and be willing to meet their needs as necessary; good communication skills; ability to stay calm under pressure.	A knowledge of sport is needed, but many people working in retail will need business skills and customer care skills. A BTEC in business studies or leisure studies would be appropriate. If you have aspirations to run a sports shop, it may be necessary to hold an HND or degree in a management-based subject.	Staff discounts to buy sports products from the shop where you work; work can be carried out as a part-time job while in school or college; you get to keep up to date with all of the latest sports products.	Usually involves working weekends and pay can be quite low.

P2

M2

D2

Sources of information

There are many of different sources of information where you can find out about the different types of jobs available in the sport and active leisure industry. Most sectors have their own websites or specific journals where they advertise jobs.

Websites

You may find the following websites helpful:

- SkillsActive (Sector Skills Council for Sport) – www.skillsactive.com
- Chartered Institute for the Management of Sport and Physical Activity – www.cimspa.co.uk
- Sports Recruitment International – www.sportsrecruitment.co.uk
- www.leisureopportunities.co.uk
- www.thefitnessjobs.com
- www.bestadventurejobs.co.uk

Press and journals

Sport and leisure jobs are often advertised in the press and trade journals, including local newspapers, regional newspapers and national newspapers. Trade publications such as *Leisure Management*, *Leisure Opportunities*, *Sports and Leisure Magazine*, *Health and Fitness*, as well as the Institute of Leisure and Amenity Management (ILAM) and promotional material from specific sport and active leisure industries.

Check your understanding

1. For each of the questions below, select the correct answer from the boxes.
   a. This type of sector tries to make a profit out of sport.
   b. A public swimming pool is an example of a facility from this sector.
   c. This sort of job requires shift work.
   d. This is an example of a sports centre in the private sector.
   e. This is an example of a voluntary organisation.
   f. You would need a degree to go into this profession.
   g. An example of this would be where a school has use of a leisure centre's sports facilities in the day time and then local clubs and fitness classes use it when the school is closed in the evenings.
   h. A person entering this job would need a degree in sports sciences.

| David Lloyd | public sector | pool lifeguard | private |
| sport and exercise scientist | PE teacher | youth football club | dual use |

Summary

In this section we looked at organisations and occupations in sport and active leisure. The key learning points include:

- the different sectors involved in sport are the public, private and voluntary sectors, as well as dual and joint use
- many different jobs are available in the sport and active leisure sector, all of which require different skills, qualifications and responsibilities
- sources of information about different types of occupations in the sport and active leisure sector include websites, newspapers and journals.

Activity

Part 1

Prepare a written report that describes the different types of organisation in the public, private and voluntary sectors and explain the benefits of each organisation using relevant examples.

Part 2

Compare and contrast the benefits of each type of organisation that you have researched in Part 1.

Part 3

Carry out research about two occupations in sport and active leisure using websites, newspapers and journals. Prepare a leaflet that describes the requirements, responsibilities and skills for these two occupations.

Part 4

Summarise information about a range of different occupations in sport and active leisure and explain the advantages and disadvantages of each occupation.

Learning aim B: Recognise current trends in sport and sports participation

Topic B.1 Reasons for taking part in sport and active leisure

Taking part in sport and sports activities can have a number of significant benefits including:

Health and fitness benefits

Studied ☐

Taking part in regular sports activities will help to keep your body fit and healthy. The health benefits include an increase in cardiovascular fitness, muscular endurance and strength, flexibility, improved posture and low fat body composition.

All of these help a person to carry out their everyday activities and reduce the risk of injury as well as reducing the risk of chronic diseases associated with inactivity such as coronary heart disease, type 2 diabetes and certain types of cancer.

Social benefits

Studied ☐

Taking part in regular sports can increase a person's self-confidence and self-esteem through setting and attaining goals such as completing a 10K race or being selected for a school football team. This increased self-confidence can help people to socialise and have the confidence to talk to and meet new people. Increasing a young person's self-confidence and self-esteem can often reduce the risk of them bullying others, since bullying is often the result of low self-esteem.

Playing sports is a very good way of socialising and helps people to make new friends, for example, when joining a badminton club, netball team, squash league or an exercise classes.

Developmental benefits

Studied ☐

Taking part in sports helps a person to develop their skills in that sport and also provides transferable skills that can be used in other sports, for example, hand–eye coordination which is required for catching in sports like cricket and rounders.

Team sports such as basketball, cricket, netball and volleyball help people to learn about being part of a team and to develop new and transferable skills about how to work as a member of a team. This in turn can help them in school, college and work environments, where they may be required to work with others. Leadership skills can be developed from participation in team sports, for example, by being a team captain.

Topic B.2 Reasons for growth in participation

Participation in sport has increased since the 1960s for the following reasons:

- increased car ownership
- increased leisure time
- increased availability of sports facilities
- increased promotion of athletes by government agencies
- growth in knowledge of relationship between sport and health
- increased coverage of sport on TV, radio and electronic media such as the internet
- Fashion – sport has become very fashionable in recent years. Sports retailers in the UK have been transformed from the kind of shop that only sold sporting goods to a place to buy sports clothing that will be worn as a fashion item, for example replica football shirts and trainers.

Figure 12.7 Sports retailing has become big business

- Increased disposable income – as salaries have increased, so too has **disposable income**, which is the money that someone has left after paying their bills and expenses. There has also been a growth in the population aged 50+ years because of healthier lifestyles and improvements in modern medicine. This has meant that a greater number of people than ever, many of whom are retired or semi-retired, now have the time and money to spend on leisure, although at the time of writing the UK is currently coming out of a recession and it is reported that disposable income in the UK is shrinking.

> ### Key term
> **Disposable income** – the money you have left after paying bills and expenses.

3

Topic B.3 Factors that affect participation

A number of factors can make it difficult for some people to take part in regular sports activities. Not everyone has equal access to sport and active leisure opportunities. Some factors that affect participation are discussed below.

Disability

Studied ☐

Sport is an excellent way to make disabled people feel involved in life, feel good about themselves and able to achieve new skills. However, there are two barriers to participation: opportunity and accessibility. A law was passed in 2004 to make sure that all new buildings are accessible to disabled people. This means providing access ramps, disabled changing and toilet facilities, doors of an appropriate width, access to all facilities, adaptations to equipment and Braille signs.

Ethnic origin

Studied ☐

Recent statistics have shown a direct relationship between ethnic origin and participation in sport. White ethnic groups have the highest participation rates, while people of Pakistani origin (particularly women) have the lowest participation rates. Certain ethnic groups are well represented in some sports but very poorly represented in others.

Sports development officers work hard to offer opportunities to people from all ethnic groups and meet their specific needs, for example by offering women-only swimming sessions for Muslim women.

Age

Studied ☐

As we get older our needs change and the sports activities we play become less competitive and less physical. Football, rugby and cricket are all favoured sports of the younger age groups while golf and walking are more popular in the 60+ age group.

Location in the country

Studied ☐

Participation rates vary across the country, with generally more people taking part in sport towards the south of the country compared to the north. The reasons for these differences include different availability of sports facilities, variations in income and differing views on the importance of sport and physical activity.

Income

Studied ☐

The amount of money a person has to spend on their leisure activities is called disposable income. This depends upon their original income and the various costs and responsibilities they have. The more disposable income they have, then the greater choice of sports activities they will have. For example, to play sport in private sector facilities can be very expensive. Private health and fitness clubs will charge as much as £100 a month for membership. Sports such as golf, tennis, sailing and skiing are very expensive to be involved in because the equipment and access to facilities are expensive. Other sports such as running or football are fairly cheap to participate in and are accessible to everyone.

Provision

Studied ☐

Some leisure centres or local areas do not provide the sports or sporting facilities for some groups of people, preventing these people taking part in their preferred sports. For example, a recreation ground may have football posts so people can play football but no rugby posts, meaning that people who want to play rugby may have to travel elsewhere, which may be difficult as they may have to rely on parents for lifts etc.

Gender

Studied ☐

Some sports do naturally attract more of one gender than the other. Exercise classes such as Zumba and aerobics usually attract female participants whereas circuits often attracts more male participants. So the type of provision of classes or sports can affect the gender that will participate to some degree. Also, some religions such as Islam do not permit certain parts of women's bodies to be seen by men, so if a Muslim woman wants to go swimming she has to go to female only sessions which have female lifeguards on duty.

Topic B.4 Trends in participation

New sports activities

Studied ☐

There are always new and emerging sports activities – when a new 'craze' hits the nation everybody wants to have a go. Examples of new sports activities include, cyclo-cross, in-line skating, kite surfing and open water swimming which has largely been brought about from the increased interest and participation in triathlons. Ultimate frisbee and handball are team games that are starting to take off in this country through inclusion in school PE lessons. Health and fitness trends continue to develop new ways to help people to get fit and some of these trends stand the test of time such as aerobics, whereas others, such as the slide aerobics class, only last a few years.

Influence of sport on fashion

Studied ☐

Sport influences fashion with many young people choosing to wear expensive trainers that are not always used for taking part in sport but are instead worn to 'look cool'. For the London 2012 Olympics, fashion and sport worked together. A well-known British fashion designer, Stella McCartney designed the Team GB kit which brought global attention to British fashion designers. Many football teams have a home and away kit which changes every season; fans buy this kit to show their support for their team.

Activities with increasing participation

The recent success of British athletes at the London 2012 Olympics has increased participation in a number of sports and active leisure activities. The continued success of British cycling in the London 2012 Olympics following success in Beijing and the first win of the Tour de France by a British cyclist has undoubtedly spurred people on to don their lycra and get out on their bikes! Similarly, the success in athletics of Jessica Ennis, Mo Farah and Greg Rutherford all winning Olympic gold medals on the same night has seen athletics clubs around the country filled with enthusiastic young people hoping to follow in these athletes' footsteps.

Activities with decreasing participation

Some activities are declining because of a lack of role models in that sport such as volleyball, or because they are expensive. Golf in particular has been affected by the recession in the British economy because many people's disposable income has been reduced.

Changing expectations of participants or spectators

After such significant British successes in the 2008 and 2012 Olympic Games, spectators are now more inclined to spend time and money going to watch and support British sporting events. The London 2012 Paralympics had capacity crowds for most events for the first time ever at a Paralympics, which clearly shows the response and change in expectations of British spectators. Expectations of participants are often high and they can therefore expect to receive funding, sponsorship and support to allow them to train and compete at the highest level.

Technological developments

As interest in sport has increased, technological developments have been made to make the sports more spectator friendly and improve the performance of the sports participants. The video referee in Rugby has relatively recently been introduced to ensure that the referee is able to make accurate decisions and that the games are played and won fairly. There is also a need for goal line technology in football to be introduced as TV replays often showing wrong decisions by the referee which causes frustration for players and spectators.

Sports clothing and footwear is continually developing to give athletes the edge by reducing drag improving and improving efficiency, for example. When only a fraction of a second is the difference between winning and losing, any new technological development is usually welcomed. This has led to the development of new fabrics and materials.

Check your understanding

1. Give three health and fitness benefits of taking part in regular sports activities.
2. Describe how taking part in sports provides a social benefit to an individual.
3. Describe three factors that affect your participation in sport and active leisure activities.
4. Name three sports that have experienced increased participation over the last few years and explain why this is.
5. Select a sport and describe how technological innovation has helped to improve the performance of the athletes.

Summary

In this section we have looked at current trends in sport and sports participation. The key learning points include:

- people take part in sport and active leisure for health and fitness benefits, social benefits and personal and skill developmental benefits
- reasons for growth in participation include increased leisure time, fashion and increased disposable income
- factors that affect participation include disability, provision, cost, ethnicity, location, age and gender
- trends in participation are affected by the introduction of new sports activities, the influence of sport on fashion
- some activities have increasing participation because of mainstream exposure while others have decreasing participation, often because they are expensive
- the London 2012 Olympics increased the expectations of spectators and participants have also been inspired.

Activity

Part 1
Carry out research and prepare a PowerPoint presentation that describes the reasons why people take part in sport and active leisure and the growth in participation in sport and active leisure.

Part 2
Describe and explain at least six factors that can affect how different people take part in sport and active leisure, giving examples where possible.

Part 3
Describe, explain and compare and contrast at least six trends in participation in sport and active leisure.

Learning aim C: Know about the impact of key issues on sport and active leisure

Topic C.1 Key issues

Social influences

Participation in sport in the UK has traditionally been divided by groups. If you consider the kinds of people who are able to take part in football, and then the type of person who is able to take part in polo, you can perhaps see that sports have a social history and reflect the class systems.

Many sociologists claim that sport allows for **social mobility**; this means that sport allows people from a working class background to access the kinds of sport and therefore lifestyles previously only enjoyed by the very rich and the upper classes.

> **Key term**
>
> **Social mobility** – a measure of how free people are to improve their position in society and to change their social status.

Economic influences

The amount of spare money that a person has may dictate how much or how little they participate in sport and exercise, the types of facilities that they use and the types of sports that they can take part in. Think about what kind of person can afford to be a member at a private gym and compare them with gym users at the local sports centre. Also consider the costs of a sport such as horse riding where the equipment and lessons are very expensive, compared to playing badminton at a public leisure centre where costs are very low and equipment can be borrowed.

Healthy lifestyles

In recent years the government has made improved health a priority and it sees sport as one of the most important ways to improve people's health. The previous focus on elite provision, in other words money going to the highest level of performance, national teams and Olympic teams, etc., has changed. The current focus for spending is nearly all related to what the government calls 'The health of the nation' – a document outlining how they aim to improve the lifestyle of the entire nation and transform us from a nation of couch potatoes to one of mostly fit and healthy people.

Role of the media

At one time, the only way sport and active leisure events could be seen was by attending the event in person. Today, most people experience sport through media coverage including television, the internet (e.g. Twitter, Facebook, NGB websites), films, books, magazines and mobile technology.

The internet has pages and pages devoted to sports fans and information on governing bodies that provide up-to-the-minute news and results services, all of which has the effect of increasing the profile and interest in sport.

Discrimination

Discrimination means preventing a specific group of people from doing something. SportEngland have promoted a series of programmes to increase sports participation among all sections of society, including the disabled, women and girls, the elderly, youth and people from ethnic minorities.

In some countries women are not permitted to take part in sport. The London 2012 Olympics was the first ever where every country who participated had women representing their country in at least one sport.

> **Key term**
> **Discrimination** – making a distinction against a person or group based on their class, sex, age, ethnic origin, etc.

P6

While many people believe that sex discrimination in the UK against women is not a problem anymore, evidence would suggest otherwise:

- Women receive 95 per cent less media coverage than men in national newspapers.
- Sporting audiences are still mostly male.
- With some exceptions, presenters, journalists and editors are predominantly male.
- Women receive less money for sporting success.
- Female sports receive less sponsorship than male sports.

Until recently the prize money for women at major sporting events was also less than for the men.

Ethnic groups

A member of an ethnic group could be prevented from joining a sporting group, perhaps because they feel intimidated or unwelcome. The UK is very much a multi-ethnic society today, but there is still evidence of bigotry and race hate in sport which should not be tolerated.

M5

Major events

The Olympics and other major sporting events can have a huge impact on people's perceptions of sport. The London 2012 Olympics and Paralympics was a huge success with both the organisation and facilities considered to be the best ever, in addition to the considerable success of Team GB.

D4

Major sports events have a far ranging impact in a number of key areas for the host country. For example, the London 2012 Olympic Games brought about a number of benefits including:

- Tourism: thousands of athletes, spectators, coaches and support staff boosted all areas of tourism, including hotels, hospitality and catering.
- Transport: public transport networks were improved to cope with the influx of participants and visitors from other parts of the world.
- Housing: much of the accommodation built for athletes and support staff will now be used as low cost housing in deprived areas.
- Environment: London 2012 was the most environmentally sustainable global sporting event yet.
- Culture and sport: a range of facilities and resources are available for sporting and cultural events in the future.

Much of this success is because the UK government developed a policy to actively support attempts to bring major games and events to the UK. These include the London 2012 Olympics, the 2014 Glasgow Commonwealth Games, the 2015 Rugby World Cup and the bid for the 2018 FIFA World Cup. These games raise the profile of the UK sport and active leisure industry and create opportunities for people to take part and volunteer at these events.

Topic C.2 Impact (positive and negative)

All of the key issues discussed in this topic can have both a positive and negative impact on the sports performer, sports providers and sports supporters and consumers.

- Sports performer: performers often have much higher profiles due to their portrayal in the media, but a negative impact of this is they come under increasing pressure to perform and may find their privacy is affected too.
- Sport providers: the success of the Olympic and Paralympic games has led to an increase in people taking up sport, but sports providers may not always be able to provide sufficient facilities to meet demand. People's participation depends on how much disposable income they have and the recent downturn in the economy may mean fewer people taking up sport, or choosing to take up less expensive sports.
- Sports supporters: taking an example of a Premier League football supporter, their experience is mixed. On the positive side the Premier League is now one of the strongest in the world and the quality of skilled play has increased, but this has led to huge increases in season ticket prices and merchandising costs.
- Sports consumers: the benefits for consumers and sport are also mixed. While the number of people spectating sport is at an all time high, participation in physical activity for some groups, particularly 18–24-year-olds, shows little sign of improvement and has not had much impact on the nation's diet and obesity levels.

Impact of the media

Studied ☐

Sport is enjoyed by many in their spare time, and many more enjoy watching sport on television and the internet. However, broadcasters, particularly the subscription and pay-to-view broadcasters, are becoming increasingly powerful in sport. For example, broadcasters often change the start times of fixtures to fit in with peak viewing times. Not so long ago, all top football in the UK was on Saturday at 3.00 p.m. Now football fixtures are moved to Sundays, earlier times on Saturdays, and even Mondays to try and attract more viewers (customers).

The media has also helped to increase participation in a particular sport or activity, for example, during Wimbledon more people tend to play tennis and when the Tour de France is on the TV and in the papers, more people tend to take part in cycling. All this helps to direct additional revenues into a sport, helping governing bodies grow the sport even more.

Impact of peer pressure

As a teenager, peers have a significant impact on a person's lifestyle choices and this is often termed '**peer pressure**'. Peer pressure is where a person's friends encourage them to change their behaviour or morals to 'fit in' with the group. Peer pressure can be positive or negative. Negative peer pressure can encourage a person to stop taking part in sports clubs and start smoking or take illegal drugs, for example. Positive peer pressure can encourage a friend to join a swimming club or take part in outdoor and adventurous activities which have the effect of increasing participation in sport.

> **Key term**
>
> **Peer pressure** – when a person's friends encourage them to change their behaviour; can be positive or negative peer pressure.

Impact of role models

A **role model** is a person that people look up to and they can also influence behaviour because people try to imitate their role models. The London 2012 Olympics has created many sporting role models, including Mo Farah and Jessica Ennis. This in turn has led to a huge increase in children joining athletics clubs around the country, which clearly has a positive effect on participation in sport.

> **Key term**
>
> **Role model** – someone people look up to and try to imitate their behaviour.

Figure 12.8 Jessica Ennis

Lack of privacy

Successful sports performers can become celebrities and stories are printed in newspapers and magazines and featured on television programmes. People follow them on Twitter and Facebook and many sports performers have their own website which provides information about their sporting achievements and sometimes details of their personal lives. This can lead to a lack of privacy and a restricted personal life because the sports performer is photographed carrying out everyday activities; their friends and associates may also sell stories about them to the media for financial gain.

Summary

In this section we have looked at the impact of key issues on sport and active leisure. The key learning points include:

- key issues affecting sport and active leisure are social influences, economic influences such as availability of disposable income, desire for a healthy lifestyle, links between sports and fashion, the impact of major events in encouraging people to get involved in sport, the need to improve access to sport for all people, regardless of disability, race or sex, and the role of the media
- the positive and negative impact of these key issues was then examined.

Activity

Part 1

Prepare a leaflet that describes and explains six key issues and their impact on sport and active leisure, such as social influences, economic influences, healthy lifestyles, fashion, major events, disability, race, role of the media and discrimination.

Part 2

Select a sport and active leisure activity or business and analyse the impact of some of these key issues on that sport and active leisure activity or business.

Real-world connection

Kevin is a freelance exercise class instructor. He has been teaching a wide range of exercise classes over a seven-year period and most years he attends a new instructor training event to help him to learn how to teach a new type of class that has come onto the market. Kevin started as a gym instructor and went on to qualify as a circuits instructor and then a resistance training instructor. Since then he has qualified as an aqua aerobics instructor, spinning instructor, step instructor, Pilates instructor, boot camp instructor and Zumba instructor. He has found that because many people get bored by the same sort of class, when a new trend arrives there is a surge in participants for that class. By regularly introducing new ways of keeping fit Kevin is able to keep participants motivated and coming back for more classes.

Unit 12 Model assignment

This assignment will assess the following learning aims:

A investigate organisations and occupations in sport and active leisure

B recognise current trends in sport and sports participation

C know about the impact of key issues on sport and active leisure.

Scenario 1

You have completed your BTEC Sport qualification and are now looking for a job in sport and active leisure. To help you to find a suitable job you need to carry out research into sport and active leisure provision in your local area and the types of jobs available.

Task 1

Carry out research using websites, local papers and visits to local sport and active leisure centres. Write a report that describes the different types of organisations in sport and active leisure. In your report, describe and explain the benefits of each organisation and compare and contrast the benefits of each.

Select two occupations in sport and active leisure that you are interested in applying for. Write a report that describes the requirements, responsibilities and skills for each occupation. You should include a summary of other occupations in sport and active leisure, describing the advantages and disadvantages of each. You should also explain the advantages and disadvantages of occupations in sport and active leisure.

Scenario 2

You are on work placement with a leisure centre manager. The centre manager wants to increase the number of customers that come to the centre and they have asked you to carry out some research and report back to them about reasons why people take part in sport, barriers to participation and trends in participation in sport and active leisure.

Task 1

Prepare a poster with illustrations and text that can be displayed around the leisure centre. The poster should describe why people take part in sport and active leisure and reasons why there is growth in this area. Your poster should also describe and explain six factors that affect participation in sport and active leisure.

Task 2

Prepare a presentation that can be delivered to the leisure centre manager that describes six different trends that can affect participation in sport and active leisure. You need to explain each trend. You also need to compare and contrast the trends in participation that you have discussed.

Task 3

There are many issues, both positive and negative, that impact on sport and active leisure.
Write a report that describes six key issues and how they impact on sport and active leisure. Try to explain and analyse the impact of these issues using examples where possible.

Unit 13

Profiling Sports Performance

Performance profiling is a method for individuals and teams to assess physical and skill-related fitness, technical, tactical and attitudinal aspects of their performance. This information can then be used to review performance and identify strengths and areas for improvement. This unit will help you develop, analyse and review a performance profile.

Learning aims

In this unit you will:

✓ understand the performance profile of sports

✓ be able to analyse and profile sports performance

✓ review the performance profiles and set goals for further development.

Assessment criteria

Assessment and grading criteria

To achieve a **PASS** grade the evidence must show that the learner is able to:	To achieve a **MERIT** grade the evidence must show that the learner is able to:	To achieve a **DISTINCTION** grade the evidence must show that the learner is able to:
P1 Describe the technical, tactical, fitness, psychological and attitudinal profiles required to successfully participate in two selected sports	**M1** Compare and contrast the technical, tactical, fitness, psychological and attitudinal profiles required to successfully participate in two selected sports	**D1** Justify the technical, tactical, fitness, psychological and attitudinal profiles required to successfully participate in two selected sports
P2 Independently design and complete performance profiles to assess performance of a team or individual in two different selected sports		
P3 Use the completed performance profiles to describe the qualities, traits and attributes for a team or individual in two different selected sports	**M2** Evaluate the qualities, traits and attributes for a team or individual in two different selected sports	**D2** Justify the completed performance profiles for a team or individual in two different selected sports
P4 Review the performance profiles for a team or individual in two different selected sports, summarising goals for future performance and development planning	**M3** Explain set goals for future performance and development for a team or individual in each selected sport, describing the development plans	**D3** Justify the selection of activities within the development plans for the performers in each selected sport

Learning aim A: Understand the performance profile of sports

Topic A.1 Performance profile

Performance profiling is a technique that is used to analyse and review the performance of an individual or a team. It is mainly used to identify individual performance within a team so that the individual's strengths and areas for improvement can be identified. Performance profiling can then be used to help an individual develop their performance and set goals.

Performance profiling can include many different aspects of an individual's performance, such as their physical fitness, technical and tactical skills, psychological skills and attitudes. You can carry out a review of your own skills, or it can be done by another person such as a sports analyst or coach.

In this unit we will be looking at performance profiling from the point of view of an analyst who wants to review the performance of individuals in sport and provide feedback on their strengths and areas for improvement.

The performance profile takes into account two types of assessment – subjective and objective. **Subjective assessment** is information taken from one person's point of view – their beliefs and opinions – and is open to more than one interpretation. Think about a disagreement you may have had with a friend about the quality of a player – you may think they are an excellent player and your friend may think they are useless. The information that you are relying on here is your own opinion rather than facts and so your friend can present their opinion and disagree with you. **Objective assessment** is factual information such as statistical data of performance and psychological profiles rather than information from an opinion. For example, you may argue that a player is excellent because they have scored 15 goals this season and created 30 chances. This information is objective rather than your own opinion. Performance profiling will use both subjective and objective assessment.

Process of performance profiling

Studied ☐

Stage 1

Choose a sports performer that you want to profile. This could be an individual from an individual sport or someone from a team sport.

> **Key terms**
>
> **Performance profiling** – a method to produce a snapshot of a person's skills and abilities at a given point in time.
>
> **Objective assessment** – obtained from factual information rather than an opinion.
>
> **Subjective information** – information according to a person's particular view.

Stage 2

Develop a list of qualities, traits and attributes that you think are necessary for success in that sport. The qualities should include aspects of physical fitness, technical, tactical, attitudinal and psychological requirements.

Stage 3

Choose the 10 qualities that you consider to be most important to the successful performance of that individual.

Stage 4

Rank the 10 qualities in order of their importance with the most important at 1 and the least important at 10. Rate the individual out of 10 for each of the 10 qualities that you have chosen, where 10 would be your idea of perfection for this individual or what is known as 'their ideal self'. The 'ideal self' is specific to each individual and how skilled they are likely to be. For example, a score of 10 would be very different for an athlete who runs for their school compared to one who competes in the Olympic Games.

Stage 5

Review the information from the performance profile and divide each quality into an area of strength (scores of 6–10) or an area for improvement (scores of 1–5).

Topic A.2 Sporting activity

A performance profile can be prepared for performers in both individual and team sports. For example, a performance profile can assess performance of individuals in golf, tennis or snooker, by breaking these sports down into their qualities, traits and attributes.

A performance profile can be prepared to assess the performance of a team or the performance of individuals within the team. For example, the performance of a football team could be broken down into technical and tactical requirements such as attacking play, defensive play, play with the ball and play without the ball. However, the performance profile can also assess the performance of players in their individual roles such as the goalkeeper, right back or central midfielder. This type of information tends to be more meaningful as performance can be broken down into the different qualities and traits that are needed to be successful in each position.

Topic A.3 Performance profile – qualities, traits and attributes

Before you can think about completing a performance profile you need to think about the qualities, traits and attributes that are needed to be successful in the sport you have chosen. To gain as much information as you can about an individual's performance, these are broken into groups that cover different aspects of performance:

- Technical requirements: these are the skills or techniques that are necessary to perform effectively at a sport.
- Tactical requirements: these are the tactics or strategies that you use to gain an advantage over your opponent.
- Fitness requirements: these are the components of fitness that are needed in different quantities to be successful at a sport.
- Psychological requirements: these are the mental traits and skills (i.e. the thoughts you have and the way you respond to situations) that you will need to be successful in a sport.
- Attitudinal requirements: attitude is how your thoughts and feelings towards an activity, person or object are shown in practice. For example, someone who is excited by sport and enjoys playing sport will show enthusiasm and positivity when playing that sport.

Table 13.1 gives examples of qualities, traits and attributes that are needed to perform successfully at a range of sports.

Table 13.1 Qualities, traits and attributes needed for a range of sports

Technical requirements	Tactical requirements	Fitness requirements	Psychological requirements	Attitudinal requirements
Passing	Movement around the court/pitch	Aerobic fitness	Arousal control	Desire to win
Serving	Variation of play	Flexibility	Anxiety management	Discipline
Shooting	Defensive play	Muscular strength	Self-confidence	Competitiveness
Tackling	Attacking play	Muscular endurance	Concentration skills	Determination
Kicking	Positioning for defensive positions	Power	Motivation to win	Positivity
Net shots	Adapting play to different weather conditions	Speed	Positive self-talk	Enthusiasm
Net volleys	Adapting play to winning positions	Balance	Mental toughness	Dedication
Crossing	Use of space	Coordination	Aggression control	
Driving	Style of play	Reaction time	Visualisation skills	
Dribbling	Decision making	Agility	Attention span	

Check your understanding

1. Explain what is meant by performance profiling and give two reasons why it might be used by a coach or analyst.
2. Match each of the qualities shown below to the correct category.

Quality	Category
Dedication	Physical
Power	Tactical
Anxiety control	Attitudinal
Attacking play	Technical
Shooting ability	Psychological

Summary

In this section we looked at what is meant by performance profiling and the qualities, traits and attributes that can be used to develop a performance profile. The key learning points include:

- performance profiling is used to analyse and review the performance of an individual or a team but it only produces a snapshot of a person's skills and abilities at one point in time
- the performance profile takes into account both subjective and objective information
- the performance profile needs to consider technical, tactical, physical, psychological and attitudinal requirements.

Activity

Select two sports and use the table below to describe technical, tactical, fitness, psychological and attitudinal profiles for each sport.

Sport 1:

Technical requirements	Tactical requirements	Fitness requirements	Psychological requirements	Attitudinal requirements

Sport 2:

Technical requirements	Tactical requirements	Fitness requirements	Psychological requirements	Attitudinal requirements

Learning aim B: Be able to analyse and profile sports performance

Topic B.1 Use performance profiling to determine current sports performance

The more information that can be collected the more accurate the performance profile is likely to be. Information can be collected from a variety of subjective and objective sources, including:

- observing performance (live and through video recording)
- views of coaches, teammates, analysts
- via an interview with the individual
- fitness testing data (VO_2 max, strength, power)
- notational analysis data (information about the strategies, tactics and movement patterns a team uses)
- statistical data from performance (pass completion, first service percentage)
- results of psychological tests.

The performance profile is produced by selecting relevant qualities, traits and attributes and rating each one out of 10.

Topic B.2 Performance profile assessment

In Topic A.3 we looked at the qualities, traits and attributes that were needed for a performance profile. The following worked example takes you through the steps to complete a performance profile for a junior tennis player, Rebecca. While other sports will have many of these traits in common, each sport will have traits specific to performance in that sport.

Stage 1:

Choose a sports performer that you want to profile.

Rebecca is a 17-year-old tennis player who is one of the top juniors in her county and has aspirations of playing tennis professionally.

Stage 2:

Develop a list of qualities, traits and attributes that you think are necessary for success in that sport. In tennis the qualities shown below are important.

Table 13.2

Technical requirements	Tactical requirements	Physical requirements	Psychological requirements	Attitudinal requirements
First serve	Movement around court	Aerobic fitness	Arousal control	Desire to win
Second serve	Choice of shots	Flexibility	Anxiety management	Discipline
Forehand return	Defensive play	Muscular strength	Self-confidence	Competitiveness
Backhand return	Attacking play	Muscular endurance	Concentration skills	Determination
Forehand shots	Positioning for first and second serves	Power	Motivation to win	Positivity
Backhand shots	Movement after serving	Speed	Positive self-talk	Enthusiasm
Net volleys		Balance	Mental toughness	Dedication
Overhead shots		Coordination	Aggression control	
Lob shots		Reaction time	Visualisation skills	
		Agility		

Stage 3

Choose 10 qualities which are most important to the successful performance of the individual.

For Rebecca I have chosen:

- First serve
- Forehand shots
- Movement around court
- Defensive play
- Speed
- Muscular endurance
- Aerobic fitness
- Concentration skills
- Arousal control
- Enthusiasm.

Stage 4

Put them in order of importance and then rate each one of out a score 10 that represents 'Rebecca's ideal self':

Table 13.3

Quality	1	2	3	4	5	6	7	8	9	10
1. Forehand shots	X	X	X	X	X	X				
2. Movement around court	X	X	X							
3. Concentration skills	X	X								
4. First serve	X	X	X							
5. Aerobic fitness	X	X	X	X	X	X	X			
6. Defensive play	X	X	X	X	X	X	X	X		
7. Speed	X	X								
8. Arousal control	X	X	X							
9. Muscular endurance	X	X	X	X	X	X				
10. Enthusiasm	X	X	X	X	X	X	X	X		

When assessing technical requirements you can gain information by recording the individual's successes and failures at each technical requirement, for example:

- Success in terms of percentage of passes completed, shots on target or first serves achieved.
- Failed achievement in terms of percentage of incomplete passes, shots off target or first serves not achieved.

Stage 5

Review the information from the performance profile and divide each quality into an area of strength (scores of 6–10) or an area for improvement (scores of 1–5).

Areas of strength:

- Defensive play
- Enthusiasm
- Aerobic fitness
- Forehand shots
- Muscular endurance

Areas for improvement:

- Speed
- Concentration skills
- Movement around court
- Arousal control
- First serve

Now that we have divided Rebecca's performance into identifiable areas of strengths and areas for improvement we can start to work on changing the areas for improvement into areas of strength.

Check your understanding

1. List five potential sources of information that could be used to develop a performance profile.

2. Fill in the blank spaces to complete the sentences about the stages of completing a performance profile.

   At stage 1 you need to choose a sports performer that you want to profile.

   At stage 2 develop a list of _____, traits and _____ that are necessary for _____ in that sport.

   At stage 3 choose _____ qualities which are most important to the _____ performance of the individual.

   At stage 4 put them in order of importance and then rate each one out of a score of 10 that represents '_____ _____ _____'.

   At stage 5 you _____ the information from the performance profile and divide each quality into an area of _____ (scores of 6–10) or an area for _____ (scores of 1–5).

P3

M2

D2

Summary

In this section we looked at sources of information that could be used to develop a performance profile and a worked example of how to complete a performance profile was presented. The key learning points include:

- information can be collected from a variety of subjective and objective sources
- sources of information include observing performance, views from coaches, teammates, analysts, data from a notational analysis and statistical data from performance.

Activity

Part 1

Using the five stages of the performance profile, design and complete performance profiles for an individual from *two* different selected sports. Copy the template below to present your performance profile for each individual.

Selected sport and individual:

Quality	1	2	3	4	5	6	7	8	9	10
1.										
2.										
3.										
4.										
5.										
6.										
7.										
8.										
9.										
10.										

Part 2

Use your completed performance profiles to describe, explain and justify the qualities, traits and attributes that are necessary for the success of your chosen individuals from your two selected sports.

Topic C.1 Review the performance profile

The fifth stage of the performance profile involved the division of each quality into an area of strength or an area for improvement. The next part is to dig deeper into the assessment of each quality and find out what it is about each one that makes it an area of strength or an area for improvement.

For example, Rebecca was rated as having a score of 8/10 for defensive play. The basis for this score is that she is very consistent at getting the ball back from the baseline and rarely makes mistakes. She also has good aerobic fitness to enable her to keep going during long rallies, takes up good positions on the back line and is accurate with her returns. On the other hand, Rebecca scores only 2/10 for her movement around court which is clearly an area for improvement. When we dig deeper we find out that her score is low because she lacks speed to get around court; her agility is poor which affects her ability to change direction, as is her anticipation of where the ball may be returned to. Breaking down the assessment in this way gives the individual specific aspects of their play to work on.

Topic C.2 Set goals for further development

Short-term and long-term goals

Studied ☐

A short-term goal is usually a goal set to be achieved in a period of up to one month. Short-term goals can be set for as short a period as one session or one hour or they could be daily goals or weekly goals.

A medium-term goal is set for periods over one month up to six months. Medium-term goals are commonly set for three months.

Long-term goals are set for six months to one year and may include season goals or one- to four-year goals. An Olympic athlete may set their goal to be achieved at the Olympics Games which are four years away.

Outcome and process goals

Outcome goals are described as being the outcome that the individual wishes to achieve. For example, Rebecca, our tennis player, would need to improve her movement around the court and she could state her outcome goal as 'To reach my opponent's returns 85 per cent of the time'. This is not a perfect goal because it is not time-referenced but the outcome is clear. The outcome goal is often set over a long time period (long-term goal).

Process goals describe the small steps an individual has to achieve on their way to their outcome goal. For example, in order to improve her movement around the court Rebecca may set the following process goals:

- To complete sprint training 3 times a week.
- To complete agility drills for 20 minutes, 3 times a week.
- To spend 1 hour a week studying the play of my opponent before each match.

These goals could all be set to be achieved in one month's time.

Rebecca's process goals are targets for development activities of specific qualities, traits and attributes and they will contribute to achieving the outcome goal. Process goals are usually set for the short term while outcome goals will usually be medium-term and long-term goals.

> **Key terms**
>
> **Outcome goals** – the outcome that the individual wishes to achieve.
>
> **Process goals** – the small steps an individual has to achieve on their way to their outcome goal.

Topic C.3 Development plan

The development plan is used to present goal setting in a clear, visual way, so that it is easily understood by the individual. The development plan could look like the example below.

Table 13.4 Example of a development plan

Name of athlete: Rebecca
Chosen sport: Tennis
SMARTER Goal: To reach my opponent's return shots 85% of the time by 30 September 2013.
Aims and objectives:
1. To improve my speed around the court so I can reach the returns more easily (physical).
2. To improve my ability to change direction at speed (agility). (physical)
3. To improve my ability to anticipate where the returned ball will be placed. (tactical)
Process goals:
1. To complete sprint training 3 times a week.
2. To complete agility drills for 20 minutes 3 times a week.
3. To spend 1 hour a week studying the play of my opponent before each match.
Time scale – to be achieved in four-weeks time.

Opportunities available:
Support from my coach
Opportunity to train at a local athletics club
Access to indoor training facilities
Potential barriers to goal completion:
Bad weather
Possibility of injury
Time constraints due to family commitments.

Check your understanding

1. Read the following goals and decide whether they are a) short-term, medium-term or long-term goals and b) process or outcome goals.
   i) Goal 1 – to complete a marathon in 4 hours in 9 months' time.
   ii) Goal 2 – to complete a total of 20 miles this week.
   iii) Goal 3 – to have completed a 10 km race in 3 months' time.

Real world connection

Shaun is a sports analyst working for a professional rugby union team. His job is to provide the team coach with information about how each individual in the team is performing and their strengths and weaknesses.

The team have a match most weekends and then come in for training again on Tuesday morning so Shaun has two or three days to a watch video recording of the match and prepare information on each individual's performance. He has to watch the match several times to observe the performance of different players and then produce his report.

Performance profiling is one of several methods that Shaun uses to present information to the team coach and it enables him to focus on many aspects of each individual's performance and to build up a profile of their performance across many matches.

Shaun has a meeting with the coach each Tuesday and then the coach uses this information to give feedback to the players and develop goals for them to work on in the coming weeks.

Summary

In this section we looked at how the performance profile can be used to review performance and set short-term and long-term goals that will help to develop the individual's future performances. We also looked at preparing a development plan that sets out the goals and development activities in a clear and visual way. The key learning points include:

- the review of the performance profile involves investigating areas of strength and areas for improvement
- a short-term goal is set to be achieved in a period of up to one month
- a medium-term goal is set for periods over one month up to six months
- long-term goals are set from six months to one year, for a season or up to lifetime goals
- outcome goals are described as being the outcome that an individual wishes to achieve
- process goals describe the small steps an individual has to achieve on their way to their outcome goal.
- the development plan is used to present goal-setting in a clear, visual way.

Activity

Part 1

Using the information from the learning aim B activity, page 358, review the performance profiles for the two individuals in the sports you selected. Summarise goals for future performance and development planning.

Part 2

Explain the goals summarised in Part 1 and describe the development plans for your selected individuals. Justify your selection of activities within the development plans for your selected performers.

Unit 13 Model assignment

This assignment will assess the following learning aims:

A understand the performance profile of sports

B be able to analyse and profile sports performance

C review the performance profiles and set goals for further development.

P4

Scenario

You have been appointed to work as an analyst with individuals in two different sports teams of your choice. You have been asked to pinpoint the strengths and areas for improvement of the two individuals so that specific development plans can be drawn up for the two individuals. You have a good understanding of performance profiling and decide to use this technique to analyse the qualities, traits and attributes of the two individuals.

Task 1

Select two sports and describe the technical, tactical, fitness, psychological and attitudinal profiles that are needed by an individual to be successful in each sport. You will need to compare and contrast the technical, tactical, fitness, psychological and attitudinal profile that each individual will require to successfully participate in your selected sports. You need to justify the technical, tactical, fitness, psychological and attitudinal profiles that are needed to be successful in each of your chosen sports.

M3

Task 2

For each of the two selected individuals you need to independently design and complete a performance profile that assesses their performance in their different sports. Then use the completed performance profile to describe the qualities, traits and attributes for each individual in their selected sport. You need to evaluate these qualities, traits and attributes for the two individuals in their different sports. You also need to justify the completed performance profiles for each individual in their selected sport.

D3

Task 3

Once the performance profile has been completed and the areas of strength and areas for improvement have been identified, review the information to prepare goals to improve future performance and present a development plan. You need to explain the outcome and process goals that you have set for future performance and the future development of the individual, then describe the development plan you have produced. You need to justify the selection of the activities within the development plans for each of the two selected individuals in different sports.

Check your understanding answers

Unit 1, Learning aim A, page 9

1.

Component of fitness	Definition
1. Aerobic endurance	**c.** the ability of the cardiorespiratory system to work efficiently, supplying nutrients and oxygen to working muscles during sustained physical activity
2. Muscular endurance	**d.** the ability of the muscular system to work efficiently, so that a muscle can contract over a period of time against a light to moderate fixed resistance load
3. Strength	**e.** the maximum force in kg or N that can be generated by a muscle or muscle group
4. Speed	**f.** distance divided by time taken
5. Agility	**b.** the ability of a sports performer to move quickly and precisely or change direction without losing their balance or reducing their time
6. Power	**a.** the product of strength and speed

Unit 1, Learning aim B, Page 20

1.

Component of fitness	Training method
Flexibility	PNF
Strength	Heavy weights with low repetitions
Power	Plyometrics
Aerobic endurance	Continuous training
Muscular endurance	Low weights with high repetitions
Speed	Hollow sprints
Elastic strength	75% 1RM and 12 reps

Unit 1, Learning aim C, Page 38

1. The fitness tests that would be suitable for measuring the components of fitness needed for my chosen sport, football, are:
- Multi-stage fitness test (to measure aerobic endurance)
- Illinois agility run test (to measure speed and agility)

2. For the multi-stage fitness test you would need a CD of bleep sounds, a flat area of 20 m, cones and a tape measure. For the Illinois agility run test you would need cones, a stopwatch, measuring tape and a flat, non-slip surface.

3. The multi-stage fitness test is valid for a sport that involves a lot of running, like football. The following can affect the reliability of this test: running surface, climate, wind speed, whether the test is performed indoors or outdoors, motivation levels of performers and group dynamics.

The Illinois agility run test is a valid measure for sports where players have to run and change direction, like football. However, the results may be affected by the shoes the participant is wearing, e.g. whether they have grip on the soles, this will affect the reliability of the test.

Unit 2, Learning aim A, page 45

1. a. The rules of sport are a set of **agreed standards** to ensure a sport is played **fairly**.
   b. The rules of a sport are set down by **national governing bodies**.

2.

Sport	Simple scoring system	Complex scoring system
Tennis		x
Swimming	x	
Synchronised swimming		x
Hockey	x	
Golf		x

3. Football:
- Referee
- Assistant referee
- Fourth official

4.
- Whistles
- Flags
- Hand signals

Unit 2, Learning aim B, page 50

1. a. Skills are different aspects of a sport that you need to **learn** and **practise**.
   b. A player with good technique would perform **skills well**.

2.

Skill	Discrete	Continuous	Serial
Skipping		x	
Ice dance routine			x
Throw-in	x		
10 m dive			x
Rowing		x	
High jump	x		

3. The aim of using tactics is to improve your chances of winning.
4.
   - Isolated practices – A skill is taken out of a sport and practised separately
   - Conditioned practices – A sport is changed to enable players to practise certain skills or tactics
   - Competitive situations – A sport is played in its full form against opponents

Unit 2, Learning aim C, page 55

1. Three reasons you need to review performance are:
   - To establish current level of competence
   - To identify what you are doing well (areas of strength)
   - To identify what you are doing badly (areas for improvement)
2. Three pieces of information that could be gained from a review of performance are:
   - Whether you were successful or not
   - The score or outcome achieved
   - How it felt to perform the skills
3. There are many sources of **feedback** about performance, including information about whether you were **successful** or not and how it felt to **perform** skills. **Video** footage enables you to **analyse** your performance more deeply. Information can also be gained by talking to your **coach** and **teammates**.
4. Two things you need to do to address areas for improvement are:
   - Set goals (short-and long-term)
   - Develop activities to improve your performance

Unit 3, Learning aim A, page 67

1. a. Personality is the sum of the characteristics that make a person unique.
   b. Traits are relatively stable ways of behaving.
2. a. False
   b. True
   c. True
3. a. Outgoing
   c. Easily bored
   f. Needs company
4.
   - Trait – Behaviour can be predicted by personality traits.
   - Situational – Behaviour is determined mainly by the person's environment.
   - Interactional – When examining behaviour, both traits and the situation need to be considered.

Unit 3, Learning aim B, page 77

1. a. Motivation is the **direction** and **intensity** of effort.
   b. Achievement motivation describes a person's efforts to master **skills** and overcome **obstacles**. It is described as **competitiveness**.
   c. Self-confidence is the **belief** that desired action can be **achieved**.
   d. Self-efficacy is self-confidence in a **specific situation**.
2.
   - Trait motivation – Motivation is an important part of my personality.
   - Situational motivation – I am motivated by the environment I find myself in.
   - Intrinsic motivation – I am motivated because sport gives me satisfaction.
   - Extrinsic motivation – The greater the reward the greater my motivation.
3.
   Specific
   Measurable
   Achievable
   Realistic
   Time-related
   Exciting
   Recorded
4.
   - Performance accomplishments – Based on success or failure in previous competitions.
   - Vicarious experiences – Based on watching other people perform the same skills successfully.
   - Verbal persuasion – Coach or teacher telling you that you can do it.
   - Imaginal experiences – Thinking about being successful and picturing it in your head.

Unit 3, Learning aim C, page 83

1. Trait anxiety describes where anxiety is a personality trait and an individual will feel anxious across many situations whereas state anxiety is anxiety in a specific situation. Cognitive describes the mental effects of anxiety, such as feelings of worry and loss of concentration, while somatic anxiety describes the physical effects of anxiety, such as increases in heart rate and breathing rate.
2. The four arousal-performance theories are:
   - Drive theory says that performance improves as arousal levels increase.
   - The inverted-U hypothesis says that as arousal levels increase then so will performance level, but only up to a certain point called the optimal point of arousal, after which any

increases in arousal will result in a steady decline in performance.

- The catastrophe theory is an extension of the inverted-U theory and says that once the optimal point of arousal has been reached performance level will drop off rapidly.
- Reversal theory says that if we view anxiety as a positive sign that we are ready to perform then its negative effects will be reduced.

Unit 4, Learning aim A, page 98

1. a. The average breathing rate for a person at rest is **12** breaths per minute.

b. The **sit and reach test** can be used to measure the range of movement in joints.

c. **Adrenaline** is released before and during exercise to increase the heart rate.

d. The technical term for breaths per minute is **pulmonary ventilation**.

e. **Synovial fluid** is released into the joints during a warm up to help increase their range of movement.

f. An adult's average resting blood pressure is **120/80**.

g. The amount of air breathed in and out in one breath is called **tidal volume**.

h. A **spirometer** can be used to measure tidal volume.

i. During resistance exercises, **micro tears** occur in muscle tissue.

j. During exercise blood is directed to **skeletal muscle**.

2.

Statement	True	False
Long-term exercise makes the heart muscle smaller		x
Long-term exercise increases the vital capacity of the lungs	x	
Long-term exercise increases a person's resting heart rate		x
Long-term exercise results in the decreased production of synovial fluid		x
Long-term exercise results in an increase in thickness of hyaline cartilage	x	
Long-term exercise makes a person's bones more likely to break if they should fall over		x
Swimming is an example of weight-bearing exercise		x
The resting heart rate of an average male is 120 bpm		x
Hypertrophy is the name given to the increase in lung size which occurs as a result of long-term exercise		x
Stroke volume is the amount of blood forced through the heart with each beat	x	

Unit 4, Learning aim B, page 102

1.

Statement	True	False
The ATP-CP/alactic acid anaerobic system requires oxygen		x
The aerobic energy system would be used to provide energy for a 100 m sprint		x
An example of a sport that uses the lactic acid energy system is a 400 m race	x	
A person competing in an iron man triathlon will mainly use the aerobic energy system to supply their energy	x	
The ATP-CP/alactic acid anaerobic system produces lactic acid		x
The energy system used to make energy is determined by the speed at which the body needs that energy	x	
Anaerobic means with oxygen		x
Lactic acid is a waste product produced by the glycolysis anaerobic system	x	

Unit 5, Learning aim A, page 117

1. a. Short-term goals are set for periods between one **day** and one **month** or they may cover a **single** session. Medium-term goals will cover a period of **one** to **six** months.

b. Long-term goals usually cover a period of **six to twelve** months or a **season**.

c. Long-term goals are usually **outcome/ performance** goals while short-term goals are **process** goals as they contribute to the achievement of long-term goals.

2. Five items that should be included in a pre-exercise questionnaire are:
- Medical history
- Activity history
- Goals and outcomes required
- Lifestyle factors
- Nutritional status

3.

Principle	Description
Time	The time length of each session
Overload	Doing more than the body is used to
Frequency	The number of training sessions per week, month or year
Intensity	How hard you work in each training session
Specificity	Targeting the component of fitness you wish to improve
Reversibility	If you do not use a fitness gain you will lose it
Type	Choosing muscular endurance, strength or flexibility

Unit 5, Learning aim B, page 122

1. Five barriers that people say prevent them from exercising regularly are:
- Lack of time
- Lack of energy
- Lack of motivation
- Excessive cost
- Illness or injury

2. a. People are motivated to exercise as it brings benefits such as improvements to **sports** performance and improvements to **health**.
   b. Exercise can improve **self-esteem** and help with **weight** management and appearance.

3.

Strategy	Description
Goal setting	Setting targets to work towards.
Making activities enjoyable	Ensuring the activities you choose are enjoyed by the participants.
Support and reinforcement	Having people or a trainer to support an individual can ensure that they exercise regularly.
Rewards for achieving goals	Providing rewards ensures that a person's efforts are recognised.

Unit 5, Learning aim C and D, page 124

1. Four pieces of information that you should record after you have completed a training session are:

- Motivation – how you felt before, during and after the session.
- How the programme was adapted – what changes you had to make during the session.
- Achievement of personal goals, aims and objectives.
- Any barriers you faced and how you overcame them.

2. Reasons why you would review each session after you have completed it could include:
- So that you can make changes for future sessions.
- To ensure that you stay motivated and interested.
- To ensure that you keep progressing and keep progressively overloading yourself.
- So that you can change or adapt any goals that have become too easy or too hard.

Unit 6, Learning aim A, page 138

1. Your spider diagram should include the following information:
   Attributes, which include:
- Skills – communication, organisation of equipment, knowledge.
- Advanced skills – activity structure, target setting, use of language, evaluation.
- Qualities – appearance, enthusiasm, confidence
- Additional qualities – leadership style, motivation, humour, personality

   Responsibilities of sports leaders, which include:
- core responsibilities – professional conduct, health and safety, equality
- wider responsibilities – insurance, child protection, legal obligations, ethics and values, rules and regulations

2. Insurance is needed in case someone is injured in the session, then the leader may be deemed to be liable and could be considered negligent if they have not given due care to the planning and implementation of their activity session.

3. A CRB check is a criminal records bureau check and it checks the criminal records of a person to make sure they have no convictions that would make them unsuitable to work with children.

4. Professional conduct means demonstrating proper personal and professional behaviour at all times and includes having the correct qualifications and experience, dressing appropriately, respecting all athletes, officials and opponents, promoting fair play and honesty and using suitable language.

Unit 6, Learning aim B, page 146

1.
a. **Young children** will need to have more helpers in an activity session.
b. A **cool down** should take place at the end of an activity session.
c. Netball is more often played by **female** participants.
d. A PAR-Q can be completed to find out about the **medical needs** of sports participants.
e. A sports leader should always ensure a **demonstration** is delivered correctly and clearly.
f. A **session plan** should be written out before any activity session.
g. The **warm-up** should take place at the start of an activity session.
h. The **aims** are what the sports leader wants their participants to be able to do by the end of the session.
i. The **game play** is the part of the activity session where participants get to put the skills learnt into a game context.
j. A sports leader may need to **adapt** a session plan if things are not going as expected.

Unit 6, Learning aim C, page 150

1. Three methods of obtaining feedback after leading an activity session are:
   - giving participants a questionnaire
   - asking your supervisor to complete a learner observation record
   - video-taping yourself.
2. SMARTER = **S**pecific, **M**easureable, **A**chievable, **R**ealistic, **T**ime-related, **E**xciting, **R**ecorded.
3. A review should be carried out after an activity section so that you can see how you performed, see what the areas are for improvement and put a development plan in place to achieve this.
4. Your development plan will depend on your individual circumstances, but it should include:
   - what your aims and objectives are
   - SMARTER targets
   - the activities you will undertake to achieve your targets
   - any obstacles that might prevent you achieving your goals.

Unit 7, Learning aim A, page 172

1.

Muscle	Location
Latissimus dorsi	Back
Hamstrings	Back of upper leg
Deltoids	Shoulder
Gastrocnemius	Lower leg
Pectorals	Chest

2.
a. True
b. False
c. True
d. False
e. True

3. During a concentric muscle contraction the muscle gets **shorter** in length as it develops tension and the two ends of the muscle get **closer** and the muscle becomes **fatter**. In an eccentric contraction the muscle **increases** in length as it develops tension to **control** movement. An isometric contraction is where a muscle contracts but its length **stays the same** and it is used to stabilise **joints**.

4.

Feature	Slow twitch (type I)	Fast twitch (type IIa)	Fast twitch (type IIb)
Colour	Red	Greyish	White
Speed of contraction	Slow	Moderate to fast	Fast
Force of contraction	Low	Medium	High
Fatigue	Slow to fatigue	Fairly resistant to fatigue	Fast to fatigue
Aerobic or anaerobic	Aerobic	Anaerobic but some aerobic capacity	Anaerobic

5.
i) c
ii) b
iii) d
iv) a
v) a

6.

Description of cartilage	Type of cartilage
This cartilage is found on the ends of bone and helps to produce smooth movements between bones	Hyaline cartilage
This cartilage comes in thick chunks and acts as a shock absorber	Fibrocartliage
This cartilage gives shape to organs such as the ears	Elastic cartilage

7.

Movement	Description
Flexion	Bending a joint
Extension	Straightening a joint
Adduction	Movement towards the body
Abduction	Movement away from the body
Circumduction	Moving a joint around in a circle

Unit 7, Learning aim B, page 187

1. a. False
   b. True
   c. True
   d. True
   e. False

2. Deoxygenated blood enters the heart on the **right hand** side via the **vena cava** and enters the **right atrium**. The blood is pushed through the **tricuspid valve** to the **right ventricle** which contracts to send blood through the semilunar valve into the **pulmonary artery** and to the lungs. Blood is oxygenated in the lungs and then returns via the **pulmonary vein** into the left **atrium** which contracts to push the blood into the left **ventricle** where it leaves the heart via the **aorta** to be taken around the body.

3. Arteries Arterioles Capillaries Venules Veins

4. i)   c
   ii) d
   iii) a
   iv) b

Unit 8, Learning aim A, page 207

1. a. True
   b. False
   c. True
   d. False
   e. True

2. ● Sport England – Promoting sports participation in the community
   ● NHS/Department of Health – Promoting active lifestyles
   ● Youth Sport Trust – Promoting sport among young people

3.

Cost	The price of tickets has increased
Availability	Tickets are almost sold out
Accessibility	The event has been moved to a bigger venue further away
Targeted groups	Some tickets are discounted to encourage children to attend
Advertising	The programme for the event features lots of adverts
Role models	One of the stars of the event is promoting it on television
Brand sponsorship	One of the stars is endorsing the footwear that will be worn in the competition
Merchandising	Souvenirs and t-shirts with the name of the event are widely available

Unit 8, Learning aim B, page 221

1.

Public sponsorship	Grant for Sport England
Private local sponsorship	A high street sport shop sponsoring a football league
Regional sponsorship	Lees Brewery Lancashire County League
National sponsorship	Rugby Union Aviva Premiership
International/global sponsorship	AC Milan sponsored by Emirates Airlines

2. a. False
   b. True
   c. False
   d. False

Unit 8, Learning aim C, page 228

1. These are just some possible answers; there are many others that you may have thought of that could be equally valid.

	Advantage	Disadvantage
Posters	Can attract attention if displayed prominently	Cannot be taken away by potential customers
Leaflets	Can be taken away by customers for later reminder referral	Can become scattered when left in reception areas
Internet/intranet	Allows extra information to be displayed	Might be difficult to attract customers to visit the page where information is displayed
Video promotion	Can provide a powerful message to sell the event	Can be time consuming to produce if done well
Press advert	Seen by lots of external customers	Can be expensive
Personal selling with cards	Allows the face to face selling of the event which can be effective	Can be time consuming
Mailshot	Allows targeted marketing to people who might be interested	Can be expensive if postal services are used

Unit 9, Learning aim A, page 235

1. a. A child aged 10 years old should take part in at least 60 minutes of moderate to vigorous intensity physical activity every day.
   b. An adult aged 40 should be active every day and do at least 2½ hours of moderate intensity activity each week, in sessions that last at least 10 minutes or more. For example, 30 minutes of exercise at least 5 days a week.
   c. An adult aged 70 should be active every day and do at least 2½ hours of moderate intensity activity each week in sessions that last at least 10 minutes or more, e.g. 30 minutes of exercise at least 5 days a week.

2. Children and adults should take part in activities that strengthen mucles and bone at least three days a week, older adults aged 65+ should take part in balance and co-ordination physical activities.

3. A 16-year-old could increase their activity levels by:
   - Walking or cycling to school
   - Taking part in a sports club at lunch time and after school
   - Taking part in sports when they meet up with their friends, e.g. badminton, football or swimming.

Unit 9, Learning aim B, page 245

1.

2.

Food	Food group
Brussel sprouts	fruit and vegetables
Eggs	milk and dairy
Olive oil	food high in fat
Bananas	fruit and vegetables
Milk	milk and dairy
Fish	meat, fish, eggs, beans
Beans	meat, fish, eggs, beans
Bread	bread, rice, potatoes, pasta
Potatoes	bread, rice, potatoes, pasta
Nuts	meat, fish, eggs, beans
Butter	food high in fat

Unit 9, Learning aim C, page 251

1. Any three health risks from:
   - Lung cancer
   - Bronchitis
   - Coronary heart disease
   - Emphysema

2. Any three health risks from:
   - Mental health issues
   - Stroke
   - Weight gain
   - Stomach ulcers
   - Gastrointestinal complications
   - Liver complications.

3. Smoking over a period of time will adversely affect health and, in most cases, will decrease sporting performances, especially in sports that use the aerobic energy system. As the aerobic energy system requires oxygen, if the lungs are damaged by the tar from cigarettes 'blocking' the alveoli, then they will not function and this will decrease the amount of oxygen that can be taken in to the body and used for aerobic energy production. Haemoglobin is in red blood cells and functions to transport oxygen around the body to where it is required in muscles, etc. Carbon monoxide is breathed in from smoking and this attaches to the haemoglobin and prevents them from working which reduces the amount of oxygen that can be transported around the body.

4. Four different methods that an individual could use to reduce their alcohol consumption are:
   - Keep a drinking diary to chart how many units are drunk per week.
   - Modify drink choices so that lower alcohol versions are drunk or they are mixed with a non-alcoholic mixer, e.g. a shandy.

Answers

- Meet with friends in a coffee shop rather than a pub so there is no alcohol available to buy.
- Go to counselling and support groups.

5. To try to overcome the addiction to nicotine, a person can slowly decrease the number of cigarettes they smoke over a set period. They could use a nicotine replacement therapy, such as a nicotine patch and/or nicotine gum.

Hypnotherapy can be used to help a person to stop smoking, this is where they are put into a state of deep relaxation and the therapist helps the person to overcome their addiction to smoking. Acupuncture is another alternative technique to help a person stop smoking which involves placing tiny needles in various parts of the body which are believed to help to a person stop smoking.

Unit 9, Learning aim D, page 255

1. a. Anabolic steroid
   b. Diuretic
   c. Beta blocker
   d. Stimulant
   e. EPO
   f. Doping
   g. Damage health
   h. International Olympic Committee

Unit 10, Learning aim A, page 263

1.

Example	People risk/ hazard	Equipment risk/ hazard	Environment risk/ hazard
Hot weather conditions			X
Adults playing against children	X		
Icy hockey pitch			X
Not doing a warm-up before a basketball game	X		
Picking up gym weights incorrectly	X		
Not wearing shin pads for football		X	
Wet patch on the gym floor			X
Chewing gum while playing sport	X		
Skiing on a dry ski slope			X

Unit 10, Learning aim B, page 269

1. a. Sprain
   b. Intrinsic
   c. Bruise
   d. Strain
   e. Concussion
   f. Symptom
   g. Sign
   h. Extrinsic risk factor
   i. Asthma
   j. Viral infection

Unit 10, Learning aim C, page 277

1. a. True
   b. False
   c. False
   d. False
   e. True

Unit 10, Learning aim D, page 284

1. a. Health and Safety at Work Act 1974
   b. Health and Safety (First Aid) Regulations 1981
   c. The Children Act 2004
   d. COSHH (2002)
   e. Hazard
   f. High risk

Unit 11, Topic A.1, page 290

1. The objects and facilities that you need to run an event are known as **physical** resources. The people that are needed and the skills that you must have available are called the **human** resources. The money that you will need to run the event is called the **financial** resources. Finding out information in advance to see what events are possible and what are not can be called a **feasibility** study.

2.

Objective	Event
A fundraising activity	Raising money to go towards the setting up of a new playgroup
Supporting local community organisation	Holding an open day at the local youth club to attract new members
A skill improvement activity	A community badminton coaching programme
A competitive activity	A 5-a-side football competition
Encouraging sports participation	A 'come and try' sports day in the sports hall

Unit 11, Topic A.2, page 292

1.
   - To raise money for the British Heart Foundation – No
   - To raise money for the NotOut Junior Cricket Club – Yes
   - To raise money for the Bees Junior Rugby Union Club – Yes
   - To improve the skill level in local sports clubs – No
   - To raise money for the Old Town Girls Football Team – Yes

Unit 11, Topic A.2, page 294

1. It is a good idea to place the names of the people responsible for a task on the records of meetings (minutes) so that the group and the persons concerned know who is responsible for which duties or tasks.
2. It is a good idea to place the date by which something must be done on the records of meetings (minutes) so that everybody is clear and agreed about the date by which something should be done.
3. It is a good idea to look at the records of the last meeting and ask around to see who has done their allocated tasks before setting new tasks. The group can check on progress about what has been done since the last meeting before moving on to make new decisions at the current meeting.

Unit 11, Topic A.2, page 296

1.

Statement	Definition
Tripping over a trailing cable to the PA system at a sports day	The hazard
Harmful	The risk of damage
Likely	The risk of likelihood
Moving the PA system beside the power point so the cable does not trail	The control measure

Unit 11, Topic A.2, page 298

1. One of the main **constraints** we have in running our sports day is that there is limited space available on the playing fields so that has limited the number of entries we can accept. However, we have been able to book the sports hall which we can use as a **contingency** in case it rains heavily and we are unable to use the playing fields. We carried out **risk** assessments to ensure the event will be safe and the promotional materials have been distributed to our **target** audience so we expect to have a good turnout.

Unit 11, Learning aim C, Page 310

1. Tim arrived for the event but, unlike the rest of the group, was not wearing the t-shirt that we had printed meaning he had not followed the **dress** code. Sally had an **autocratic** leadership style as she did not consult with the others before issuing instructions. Jason, on the other hand, has a **democratic** leadership style because he consulted and listened before he gave instructions. Ali spoke clearly and well throughout, showing good **verbal** communication but let himself down because he was often slouching with his feet up and had his hands in his pockets. This showed poor **non-verbal** communication on his part.

Unit 11, Learning aim D, page 314

1.

Increase the numbers of youths playing football in the borough within two weeks	not measurable
Increase by 25 the numbers of youths playing football in the borough	not time bound
Increase the numbers of youths playing football so that everybody in the borough plays football at least six times a week within two days	not realistic

Unit 12, Learning aim A, page 332

1. a. Private
   b. Public sector
   c. Pool lifeguard
   d. David Lloyd
   e. Youth football club
   f. PE teacher
   g. Dual use
   h. Sport and exercise scientist

Unit 12, Learning aim B, page 339

1. • Cardiovascular fitness
   • Muscular endurance
   • Muscular strength
   • Flexibility
   • Improved posture
   • Low fat body composition

2. When a person takes part in regular sports their self-confidence and self-esteem can be improved through setting and attaining goals such as completing a 10 km race or being selected for a school football team. This increased self-confidence can help people to socialise and have the confidence to talk to and meet new people. By increasing a person's self-confidence and self-esteem they are also less likely to bully others, as bullying is often the result of a person suffering from low self-esteem.

   Playing sports is also a very good way of socialising and helps people to make new friends through joining a badminton club, netball team, a squash league or going to exercise classes and meeting the other class members.

3. Factors could include disability, ethnic origin, age, location and income.

4. Athletics – from the success for the GB team in the Beijing and London Olympic games lots of children and adults are joining athletics clubs and many now have full groups and people are on waiting lists hoping to join the club.

   Cycling – from the success of Bradley Wiggins winning the Tour de France and the GB cycling team doing so well in the last two Olympics.

   Zumba – is a new aerobics class which has lots of dance moves in it which helps to motivate people (mainly females) to take part.

5. Tennis – new tennis rackets made out of light-weight materials and strong strings have increased the speed that the ball can be hit at, which increases the performance of tennis players. Shoe technology has also improved, which helps the player to grip the surface when having to quickly change direction to reach the ball to make a shot.

Unit 13, Learning aim A, page 353

1. Performer profiling is a method used to assess a performer's skills and abilities at a given point in time. It can include physical fitness, tactical and technical skills and psychological attitudes, and can combine subjective and objective assessment. It can be used by a coach to review performance and to indentify strengths and areas of weakness.

2.

Quality	Category
Dedication	Attitudinal
Power	Physical
Anxiety control	Psychological
Attacking play	Tactical
Shooting ability	Technical

Unit 13, Learning aim B, page 357

1. Five potential sources of information that could be used to develop a performance profile are:
   • Observing performance
   • Views of coaches, teammates and analysts
   • Data from fitness testing
   • Statistical data
   • Scores from psychological tests

2. At stage 1 you need to choose a sports performer that you want to profile.

   At stage 2 develop a list of **qualities**, traits and **attributes** that are necessary for **performance** in that sport.

   At stage 3 choose **ten** qualities which are most important to the **successful** performance of the individual.

   At stage 4 put them in order of importance and then rate each one out of a score of 10 that represents 'their ideal self'.

   At stage 5 you **review** the information from the performance profile and divide each quality into an area of **strength** (scores of 6–10) or an area for **improvement** (scores of 1–5).

Unit 13, Learning aim C, page 361

1. i) Long-term goal. Outcome
   ii) Short-term goal. Outcome
   iii) Medium-term goal. Outcome

Index

Picture credits

The authors and publishers would like to thank the following for the use of photographs in this volume:

Figure 1.2 Maridav – Fotolia; Figure 1.10 deusexlupus – Fotolia; Figure 1.11 Elenathewise – Fotolia; Figure 1.20 © Marcin / Sylwia C. / Fotolia.com; Figure 2.1 Bob Martin /Sports Illustrated/ Getty Images; Figure 2.2 VI-Images via Getty Images; Figure 2.3 Corbis RF / Alamy; Figure 2.4 Stefan Schurr – Fotolia; Figure 2.5 INDRANIL MUKHERJEE/AFP/Getty Images; Figure 2.6 Stu Forster/Getty Images; Figure 3.2a Rex Features; Figure 3.2b ODD ANDERSEN/AFP/GettyImages; Figure 3.6 Vibe Images / Alamy; Figure 4.3 Agencia EFE / Rex Features; Figure 4.4 PM Images/ Image Bank/Getty Images; Figure 6.1 .shock – Fotolia; Figure 6.2 Alistair Berg/Digital Vision/ Getty Images; Figure 6.3 Monkey Business – Fotolia; Figure 7.10 David Rogers/Getty Images; Figure 8.1 Carlos Mira/Actionplus; Figure 9.1 yellowj – Fotolia; Figure 9.2 anoli – Fotolia; Figure 9.3 ExQuisine – Fotolia; Figure 9.4 © Crown copyright, Courtesy of Department of Health in association with the Welsh Government, the Scottish Government and the Food Standards Agency in Northern Ireland; Figure 9.5 ARTHUR GLAUBERMAN/SCIENCE PHOTO LIBRARY; Figure 9.6 © Mark Sykes / Alamy; Figure 9.7 Max Tactic – Fotolia; Figure 9a © Crown copyright, Courtesy of Department of Health in association with the Welsh Government, the Scottish Government and the Food Standards Agency in Northern Ireland; Figure 10.1 audioscience – Fotolia; Figure 10.2 DR M.A. ANSARY/SCIENCE PHOTO LIBRARY; Figure 10.3 auremar – Fotolia; Figure 10.4 Martin Rose/Bongarts/Getty Images; Figure 10.5 PA Photos/AP Photo/dapd, Christof Stache; Figure 10.6 David R. Frazier Photolibrary, Inc. / Alamy; Figure 10.7 Eileen Langsley Sport / Alamy; Figure 10.8 WILLIAM WEST/AFP/Getty Images; Figure 12.4 Juice Images / Alamy; Figure 12.5 LLUIS GENE/AFP/Getty Images; Figure 12.6 RIA NOVOSTI/SCIENCE PHOTO LIBRARY; Figure 12.7 Robert Stainforth / Alamy; Figure 12.8 Rex Features; page 371 © Crown copyright, Courtesy of Department of Health in association with the Welsh Government, the Scottish Government and the Food Standards Agency in Northern Ireland

Every effort has been made to trace and acknowledge ownership of copyright. The publishers will be glad to make suitable arrangements with any copyright holders whom it has not been possible to contact.